Joint winner of the 2020 Prime Minister'
Shortlisted for the 2020 Victorian Premier
Shortlisted for the 2020 Chief Ministe.
Longlisted for the 2020 Stella Prize
Longlisted for the 2020 Colin Roderick Award

'*Songspirals* carries millions of stories, because each story in its pages is connected to another, and another, and another . . . This book is vital, important, and timely. If there was ever a moment to reconsider what it means to be connected to each other and to the place we live; to the past, to many possible futures, and to how we might simultaneously grieve, love, and heal, that time is now.'

—Victorian Premier's Literary Awards judges' comments

'. . . a glimpse into a profound way of learning about country, culture and family . . . This generous, rich narrative helps readers slow down and open up to deep learning.'

—Stella Prize judges' comments

'This insightful book reveals the deep spirituality of these song spirals and their creators. This book marks a major contribution to our understanding of contemporary Indigenous culture.'

—Prime Minister's Award judges' comments

'Just read this extraordinary book.'

—*Good Reading*

'If you want to learn about Aboriginal ways of loving and honouring their land, Country and kin, paying careful attention to the wise words contained in this book will be an education you won't forget, for it is potentially transformative. The telling is dramatic, lyrical and awe-inspiring.'

—*Aboriginal History*

'This book is a gift, offered in the hope of creating new understandings.'

—*Overland*

About the Gay'wu Group of Women

Gay'wu Group of Women is the 'dilly bag women's group', a deep collaboration between five Yolŋu women and three non-Aboriginal women over a decade.

Sisters Laklak Burarrwaŋa, Ritjilili Ganambarr, Merrkiyawuy Ganambarr-Stubbs and Banbapuy Ganambarr are elders of the Yolŋu people of North East Arnhem Land. Each is a community leader in her own right. Laklak is a caretaker for the Gumatj clan, founder of the family's successful tourism business Bawaka Cultural Experiences, and has been awarded an honorary doctorate from Macquarie University. Merrkiyawuy was principal of Yirrkala School and is now Director for Yolŋu Education. Ritjilili works for Miwatj Health and Bawaka Cultural Experiences. Banbapuy is the main spokesperson for the family, an author, artist, weaver and teacher. Their daughter Djawundil Maymuru has been on the board of Laynapuy Homelands Aboriginal Corporation and is a key member of Bawaka Cultural Experiences.

The sisters have collaborated on a series of cultural and research projects with Associate Professors Kate Lloyd and Sandie Suchet-Pearson from Geography and Planning at Macquarie University, and Associate Professor Sarah Wright, Future Fellow in Geography and Development Studies at the University of Newcastle. They are all co-authors of *Weaving Lives Together at Bawaka, North East Arnhem Land* and a book for young adults, *Welcome to My Country*.

SONG SPIRALS

Sharing women's wisdom of Country through songlines

GAY'WU GROUP OF WOMEN

Laklak Burarrwaŋa
Ritjilili Ganambarr
Merrkiyawuy Ganambarr-Stubbs
Banbapuy Ganambarr
Djawundil Maymuru
Sarah Wright
Sandie Suchet-Pearson
Kate Lloyd

ALLEN&UNWIN
SYDNEY•MELBOURNE•AUCKLAND•LONDON

First published in 2019

Allen & Unwin
83 Alexander Street
Crows Nest NSW 2065
Australia
Phone: (61 2) 8425 0100
Email: info@allenandunwin.com
Web: www.allenandunwin.com

A catalogue record for this book is available from the National Library of Australia

ISBN 978 1 76063 321 9

Internal design by Bookhouse
Map by Guy Holt
Index by Garry Cousins
Set in 12/17 pt Sabon LT Pro by Bookhouse, Sydney
Printed and bound in Australia by McPhersons Printing Group

15 14 13 12 11 10 9 8

The paper in this book is FSC® certified. FSC® promotes environmentally responsible, socially beneficial and economically viable management of the world's forests.

Contents

DEDICATION

We dedicate this book to our grandfather, our mother's father, our ŋathi, Djulwanbirr Mungurrawuy Yunupiŋu. Djulwanbirr is his deep name, a name that we only use in certain significant contexts. Our mother was his first child. He was the teacher for Mum, he taught her everything, taught all of his children. He was a strong leader, a Gumatj clan leader, a master of ceremonies. He was a powerful leader who made sure that Yolŋu people and his own clan were safe. He always negotiated with non-Indigenous people and other clans. He used to tell us bedtime stories around the campfire. He was a family man with a good heart. We have very fond memories of our grandfather because he loved his grandchildren deeply and treated us all equally. He was involved in our activities. When we had our school fete he was there, at the church choir, at everything.

Djulwanbirr Mungurrawuy Yunupiŋu, grandfather of Laklak, Ritjilili, Merrkiyawuy and Banbapuy.

(*The Buku-Larrŋgay Mulka Art Centre archives and courtesy of Ian Dunlop*)

We also want to dedicate this to our grandfather because of his yumalil, his sweet harmony, his sweet voice. He passed it down to our mothers and their daughters and sons. It makes people cry, it touches their heart. Now it is our responsibility to teach and share.

Respecting Country

We sisters, Laklak Burarrwaŋa, Ritjilili Ganambarr, Merrkiyawuy Ganambarr-Stubbs and Banbapuy Ganambarr, together with our daughter Djawundil Maymuru, speak from our place, our Country, Rorruwuy, D̠ät̠iwuy land and Bawaka, Gumatj land, Yolŋu Country, in North East Arnhem Land in Australia. When we talk about Country, we are using an Aboriginal English term that refers to specific places, specific Aboriginal peoples' homelands. There are many, many Countries within Australia, many peoples, many languages, many Aboriginal nations. To talk of Country means not just land, but also the waters, the people, the winds, animals, plants, stories, songs and feelings, everything that becomes together to make up place. Country is alive for us, it cares for us, communicates with us, and we are part of it.

Kate Lloyd, Sandie Suchet-Pearson and Sarah Wright speak also from their place, as ŋäpaki (non-Indigenous) women, living on unceded Aboriginal land in New South Wales. They would specifically like to acknowledge Gumbaynggirr Country, Darug

Country and Awabakal Country, where Kate, Sandie and Sarah live and work and where we have all worked together at various times as a collective. Kate, Sandie and Sarah thank from the bottom of their hearts the Elders, past, present and emerging, particularly those who have mentored, taught and guided them, including Aunty Shaa Smith, Uncle Bud Marshall, Yandaarra, Uncle Michael Jarrett, Uncle Lexodious Dadd, Aunty Corina Norman-Dadd and Aunty Sandra Griffin. Kate, Sandie and Sarah want to acknowledge and celebrate the strength of the cultures and ongoing connections with Country that, in the face of many deep and violent colonising atrocities, continue to survive and thrive every day in the places where they live and work.

We sisters and Kate, Sandie and Sarah as the Gay'wu Group of Women would also like to acknowledge the Countries—the places, people, beings, songspirals and stories—where our words travel, the many different places where they will be shared and read. As we share our knowledge with you, we respectfully offer this in relationship with you and the stories, laws, songs and histories of your place.

When the British came they didn't see, or they ignored or refused to see, the songspirals, the Law, the culture that is here. And they claimed the land. They had only been here for the shortest time and they claimed it. But the land was already claimed. We have boundaries, clan boundaries, we have Law, culture and language. We know which clan belongs to which land.

This book is important and powerful because it comes out of Yolŋu minds, Yolŋu hearts, Yolŋu mouths. It is us, speaking for ourselves.

SONG
SPIRALS

Djalkiri

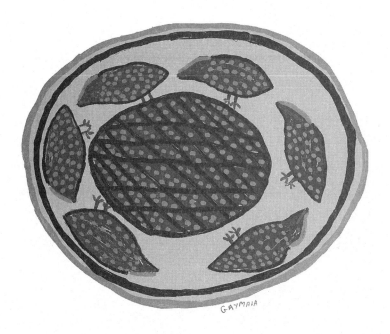

GAYMALA

Previous page: Gaymala Yunupiŋu, *Djirikitj* (1998).
(The Buku-Larrŋgay Mulka Art Centre archives)

Ŋarra yukurra nhäma moṉuk gapu, gäma yukurra
    ŋarranha bala ŋuylili barrku gulula,
Ŋarra yukurra Dhäwuḻwuḻyun Yiwarrnha.
Ŋupan Marrawuḻwuḻ Gunbiḻknha,
Ŋilinyu yurru märina rrambaŋina Mirrinyuna
    Marrawaṯpaṯthun.

I can see the salt water carrying me, moving together
    with the current;
Carrying me further into the depths of the ocean,
    where the foundation of my bloodline lies.
Here my grandmother and I, together we paddle,
    following the sea breeze, to finish our journey,
    across the calm, mercurial waters towards the
    horizon, our final destination.

We want you to come with us on our journey, our journey of songspirals. Songspirals are the essence of people in this land, the essence of every clan. We belong to the land and it belongs to us. We sing to the land, sing about the land. We are that land. It sings to us.

Songspirals are often called songlines or song cycles. In this book, we call them songspirals as they spiral out and spiral in, they go up and down, round and round, forever. They are a line *within* a cycle. They are infinite. They spiral, connecting and remaking. They twist and turn, they move and loop. This is like all our songs. Our songs are not a straight line. They do not move in one direction through time and space. They are a map we follow through Country as they connect to other clans. Everything is connected, layered with beauty. Each time we sing our songspirals we learn more, go deeper, spiral in and spiral out.

We invite you to read this book to find out more about songspirals, and particularly about milkarri. We Yolŋu women from North East Arnhem Land in northern Australia, we cry the songspirals, we keen the songspirals—this is what we call milkarri. Only women keen milkarri. Milkarri is an ancient song, an ancient poem, a map, a ceremony and a guide, but it is more than all this too. Milkarri is a very powerful thing in Yolŋu life.

When we sing through the tears of milkarri, it comes from deep inside us. We feel the song and let it flow. Milkarri is a chant, a soft tremulous voice deep with emotion, sometimes grief, sometimes joy, pierced with loss and pain, often all of these and more. It is hard to translate the concept of milkarri into English and so we are writing this book to explain it to you.

We start with the song, the poem, the milkarri that Mum did for us in the hospital just before she passed away. She is our mother, so this is a good place to start. She saw herself carried by the salt water. She felt it, she was it. She moved together with the current out to the depths of the ocean. She was getting ready for her final journey and she wanted to share milkarri with us. She wanted us to share it with you.

Songspirals have been here a long time. Forever. They are Yolŋu Law. They bring us into being and they link us to the land, to Country. They come from the land and they create it too. It's not just that songspirals created our land a long time ago, but they keep on creating it, and us, and everything in our Country. We are still doing milkarri of the songspirals. Our mother was famous and respected for her milkarri. Milkarri is another way of healing people, healing self. That's why she did milkarri when she was sick. Using the deep names of people or places heals your body.

We have written this book as Gay'wumirr Miyalk Mala—Gay'wu (Dilly Bag) Group of Women—and as the Bawaka Collective. We are the four daughters of Gaymala Yunupiŋu, Dätiwuy women from Rorruwuy homeland in North East Arnhem Land—Laklak, Ritjilili, Merrkiyawuy and Banbapuy—and in this book we honour our mum. Mum's artwork of the quail, *Djirikitj*, is the image used at the start of this introduction. It shows renewal and sacred fire. The six baby quails on her screenprint are us four sisters, our brother, Djali and our oldest sister, Wulara, who passed away as a little girl. To our mum, we are the new generation.

We are Elders and caretakers for Bawaka homeland in North East Arnhem Land, and we work together with our daughter Djawundil. Our collective also includes three ŋäpaki, or non-Indigenous, academics, Sarah, Sandie and Kate from Newcastle and Macquarie universities in New South Wales, who have been

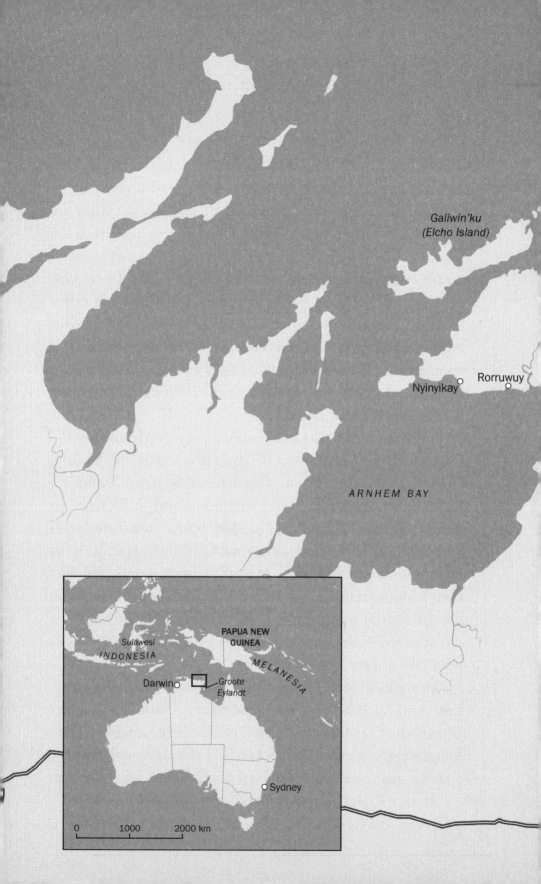

Galiwin'ku
(Elcho Island)

Nyinyikay○   ○Rorruwuy

ARNHEM BAY

PAPUA NEW
GUINEA

Sulawesi
INDONESIA

M E L A N E S I A

Darwin○   ○Groote
Eylandt

○Sydney

0   1000   2000 km

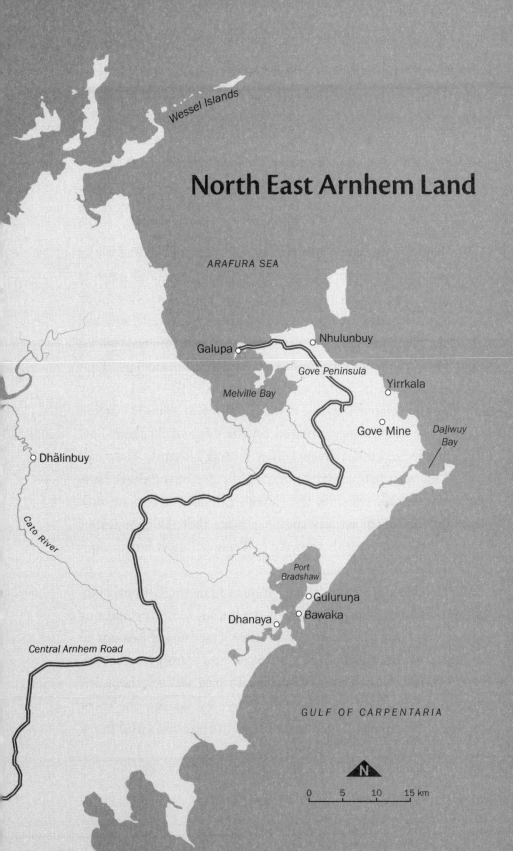

North East Arnhem Land

Wessel Islands

ARAFURA SEA

Galupa ○

Nhulunbuy

Gove Peninsula

Melville Bay

Yirrkala ○

Gove Mine ○

Daḻiwuy Bay

Dhälinbuy ○

Cato River

Central Arnhem Road

Port Bradshaw

Guluruṇa ○

Dhanaya ○

Bawaka ○

GULF OF CARPENTARIA

N

0   5   10   15 km

adopted into the family as granddaughter, sister and daughter respectively. We have written this book as a collective who have been working together for over twelve years. What we share is led by Country and by the songspirals. We have written these words together, but they are mostly a sharing by us four sisters, Laklak, Ritjilili, Merrkiyawuy and Banbapuy. So in this book, when we use the terms 'we' and 'our', we talk as us sisters. In this, we can only speak for our place, our stories.

We begin with our djalkiri, our foundation. Our djalkiri makes us strong, it emerges from the soil as the land gave us our tongue, the words to speak. We are four sisters and our homeland is Rorruwuy, the place of sharks, the waterspout, and namal the black stingray, the really big powerful stingray with a sharp barb. It is a place of muddy water, ritjilili manybarr. That is in the songspirals. Rorruwuy is a homeland for the Dätiwuy clan and the related Ŋaymil clan, for the Ganambarr nation. It is a small community situated on the edge of Arnhem Bay. Our knowledge comes from Dätiwuy and Ŋaymil. They call us the Mel'mari people, which means the eye of the shark. It is where the shark lives. It is the shark's domain. When we talk about our children, we say they are born there in that water. That is in the songspirals too. We call our children binydjalŋu, the children of the shark.

We also look after Bawaka, a homeland of the Gumatj clan. We look after that land because it is Gumatj Country and our mother was Gumatj. We also look after it because it belongs to the Burarrwaŋas and Laklak's husband and family lived there. It is the clan land of Laklak's husband's mother's mother—his märi-pulu clan. Bawaka is watched over by Bayini, the spirit woman of Bawaka. It is a place of beautiful beaches and bäru, crocodile, sitting on the edge of Port Bradshaw off the Gulf of Carpentaria.

We are all women and this is our gay'wu, our dilly bag. We were given our gay'wu by the Djan'kawu Sisters, ancestral beings who create Country, the people, animals, plants and birds. The Djan'kawu Sisters gave us our knowledge, language and Law. We weave our gay'wu and use them to hold bits and pieces for the children, to hold the foods we gather, to hold our knowledge, to hold our dreams and lives and ceremonies. Gay'wu is for all women. Our gay'wu includes our mother, who has passed away, and our ancestors, as well as the young ones not yet born. It also includes Country, who guides us, and the songspirals, which have knowledge and life of their own. Ours is a story of lives entwined and of new places of being, becoming together and belonging. We have written this book together, learnt together and we continue our journey together.

We draw upon women's and men's knowledge in this book. Although milkarri is for women, and we share much women's knowledge, men's and women's knowledge balances each other. It is entwined, it is not separate. Each complements, connects, nurtures and teaches the other. Marri'marri Burarrwaŋa and Djerrkŋu Yunupiŋu, two of our mums, were generous in sharing, and of course our mother, Gaymala Yunupiŋu. They are leaders of the Gumatj clan. Our daughters, granddaughters, grandmothers, mothers and aunties have all helped us. In their various roles for different songspirals, men have also been an important part of the sharing. They include Djamu Yumbulul, Waykarr Gurruwiwi, Witiyana Marika, Gitjpurrwala Ganambarr, Manydjarri Ganambarr, Djali Ganambarr, and our sons, Djäwa Burarrwaŋa, Rrawun Maymuru, Ŋoŋu'

Ganambarr, Nalkuma Burarrwaŋa, Dhalpalawuy Garmu and Bambuŋ Pearson.

Country is the keeper of the knowledge we share with you. Country gives the knowledge for this book. It guides us and teaches us. Country has awareness, it is not just a backdrop. It knows and is part of us. Country is our homeland. It is home and land, but it is more than that. It is the seas and the waters, the rocks and the soils, the animals and winds and people too. It is the connections between those beings, and their dreams and emotions, their languages and their Law. Country is the way humans and non-humans co-become, the way we emerge together, have always emerged together and will always emerge together. It is all the feelings, the songs and ceremonies, the things we cannot understand and cannot touch, the things that go beyond us, that anchor us in eternity, in the infinite cycles of kinship, sharing and responsibility. Country is the way we mix and merge, the way we are different and yet become together, are part of each other. It is the messages, languages and communication from all beings to all beings. And Country is the songspirals. It is milkarri.

Milkarri connects us to our clan, our family and our homeland, to the waters and rocks and winds and animals, to everything. When we do milkarri, as soon as we hear it, the tears just come, because the words and the meanings are so deep that the land is talking. It is in our cry, the sounds of our keening. The land is crying for her people and the people are crying for the land. Country cries too. It has its milkarri. We keen milkarri for Country and Country keens its milkarri with us.

Songspirals are all about knowing Country, where the home-lands are, the essence of the land and water and sky. They map

the land but in a different way, a deep mapping.
spirals, we travel through the land and through th
see it, know it, feel it, sing it, come into being with   и
a Yolŋu person has never been to that Country, they see it in
their spirit. It helps us find our way. We learn the land itself,
where those places are, what they mean and how they connect
to other places and beings. It is telling a story, singing. We are
telling another person and that person is sitting down and they
are listening.

The songspirals locate a place, locate Country, and they
take us there. They connect us to that Country and to the
person who was there and has passed away, to the ancestors
and to those yet to come, and they connect that Country to
other Countries, to other clan homelands around it, in a great
pattern of co-becoming and co-emergence. Through songspirals,
we know where we are and we know who we are.

In this book we share five songspirals with you: Wuymirri,
the Whale; Wukun, the Gathering of the Clouds; Guwak,
the Messenger Bird; Wititj, the Settling of the Serpent; and
Goŋ-gurtha, the Keeper of the Fire. Each of these songspirals
reaches out and connects clans and peoples and Country across
North East Arnhem Land, across northern Australia, across
Australia, to the centre and down south, and even north into
the currents of the Arafura Sea and to the islands of Melanesia,
Polynesia and beyond. They connect us down through the soil
and up into Sky Country, into space.

We translate the five songspirals for you and share some of
their poetic meanings. But we will not, and cannot, share all

their meaning. That would not be right. Some of the layers of meaning in songspirals are too deep and sacred to share. We also cannot share the songs of other clans, and we can only talk from our own perspective. Yolŋu have thousands of songs. Other clans, other leaders, other caretakers will have different knowledge. We respect that. We can only share what is our knowledge.

We also share some stories of our family, about our mum, about our eldest sister, Laklak, about how we work together as miyalk, as women, and about some of our inspiring daughters and granddaughters and how they are keeping the songspirals alive. The deep and sacred knowledge in songspirals is everywhere. It is in our lives and in us. It is about us. It doesn't stand separate but is entwined in our everyday lives. We show you this by inviting you into our lives. As we sit on the beach with our family, fishing and gathering oysters, that is the songspirals. As we laugh or argue or mourn or love or cry, that is the songspirals. As our grandchildren perform in their rock bands or dance or share in different ways, that is the songspirals. We also introduce different themes that we deepen as the book unfolds. These too are guided by the songspirals.

When old people hear women doing milkarri, they say, 'Ahhh, they are telling a story.' Through milkarri the women are taking us back to a place, to Country, to a person, to everything that lives there and that lived there. It touches our soul. They know that Country. When people die, when a person dies, we sing about that person's life. We sing about going hunting, finding a tree, gathering under it; about a person going down to the beach, looking out to the horizon, making a fire. That is what women sing through the tears of milkarri, what we do in our songspirals. We are singing a picture but that picture is alive, that Country is alive, that person's being is linked to that Country, it can't be separated from that Country. Every songspiral is a song, a ceremony, a picture, a story, a person, a place, a mapping, some things that we did, that we do and that we will always do, and it is all of those things together because those things are really the same. And it is more, much more. It is knowledge and language and Law.

In this book, we tell you about songspirals and milkarri. Many ŋäpaki, non-Indigenous people, talk about songlines but they don't know what they really are. Most of the books written about songlines have been written by white people, and mainly white men. That is why we decided to write this book. Often when we read about Yolŋu, it is not from Yolŋu people. The words are not chosen and controlled by us. They often leave things out or get things wrong. Sometimes we are offended by what other people write about us. We also find that most of what's written talks about men's knowledge and doesn't pay attention to or value women's knowledge and milkarri. So, we decided we would write this book ourselves as Yolŋu women.

We share songspirals with you and we ask that you treat them with respect. Respecting the knowledge means not writing about things that you don't understand, not putting things into your own words. The words in this book are our knowledge, our property. You can talk about it, but don't think you can become the authority on it. You can use our words for reflection. You can talk about your own experiences and think about how to take lessons from our book into your life. You need to honour the context of our songspirals, acknowledge the layers of our knowledge. You can talk about the very top layer but you need to be respectful and aware of the limits of what we are sharing and what you in turn can share.

We will go deeper into what songspirals mean and why milkarri is so important. We will help you understand. We do this to educate people and open their eyes. We want you to realise that, yes, Yolŋu have a place to belong. Yolŋu have culture and language, and we obey our rules and follow our system. We are Yolŋu, we exist. We are Australian and we have a culture. We are still here. We need to keep our culture by doing what we have to do. We want people from different backgrounds, different cultures to walk with us, to learn our culture, to understand milkarri.

Sometimes we feel that Australia can be, or is, a racist country. We see ŋäpaki saying to our neighbours, 'Get out, you don't come from here, you come from another country, you are from another culture, another religion, a different belief.' A few Australians welcome people and that's what we've always done. The true Australians welcome people.

We need to keep our culture by getting other people to walk with us. We want you to touch, and hear, our world. Because when children are little, they learn from touching, feeling, doing. But when we talk, talk, talk, they don't learn. We invite you to sit on the ground with us. We can balance both cultures, we can share. We will treat you as family.

As we bring this book to you, we are also sharing and learning among ourselves. We cannot let this knowledge fade away. It has been here for so long and it is still here. That is why this book is so important, to pass knowledge down between the generations and to continue the spirals. We are all learning. This book is a journey for us too, a journey of intergenerational learning. We have learnt from our sisters and our mothers. Our mothers have given this to us. Now we need to bring it out from ourselves. And from ourselves to you. It needs to happen now and we want you to walk with us on this journey.

There are important roles, responsibilities and rules around the sharing of songspirals. Songspirals are a process. They are not a thing, they are not static. Songspirals must be done in the right way, in order. In this book, we share five songspirals under the authority of the appropriate Wäŋa Wataŋu, the custodian, the landowner clan. This is the clan who belongs to Country and to whom Country belongs. The songspirals that are included here are ones that are closely related to us, where we have direct connection with the line of authority. In this book, we acknowledge the Country, the landowners, the Wäŋa Wataŋu, for each songspiral who have helped guide us and who have allowed this sharing.

Our translations into English have been made by us sisters, mostly by Banbapuy, who has a gift with beautiful words in English, and with our son Rrawun Maymuru. We have discussed these translations together and with the custodians of each song. We have worked carefully on the writing down of the Yolŋu matha words, and the way they are translated, written and punctuated in English, to make sure they give a strong sense of what the songspirals mean to us. The translations are not '*the* songspiral', as if the whole songspiral could be captured in words and fixed in a book. No. The words are those that were shared in a particular context, a particular time and place, by a particular person who has the authority to do so. Country shapes what is shared. The songspirals are ancient but fresh. They are always sung. The Rom, the Law, behind the songspirals never changes, but the spirals, and the words in them, are always in emergence.

People might think that the land doesn't speak, nor the rivers, the animals or the winds, but they do. We feel the land, the sea and the rivers, and they tell us many things. The songs speak, the people speak for the land. That is the song. The ocean that comes in and out, that is the song. The people shape the land, the different habitats, through singing.

The language of the songspirals is deep and complex, with many layers and meanings. These always go back to the land, the sea and the sky. Sometimes, the words may say one thing but the deeper meaning is different. In this book we sometimes use several phrases to evoke the feeling of the song. Sometimes we have chosen English words that do not have the same literal meaning as the Yolŋu matha, our language, but give a better sense of what is being conveyed. These are difficult decisions.

English is like talking backwards. The way we talk in Yolŋu matha is straight and direct, and yet one word can have many layers. Yolŋu people with deep knowledge know this. For the people who belong to the land, who own that land and know it in a deep way, it is not complex. They know the meanings from living on the land, from their relationships and from the songs—generation after generation after generation. We have shared what we feel we can, in the way we feel is best. The songspiral is the present, past and future. That is why we cry. Because we are here.

We are not sharing the deep understanding but we are sharing the open, public understanding of the songspirals so that other people can understand how Yolŋu people, the land, the sea, the sky and the rivers are connected. What we share is the sacred heart of Country. Reading this book is not just about reading and relaxing, it is harder and deeper, but it will give you a chance to understand our culture. It is our life.

Part 1
....
Wuymirri

CHAPTER 1

Mum

Our mother, Gaymala, became Wuymirri, the Whale, as she lay in hospital. This was back in 2005. She was sick and knew she was going to pass away soon. She started talking in her sleep and Banbapuy, our youngest sister, was there. Banbapuy quickly wrote down the words. In this verse Mum was talking in Gumatj, her clan language, about her märi-pulu, her mothers' mothers' clan. She was speaking as the spirit on that journey. They are the words that started this book:

Ŋarra yukurra nhäma moṉuk gapu, gäma yukurra
    ŋarranha bala ŋuylili barrku gulula,
Ŋarra yukurra Dhäwuḻwuḻyun Yiwarrnha.
Ŋupan Marrawuḻwuḻ Gunbiḻknha,
Ŋilinyu yurru marina rrambaŋina Mirrinyuna
    Marrawaṯpaṯthun.

*I can see the salt water carrying me, moving together
    with the current;*

3

Carrying me further into the depths of the ocean,
where the foundation of my bloodline lies.
Here my grandmother and I, together we paddle,
following the sea breeze, to finish our journey,
across the calm, mercurial waters towards the
horizon, our final destination.

Mum's words speak of the part of Wuymirri's journey where she, as the Whale, dives down into the depths of the ocean, knowing the hunters will soon be coming. Mum is describing what happens and also describing herself, where she will go, soon. She isn't saying that she is dying, that she will go away. She won't tell us that. But she is using the deep meaning of the language. We know this because she taught us the meaning of this language as she brought us up.

When we heard those words we knew straight away that we had to take her away from the hospital. When people are sick, or dying, we talk about being on the journey. This is the message they give to the family and the family knows straight away, it is time.

Our dhäruk, our language, has many, many layers. One layer is the language used for everyday talk. A second layer is for more formal interactions, for approaching people in the right way. It is used to make people in a ceremony understand what to do and how to relate to each other. If a conflict is going on, the second language is a way of getting the families back together, to remember how they relate to each other. The third layer, the deepest layer, is the hidden language and is only for those who understand, the ones who are taught, only those who have reached that level. This is the level for keening and singing. It is much deeper. We are speaking the same language

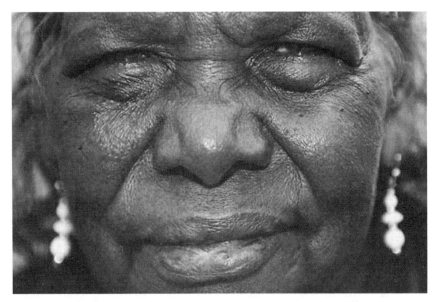

Gaymala Yunupiŋu, mother of Laklak, Ritjilili, Merrkiyawuy and Banbapuy.
(The Buku-Larrŋgay Mulka Art Centre archives and courtesy of Peter Eve Monsoon Graphics)

but with different words. When you understand the second layer, you understand what the Elder was talking about, you have the knowledge to understand the hidden language. Mum was one who could speak and keen milkarri with the hidden language, the deepest layer, she was the liya-ŋärra'mirr.

She was telling us in a different way that the time had come close. She didn't say the hunters were coming. She said, using deep language, 'I am going now with my grandmother, we are paddling into the ocean, we will dive into the depths of the ocean.' She was letting us know the hunters would hunt. But she didn't need to say that last part. We knew straight away. So we took her out of the hospital. She needed to be at home.

The language that is in us, it is so deep. It is a beautiful way to describe things, from the beginning of life, to the end of life's journey. It is very beautiful and very powerful. These song-spirals have been sung and cried through the tears of milkarri forever. Songspirals are about a particular person, their deep and true being. But they are not only about that person, they are also about the person's connections, their connections with nature, their connections with places, their relationships. Mum's spirit went back to the ocean. And she went with her grand-mother. Her mothers' mother is her märi, she is the gutharra, grandchild, and this relationship is märi-gutharra. That is our backbone, quite literally our backbone. For us, our backbone is our mothers' mothers' clan. We point to our backbone as a visual sign of this important kin relationship. Everyone has their backbone. That is why she was with her grandmother. Her grandmother carries her.

Wuymirri, the Whale Songspiral, is a Warramirri song-spiral, our great-grandmother's songspiral, and one we share with you now. We share it to start our book and to start our journey together. You can see how important it is to us, how our mum's life and death help to keep that songspiral alive. You can see how that songspiral keeps Mum and us alive too, how our hearing and keening the Wuymirri songspiral for this book keeps Wuymirri alive, and Country. As you read and learn, as you sound out those words, you become part and parcel of the songspiral, part and parcel of bringing the world into existence.

Songspirals are always personal and always about Country, about places and our relationships with them. Songspirals sing the actual land and the sea. Wuymirri talks about the whale, it talks about the boat that journeys through the water. It talks about the places that the whales and boat pass through, the journey's route. And in that is the route of our lives, our beings, our connections with Country.

For us, this songspiral and this book are intensely personal, emotional and meaningful. They are for Mum. They are for all mothers, any mother, Yolŋu or ŋäpaki—Indigenous or non-Indigenous. Every mother, whether black, white or from a different background, cries with sorrow, love, happiness, joy and heartache. These are always expressed with tears. Tears represent a being or a belonging, a beginning or an end, a journey. When there is a newborn we cry, because there is a new being; we cry happy tears and also sad, as we think of the generations that have gone.

All the women who have written this book are mothers, we feel that connection. We feel those emotions. In a Yolŋu world, we are all mothers, in relationship with things as a mother, and that includes men too. Men are in a child–mother relationship with other beings, both as a child and as a mother. We call this the yothu–yindi relationship and we will tell you more about that later. We understand how urgently, critically and fundamentally important it is to bring life, to sustain and nurture life. Just as our grandmothers are our backbone, the songspirals are our anchor.

When women keen the milkarri of Wuymirri they are telling a story. Wuymirri is about a journey. It is the last journey of a person's soul. It is about a whale, but it is also about sitting there, being on the boat, going along, singing about those places. Looking at the things the person saw in their life. It is the spirit's final journey. It is looking, travelling, for the last time; watching the whales, out in the ocean.

We share Wuymirri with you to give you a sense of its meaning. Remember, the translation is partial, it tells what it tells, not everything. We go through each stanza to give you a sense of some of the layers, the complexities of the language and meaning. The meanings of this song are deep and intense, so we will devote a full chapter to each stanza, explaining a small part of its deep meaning.

We are sharing Wuymirri because of our connection to our mother and her märi-pulu. There are a lot of people who are connected to Wuymirri and we acknowledge them and the different parts we all play in keeping Wuymirri alive. We are connected to this songspiral because our great-grandmother Bamatja and her brother Daymaŋu are of the Warramirri clan. Our mother keened the milkarri of Wuymirri because she had the authority as the Gutharra, granddaughter, of Bamatja. Bamatja and Daymaŋu are her backbone.

The Wuymirri we share now is in Gumatj language and comes from a recording of our mum doing milkarri of it a long time ago. Our mum's younger sister Djerrkŋu helped us transcribe and translate it, and we all sat around the recording together, listening to it so carefully, playing it over and over again on our smartphones, learning and teaching so much. As she is the sister of our mother, Djerrkŋu is our mum too. In our gurruṯu, our kinship system, all our mother's sisters are our mothers and all our father's brothers are our fathers. So that means that all our mother's sisters' children are our brothers and sisters and all our sisters' children are our children too.

Djerrkŋu shared her own versions of Wuymirri in Gumatj and Warramirri clan languages that we include at the end of this part of the book. We sat, too, with Djamu Yumbulul, the Wäŋa Wataŋu (custodian) of this songspiral, who guided us, gave his permission, and shared more deep insights and understandings, and Gawiniyawuy Waŋgurra, our niece, another direct descendant of Bamatja, our Warramirri great-grandmother from the Wessel Islands, a chain of islands extending north into the Arafura Sea towards Papua New Guinea.

The language of songspirals is deep and complex, not the language of our every day but of ceremony. This is language that doesn't change. It must be the oldest language. Gaymala has the deep knowledge needed to be able to communicate many layers. Our mother is crying the ancestral boat, an ancient Macassan boat, and beneath the boat is the whale. She is singing about the boat, and as she does so she sings herself as a navigator, as someone with deep knowledge. And she is singing about the boat passing the land. She knows whom those lands belong to. She is singing about herself, and about what is beneath, the whale. The whale is following her, she is passing through the whale sanctuary. She is interpreting the whale's movement. When she shared her milkarri in the hospital, as she knew she was dying, she cried milkarri of the whale, she was the whale. So all the words have two, three meanings—where she was, where she was standing and where she will go.

For ceremony, we need to gather the families, the ones with the right connections and relationships. Before the ceremony starts, before we put ochre on our body to dance the songspiral, we must wait for the guidance of the Djungaya.

Each songspiral has many Djungaya. The Djungaya could be a woman or a man. The role is passed down through a family, we get it through our family line from our mother. For a particular ceremony, a Djungaya with the appropriate knowledge is chosen. In this role, the Djungaya will make sure the clan is not doing the songspiral the wrong way; the song must be on the right track, in order. They are the caretaker for the songspiral and director for the ceremony. The Djungaya are messengers who coordinate the ceremony. They direct the use of the clay for the bodies of the dancers. They protect the clans by making sure the right order is followed. Even if the Djungaya is a younger person, if they have the knowledge they can still direct the songspiral. We need the right dance, the right song, someone who knows the right ceremony. In our family, the Djungaya for this songspiral are our son Djäwa's wife, Rita Wopurrwuy Gondarra, and her brothers and sisters.

There are other vital roles too for the songspirals. The Gutharra are the grandchildren of the land through the maternal line, the daughters' children. The Gutharra are there to strengthen the backbone of the märi-pulu, the grandmother clan. The grandchildren may be old or young, women or men. It is gurrutu, a kinship relationship. In a public ceremony the grandmother clan will say, 'Manymak Gutharra, Grandchild, thank you for coming and strengthening your märi-pulu, your grandmother clan.'

The Gutharra, the grandchildren of the clan, from our family include Rita's children, Rriwit, Dimathaya and Butjarri, as well as some of our other grandchildren, Maminydjama, Yambirrwuy, Nyinanyina and many others.

The most fundamental role is the Dalkarra or Djirrikay, the trustees of knowledge for the ceremony. Dalkarra is from the

Dhuwa moiety, and Djirrikay is Yirritja moiety. We will explain what these moieties, these groups, are in the next chapter. The role of the D̲alkarra and Djirrikay is to announce, in the presence of all, the sacred deep names, the ritual recitation of power names, Birkarr'yun. D̲alkarra and Djirrikay hold the power. They know the rules. They are like the top of the university, the leaders. The D̲alkarra or Djirrikay are there as the professors, the doctors, to ensure that the power remains tight, that the songspiral is not loosened. They understand the spirit of the land, sea and river. The D̲alkarra or Djirrikay could be the Wäŋa Wata̲ŋu or the Gutharra. They could also be the Djungaya.

For the songspiral we must recite the deep names, the sacred names and meanings. If we don't have the sacred names, we have nothing. We can't fool around with the songspirals. For Wuymirri, we must call out mami̲dal, which signifies the deep connection between the hunter and the whale, between the hunter and the hunted, the respect. Only the select few can hunt whale, only the Warramirri clan, because of the ways the whale and the clan are related to and reflect one another. Mami̲dal is the hunter's feeling about the whale and about catching it, and the whale feeling the hunter too. The feelings between the hunter and the whale are very strong, the two are bound in one. Mami̲dal also signifies the power of the whale beneath the sea. We also have the deep names of the body parts: bintha and dhaŋbulyun, which are the head; bi̲la, the tail; warriwa̲tpa, the fins and the whale paddling beneath the sea. The fins of the whale are like the paddle of the hunter. Warriwa̲tpa means the same thing on different levels: one is the hunter paddling and the other, deep beneath, the whale.

We claim the spirit of the land and the journey of the ocean and the pure river that flows. We have the important roles, the Wäŋa Wataŋu, the Djirrikay or Ḏalkarra, the Djungaya and the Gutharra. When the Rom (the Law), the movement of the song, the energy and the power come together with the sounds and actions of the dancers, with the yiḏaki (didgeridoo), the biḻma (clapsticks), the sounds of the women keening milkarri and the deeper timbre of the men, the Djirrikay or Ḏalkarra is ready to call out the names: where the journey will start and where the journey will end.

This is an important gift that we share with you, it was a precious sharing of milkarri by our mother, Gaymala. It is a particular honour to be entrusted with the responsibility to appropriately give and receive the knowledges and responsibilities that come with these songspirals. We hope that you appreciate the generosity and trust that is being placed in you.

1.
Ŋuruku miyamanarawu Dhaŋgaḻa aaaaaaaa . . .
Waṉa nyerrpu miyaman ŋunha marrtji Baŋupaŋu.
Miyaman marrtji Balwarri Nepaway, Maywuṉdjiwuy.

Of that body of water I sing, I sing of the body of water.
The arm of the paddler is knowledgeable, over there is Baŋupaŋu.
I am singing about Balwarri, the whale, Nepaway, the open sea.

2.

Bawaywuyŋu miyamara Dhululwuyŋuru;
Bawaywuyŋu miyamara Rrawululwuyŋuru;
Ŋuruku miyaman ŋarra marrtji Rrawulwulwuyŋu.

Of the place between sunrise and sunset I sing,
Where the whales swim with open mouths, scooping
    water, filtering fish;
A pod of whales, flipping and jumping, playing and
    roaming;
A gathering of many people;
For that I sing towards Rrawulwul, the place where
    the whales are feeding.
I sing for those people, the ones far away.

3.

Nhinana ŋarra Rrawulwulwuyun mala maypa.
Aa'a—Dhululŋura Balwarri, Balwarri,
Nepaway, Baway'yu miyaman ŋunha marrtji
    Dhaŋala.

I sit comfortably, feed comfortably as part of a big
    pod, filtering food, sifting the water through my
    mouth, one among many whales.
Oh, dear whales, whales, the open sea, between
    sunrise and sunset, singing of that place over there,
    eastward, always to the horizon.
I sing towards Dhaŋala, I see myself, standing tall
    and straight like the mast of my boat, a flag, my
    journey, Dhaŋala.

4.

Ṉuruku ŋarra miyaman Ṉulpurrwuyŋu,
Dhuḻuḻwuyŋu, Balwarriwuyŋu, ŋeee—miṯji maypa
  Balwarri.

For that I am singing Ṉulpurrwuyŋu;
I sing of the body of water.
Dhuḻuḻwuyŋu, Balwarriwuyŋu, a place of many
  whales;
Yes, a clan, a pod of many whales.

CHAPTER 2

Country

Ŋuruku miyamanarawu Dhaŋgala aaaaaaaa . . .
Wana nyerrpu miyaman ŋunha marrtji Baŋupaŋu.
Miyaman marrtji Balwarri Nepaway, Maywundjiwuy.

Of that body of water I sing, I sing of the body of water.
The arm of the paddler is knowledgeable, over there is
    Baŋupaŋu.
I am singing about Balwarri, the whale, Nepaway, the
    open sea.

When Yolŋu people sing of water, we are singing our deep
knowledge of water. We are singing our connection to water.
We sing of that body and of our own body, our own bodies
of water. For we are not singing of something that is separate
from us. We are not singing about water but singing water itself.
Of that body of water we sing. We sing of the body of water.

15

Ŋuruku miyamanarawu Dhanggaḻa aaaaaaaa.

And when we sing of that water, we remake that water, and we remake ourselves and our connections with water and all else that is Country.

Songspirals are many things. They are a story, a big story. They are ceremony with a story in it. They are not a made-up story. Wuymirri is telling a story about that body of water and the whales we see as we journey in our boat, as whales and as ourselves.

When women cry milkarri our tremulous voices sing a story about pain, heartbreak, hope, loss, anger, frustration, happiness and love. When we say love, we are talking about what binds us together. We are talking about loving our family, our land, our life, and loving who we are and where we come from. Yes, because when we cry milkarri for our Country, us women are claiming our self and the land, we are one.

We're going to be talking about Country a lot as we talk about keening milkarri, because keening milkarri helps create Country. Milkarri enlivens Country, brings it into being again and again as we all unfold together through songspirals.

We sing and keen milkarri for everything, and it is the singing and doing milkarri that brings everything into being. We cry milkarri for everything, from the smallest living creature that lives in the earth to the furthest stars that we can see, for maggots and flies, for the soil and the deep roots. It's a big responsibility.

We let that feeling flow through us. Let our body be that body of water of which we sing. Let our singing and crying milkarri be that body and our body, and know that we and Country are one, that we are Country, that we must do milkarri, name Country, harmonise with Country so that our knowledge, our sound, the vibration inside us brings Country alive, makes it sacred again and again and again. Of that body of water we sing. And that water sings us.

We cry milkarri in Yolŋu matha, the family of languages of our homelands. Each clan has their own Yolŋu clan language. It is Yolŋu matha that names the deep names, the true names, of the water and the places, the beings and becomings of our songspirals. Language is like water flowing in the river, picking up all the sediment, the rocks, the leaves and the sand. It moulds it all with the clay. That is how Yolŋu matha is. That is how we are, how our songspirals are. There is never just one Yolŋu person, separate from family or from Country. Everyone and everything is always connected, always in relation. And in the same way, we sing not just the water but all the things that flow with the water.

Our water is never just one water. We name the tides, the currents, the muddy water and the clear, the shallow water and the deep, the salt and the fresh. And it is important to us when these things come together. When the salt water meets the fresh, that is Garma, two knowledges mixing and mingling.

Underpinning this pattern of connection and balance are the two moieties, Yirritja and Dhuwa. Everyone and everything is either Yirritja or Dhuwa. Yirritja and Dhuwa are important to Yolŋu and for songspirals, for everything. They are a pattern, a wholeness that underpins and makes up the universe. This is a foundation for us. Yirritja and Dhuwa are two complementary aspects of our world, of Country. Together they make a whole. Yirritja and Dhuwa together make up the world.

There are Yirritja waters and Dhuwa waters, just as there are Yirritja people and Dhuwa people, Yirritja animals and Dhuwa animals, Yirritja sunsets and Dhuwa sunsets, Yirritja songspirals and Dhuwa songspirals. Yirritja is the mother of Dhuwa and Dhuwa is the mother of Yirritja. It is a cycle that goes from one to the other. It goes from mother to daughter to granddaughter. Our mum, she was Yirritja. So that means we sisters are Dhuwa. Djawundil, our daughter, is Yirritja. Her daughter is Dhuwa again. That is the cycle.

It is the cycle between generations, and it is a cycle in nature too that shows where and how we fit. So, like the relationship between mother and daughter, where Dhuwa is the daughter of Yirritja and Yirritja the daughter of Dhuwa, there is a relationship between the muddy water, Ritjilili, which is Dhuwa, and Mungulk, the water that runs down from Dhälinbuy, our grandmother's land, which is Yirritja. The waters meet as mother and child. They respect each other. In the songspirals, Yirritja and Dhuwa waters talk to each other. We sing of the currents and the waters passing over each other, the little waves and foams. Yirritja water is clear, on the top. Dhuwa water is muddy, where the sharks roam.

All things are Yirritja and Dhuwa, all things are in that cycle of mother and daughter. And we are Yirritja and Dhuwa. That means we are in a relationship with all things as mother and daughter. We have a yothu (child) water and a yindi (mother) water. All animals and rocks and winds, all things in Country, are Yirritja or Dhuwa too, such as our Yirritja homeland, Bawaka; and Guluruŋa, our Dhuwa homeland at the point jutting out into Port Bradshaw. We always have a relationship with them. Maybe they are the same moiety as us or maybe they are our mother or daughter, so we are caretaker for them. We always know.

This songspiral we are singing now, of the whales and of travelling, is a Yirritja song. That means we are the mothers for this song. We are the mothers because the Whale song connects with Bamaṯja, our daughter through gurruṯu. This song is Yirritja, and we are Dhuwa, so here we sing the songs of the children, in their tune and with respect to them. That was what Mum was sharing with us in hospital.

And that is what we are doing here. We are holding and taking care of this songspiral for our mother, for all our mothers. And for our children.

We start from Bawaka, with the boat, a canoe, that takes us on this songspiral. We could start from many places, as long as they are Yirritja places and are related to the right clan. We could start at Daliwuy Bay or Dhanaya, with that boat. The boat is sailing forever, not coming back. We are sailing to infinity, going on and on and on.

This is a traveller's story, a traveller's song, a navigator's song. This is what a family would do in a canoe. The one in the front would know the way to go and know if there are rocks they can't go through. They know their way. The eyes are looking and the hands are paddling.

'The arm of the paddler is knowledgeable, over there is Baṉupaṉu.' When we sing that the arm of the paddler is know-ledgeable, we are saying that the paddler knows where all the places are. This is a deep knowledge, held in their body, in their arm. They name those places, they know those places and so

19

they enliven them. They honour them. They bring them into being, again and again.

The paddler is looking at those places, they know the places are just around the corner, over there. Even with the speedboat as we go out today, fishing or doing other things, we name the places, we know they are there. We know they always have been there and always will be there. It is an acknowledgement of those places. They are still there, were there all the time, are always there in the songspirals.

So our songspirals are in many times. They are in the past and the future. They are in the present. They are eternal stories that talk of our journey after death. And they are everyday stories that talk of us fishing in speedboats. Because—and this is important—the everyday is eternal too.

For Yolŋu, there are layers of depth and meaning in everything. In a songspiral, we cry about getting wet in the rain or feeling mädirriny (the south wind) and so many things that happen on Country. These are not inconsequential. The wind does not just blow. It communicates, it tells us things, it has its own story and Law, its own ceremony. The wind is its being and its becoming. It co-becomes with us and with Country.

So when we sing of a wind in a songspiral we are evoking all those things and more. Fishing and sitting and feeling the breeze are everyday things, but they are also sacred things, deep things, knowledgeable things, meaningful things. Sacred, yes, but not like a religion, not in a way that means they are more special or more linked to our creation and our being than anything else. Everything is sacred. We do not *believe in* this or that. We are those things. Songspirals are those things. Songspirals are life.

When someone sings this song, they are singing about the paddler seeing those places. So the singer is also with the paddler. The singer sees it, the singer is there. They are that water, and that paddler. We travel along the land. We travel along the water. They are thinking about those places, the trees, that raŋi (beach) where the paddler was born, where they grew up. It is all about remembering the paddler, telling a story about who they are, about their place and their journey, which is our journey too. Even a person who has never been there goes there, through those songs.

We sing, 'Over there is Baŋupaŋu.' We sing, 'The arm of the paddler is knowledgeable.' The paddler, that is us, knows the deep names, of places and of clans. Every clan has a deep name. Every clan has an essence. For example, that gum tree behind us is different from another type, from the other gum trees in Australia and the world. They are all one, but the leaves and the trunks are different, the soul within them, the essence. Every clan is like that. We are all one, the same, Yirritja and Dhuwa, but the deep name is different, the source is different. So in the songs, when we chant, we have to chant each clan. For the D̲ät̲iwuy, it is Djurdjurŋa, Birrwanga, Gal̲irriŋbuŋ, and for the Ŋaymil, it is D̲ar'miny, Gamburrtji, Bul̲ukmana.

We are reading the sea, we name the islands. We call out place names, islands, and this is deep knowledge. In the dance we have a paddle. We use it to point to the places. And we sing this stanza over and over, with different places.

We are singing about Balwarri, the whale; Nepaway, the open sea. We sing about travelling, in and with the boat. We see whales on the horizon, see the waterspout. We are that traveller and then we are the Whale. We see each other as we go past.

These songs, they are sung by different clans. There are strong rules about who can sing what, but there is overlap too. For each clan, there are some things in the songspirals that are shared, some that are different. We are in relationship with each other through the clans and through Yirritja and Dhuwa. Some animals belong with a specific clan, some insects and trees, but other clans can sing them too because they are also related to them through gurrutu. And the songspirals, they travel, they speak to each other. Another clan might start a different part of a songspiral, the next part in a journey. Every clan's tune is different. The words can be the same—if they are all singing the Whale, that may be the same—but there are parts that the clan doesn't have authority for, so they don't sing it. Our songs spiral out, they link us together.

Songspirals connect our homelands. That is how they link us far and wide. Even when we are singing about one homeland, like Bawaka, it extends beyond that because our eyes can see out and we can sing about that as well. That land over there might belong to someone else but we sing about people walking along, the beach we can see, their feet touching the water.

Like the Whale, the songspiral travels far. Nepaway, the open sea. Songspirals are about the journey of animals and spirit beings, those beings who can be person, animal or both. The animal created something here and then it went to that land, so the clans share that animal. Our places have been created by animals or beings who travel. That is how the songspirals reach out, spiral out. Another clan will take up the next step of the journey, of the whales or the hunters or the ones on shore, watching. This way, our songspirals connect and travel, all the way across the Pacific and to Asia. We are not isolated.

We come from our place and we make our place and we are our place. That is what we mean by Country. It is the way we are connected, as yothu–yindi, child and mother to all beings and becomings. We keen milkarri and we bring ourselves into being, as we do Country. We follow and remake the paths of the whale and the open sea. Mother and child, they sing and they dance and they do milkarri. Our Country is land and it is sea.

Country is home, it sings to us and nourishes us. It is the feeling of home, the feeling of the seasons that communicate with us. It is all the beings of home. It is everything that we can touch or feel or hear or sense, and it is everything beyond that too. It is everything that belongs in Country, with Country and as Country, including us. And it is the relationships between all those beings too. We come into being together.

Mum was the first child and daughter for Mungurrawuy Yunupiŋu, and her father taught her everything about the songspirals, the places, the deep language, the deep names, the ceremonial designs. She learnt from her father the way we younger sisters now learn from Laklak or Djerrkŋu. Sitting with them and doing milkarri. Sometimes, Mum would help her brothers out, telling them the place names, correcting them, telling them how to sing and what not to sing. Mum used to tell the men, 'Don't sing that way, that is not right. Follow me.' She had such deep knowledge.

Mum was so very strong. No one would tell her what to do. She learnt that from her father and her mother. We daughters learnt from her. She would make the women and men shut up every time she was talking. Mum told us stories. Every time we heard her keen milkarri we would cry tears full of emotion. Us crying would make her feel proud. She was like her mother, very beautiful in the heart.

Mum taught us to weave. Sitting down talking, we watched her and started weaving. Stories were woven into the dilly bag. She used to tell us funny stories or tell us where to go to get the pandanus to weave our baskets or dig the roots to make our dyes. Mum was one of the first women to do screenprinting at the Buku-Larrŋgay Mulka Art Centre in Yirrkala, not only producing beautiful art communicating culture, but artworks to sell near and far. Merrkiyawuy's husband, Will, is a Gumatj man who looks after the family and is a good hunter; he works at the Art Centre and he encouraged her. Now her artworks enrich this book.

Mum was a good hunter; her father and mother taught her. She taught us to look for beehives, looking up in the trees for yarrpany, the Dhuwa bees, and down on the ground for barŋgitj, the Yirritja bees, which nest there. We'd look up and down to see the two kinds of bees and their hives. When we went out hunting mud crabs, she would show us how to be still and look for their outline. When we looked for mussels she would show us how to see their breathing holes. She showed us how to look for snakes, for the tracks as the snakes move around. She told us how when she was young clans weren't allowed to go into another clan's land. If you see a pond of water, she taught us to use it like a mirror. Don't drink right

Nanukala holding her grandmother Laklak's dilly bags. *(Authors' collection)*

away, but lean down and pretend to drink in case something is going to attack you.

She took us out every time she went hunting for food or gathering pandanus, and she would always have her grandchildren with her too. That way we learnt how to be independent, not to be lazy, how to take what people offer, how to have strength for our children. When she collected food, she saved it in a basket and shared it. She taught us to do this too. Now we are putting our knowledge in this gay'wu, this dilly bag, and we share it—mother to children to grandchildren—and we ask you to share it with your family.

During the land rights days in the 1960s and 70s, all the mums, especially our mum, travelled around with the anthropologists who were helping with land claims, naming places, singing songs, and showing them which clan groups belonged to which area. They went everywhere camping. It was hard work. All this hard work eventually helped us get our land rights. Mum knew so many places, as she had travelled around with her father so much. She was number one daughter of the Gumatj clan. All the second daughters were taught by her. They had to sit down, listen to stories, cry milkarri.

Mum had the idea of doing milkarri at the Yolŋu Garma Festival. This was when Garma was starting in the late 1990s. It was small and run by the family then, without any buildings or electricity. Garma is about celebrating and sharing culture and is now one of the best-known Indigenous festivals in Australia. Mum used to cry milkarri, for the dawn, for the land. We would wake up listening to her crying milkarri, so beautiful. Mum then had the idea of making it an ongoing part of Garma. In Yolŋu Rom, when people come from a far Country we welcome them crying milkarri; that is respect, and with her guidance it has become a really important part of Garma. In 2003, when the Art Centre created the Gapan Gallery, an outdoor gallery showcasing the community's art, Gaymala keened milkarri to open it, welcoming people to Garma. We still do it today, opening the Gapan Gallery with milkarri and doing the dawn milkarri at every Garma Festival. But now people join in from different clans. Even young people are starting to do milkarri. Mum said when I am gone I want my sisters to carry the milkarri on, greeting the dawn. And we have carried this on, and it remains so beautiful.

When Mum passed away, the church service was full of people. Yolŋu and ŋäpaki, so many, we weren't expecting it.

Our mother, as she sang to us in hospital, sang that body of water, was that body of water, was the boat, was the whale travelling through time, travelling down towards the deep blue ocean and coming to a place where the other whales are playing and roaming. This was our mother. She is still our mother, singing of the whale, the open sea. Country is her and she is Country and so are our tears both then and now.

CHAPTER 3

Mapping

Bawaywuyŋu miyamara Dhuḻuḻwuyŋuru;
Bawaywuyŋu miyamara Rrawuḻwuḻwuyŋuru;
Ŋuruku miyaman ŋarra marrtji Rrawuḻwuḻwuyŋu.

Of the place between sunrise and sunset I sing,
Where the whales swim with open mouths, scooping
*   water, filtering fish;*
A pod of whales, flipping and jumping, playing and
*   roaming;*
A gathering of many people;
For that I sing towards Rrawuḻwuḻ, the place where
*   the whales are feeding.*
I sing for those people, the ones far away.

We sing of special places, particular places. Nothing is abstract
or general. Of the place between sunrise and sunset we sing,

of the way of Baway. The way of Baway is a place to the south of Yirrkala, between Groote Eylandt, an island in the Gulf of Carpentaria, and the mainland. It is a region between sunrise and sunset where there is nothing except the ocean. We talk of all of Arnhem Land, our Country, with care and attention. While Baway is the middle, Miwatj is the head and these are the people of the sunrise, and Yaŋara, in the middle of Arnhem Land, is the tail, the sunset.

The whales surface and play, circling, breaching. The whale hits the surface of the water with its tail. This is the path for the whale.

As we share with you about the place between sunrise and sunset, where the whales swim with open mouths, we are sharing a version of Wuymirri that Mum did at a funeral, for her grandson who passed away. She was the first Gutharra, because she was the eldest child. She has liya-ŋärra'mirr; this means knowledge inside the head, and Mum had that knowledge.

As Mum was doing milkarri for her grandson, it is he who is singing as he is paddling that journey. It is the paddler singing the song, but the paddler is looking through Mum's eyes and she is singing. She is the eyes of the paddler; it could be in the past or in the future, but it is also the grandson who has passed away, in spirit, so Mum is guiding him along. It is the perspective of the ancestral being.

We use first person and say, 'I am now seeing . . .' as it is more respectful. It does not impose the story on another person or assume anything of them. If we used second person, saying, 'You are seeing a whale', it would be less respectful, as it is telling someone what to do. To say 'I am seeing' invites others who understand and follow Yolŋu Law to sing the journey, to be that person too.

When a woman cries milkarri, everyone stops what they are doing. Milkarri is what is happening. The person listening to that milkarri can put their own father in that boat and visualise their father or sister or anyone who has passed away, paddling that journey. When it comes time for a person to pass away, they themselves will have already travelled that journey many times. They took the journey accompanying loved ones who had passed. Now it is their turn and others will accompany them.

When we sing, we are with them, we are part of it. We don't usually see our self but we see the land. Perhaps we are beside or underneath, or flying above them, accompanying them. We are in another dimension. The time is now, when we sing. We go to that dimension. It is the milkarri. The milkarri is so strong, we cry and sob, it takes the body, it transforms. The dead person is there, almost like a hologram, an avatar. It's that spirit's journey. We can see it in our mind, yet it is real. That is why people join in, why they cry: they can see it.

We sing whales swimming with their mouths open, scooping water, filtering fish. We have travelled with them, as them. Now we are part of a pod, flipping and jumping, playing and roaming, feeling the water on our skin. As we play, we know the places. We sing Dhawulwulyun, over there, where the whales or the manta rays are feeding, diving with their mouths open, going down. As we sing, we are connecting, remaking, and when we arrive at a place we sing towards the next place, connecting with it, remaking it. Forever.

The way of Dhawulwul, where the whales are feeding, where there is krill, where the clouds sit on the horizon. Rrawulwulyun is in the distance, far away where the people are. There are so many of them. So many people at that place, a group of people. We sing for those people, thinking of those people. The ones far away, visualising them.

At the same time Rrawulwulyun is also an action. The action of the whales when they open their mouths and filter the water to get the fish. The whales are there, flipping, jumping, playing and roaming on their journey. It is the water going into the air from the whale's spout that makes the cloud, the clouds on the horizon that show the whale's journey. Sometimes we paint the whale with triangles, the clouds on the horizon.

As we sing, as we cry milkarri, we tell a story. We tell of the contours of the land, the contours of ourselves. Songspirals are a map of Country. We are seeing Country as we fly over it. When we sing or hear milkarri, we fly. We see our self flying through the land, like a bird. We see our soul, sand, land, soil, the grass. The vision of the ground from above, the landscape we travel past; our mind is like Google Maps, we see all through the song.

When we do or hear milkarri, we travel through Country, the song takes us there. We see everything—the soil, the rocks, the leaves, the sea, bäru (the crocodile) making a nest, lightning, everything. The songspirals tell us where everything is, the best place to get fish, to get a spear, gara. They tell us where not to go and where best to go. They describe where the ganguri (yams) and other root crops are, where you can find fresh water, where you can find the kangaroo, the emu. Sometimes milkarri tells us where special areas are. This is the map they make for us, the map of Yolŋu people. Songspirals describe everything, so that you see it, you know where it is, you could go there and gather it. Songspirals are a route. Songspirals walk through the land. Songspirals tell you which is the shortest route, which is the longest, one place to another. Songspirals weave Country together. Songspirals are our foundation.

That's how Yolŋu people see things. That's what we learn when we are children. We learn this map. Instead of driving across the landscape, we learn from walking and telling stories: mums, uncles telling us 'this area is Yirritja', 'this area is Dhuwa'. All across Arnhem Land we learn what is Yirritja and what is Dhuwa. The songspirals teach us this. Our Elders teach us this. We have to walk with the map in our head. We are mapping the land. With the song, it gets us to the place we go.

Women learn by crying milkarri. When we cry our milkarri we are singing the map. We are singing about the dangers, the goodness on the land, what we will find, how we are going to find it, how we are going to survive. The manikay, the ceremonial singing, with the contributions of women and men; the buŋgul, the ceremonial dancing; the ochre body painting, its design; the yidaki; the bilma—they all have to be right. The women's tremulous voices keening the words, the men with their lower-pitched singing, the richness of sound and movement and emotion, the rising dust and sand, the vibrations through the air, the beings of Country coming together as one. This is the land that is never shown to the rest of Australia. We are sharing a layer of this with you through the milkarri in this book. It is in the milkarri, in the bilma, in the movement of the dancing. It is all a map for Dhuwa and Yirritja.

Songspirals are a bit like a Yolŋu GPS; well-trained people use them. When we are lost somewhere we will follow the stars. We will follow the stars and also we will follow the wind. If we are lost somewhere in the bush, if we see leaves blowing from the east, it could be telling us that we are in this area and that our family is this way. Without the songspirals we couldn't know Country. That's why ancestors gave us everything for our survival. Like the fire—when we see the fire we know where we are going. As we will share with you later, the fire guides us.

That's why it's important that we are sharing the stories in this book. It's already written through our blood. Our ancestors recorded everything through the songspirals.

That's why we have to learn. Songspirals are a university for us. They are a map of understandings. We have to learn how to walk on the land. Sometimes the songspirals tell us to avoid an area where we have no authority to walk on that land; this might be to protect us from danger or sickness. That's why Elders say to always be aware and learn the map through the songspirals before we journey through those woods, those rocks. We need to understand Country for our own safety.

When we're painting the songspirals, on our bodies or on bark, canvas or screenprints, we have to make sure we put the animals in exactly the same area, the same way we sing it. If a place is in the north, we put it in the north; if an event happens in the east, we put it in the east. The art is a map that tells new generations where the sacred areas are, where the riŋgitj (sacred place or embassy) is that belongs to that area. Part of our learning is to paint the songspirals the right way. The paintings are a picture of the songspiral, a map of Country in a deep and spiritual way.

When women keen milkarri, we are telling the story, we think back to our family, what we've done. We keen milkarri about the spirit, about the soul, about seeing our children and the land, about tens of thousands of years, about hundreds of thousands of years, about forever. We see the spirits; they are still here. So the songspiral is the journey of all animals, spirit beings, that passed through a place. And it is a journey that connects people and places. Mum's song, Wuymirri, is a long songspiral that goes to Papua New Guinea and into the Pacific, to Fiji and beyond. Every place shares things with other places through the connections of the songspirals, but the combination of beings that pass through any one place at any one time is always unique.

Mum lived with her grandmother, her märi, on the Wessel Islands when she was small. She travelled around a lot with her mother and father in the canoe. She went from place to place, hunting and gathering, with her parents, moving around. That is how she learnt so much. Her father would tell her, 'This is the place and this is the song that belongs here', singing to her, telling her who the place belongs to. She didn't only know the surface name of the place but the deep name of the place too. That's why she knew every place, every Country around here. She travelled around until she was about twelve and then she went back to the mission at Yirrkala. The Methodists had established a mission at Yirrkala in the 1930s, drawing the clans from nearby areas into the mission.

In the mission days, things were different. If she went to school at all, it would have been just a week or two of a religious school and then they'd go off again in the canoe, paddling. Just her, her mum and dad, her brothers and sisters. She had four sisters, including Djerrkŋu, who helped sing this Wuymirri here. She had one brother, and also brothers and sisters from other mothers. Her father had four wives. The amazing part is that he kept them all together. That is unusual, that is how strong he was. They were a big family then. Her father's sons include M. Yunupiŋu and G. Yunupiŋu, famous men. They have the same father but different mothers, all Gälpu mothers.

We wonder how they all fitted in the canoe. In a book by anthropologist Donald Thomson he describes how he saw the family pack up and go together like an army. That is what made us so close together and what keeps us strong now. We sisters always look after all the mothers, as there aren't many left. We bring them mud mussels and other foods when we go hunting.

It is one of the rarest things we've seen, a man with so many wives keeping them all together. We say that's why we're here, because of our grandmother and grandfather, because they had so many skills. Our grandfather always had time to sit down and tell stories to the grandchildren. And he loved dogs. We had hundreds of dogs following the family.

Mum's marriage was a promised marriage and she went to Rorruwuy, a long way to the west of Yirrkala, to be with her husband. She had us five girls and one son. Mum also raised Witiyana, her sister Djerrkŋu's son, as well as Guluwu and Gärŋarr. Witiyana is so strong and has now travelled the world. That is what happens. If you don't have children, or your children have grown up and are no longer in the house, you raise others. It is the same rule now. She had to raise one son so the son would carry on the songspirals, the stories. Mum and Dad then separated. My grandfather was worried about us and sent a message to Mum to come to Yirrkala. Mum decided it was time to go, so we walked together across Arnhem Land to get there. She wanted us to get an education.

Mum died first, on 10 March 2005, and Dad died soon after, on 2 April 2005. Their coffins were together in the morgue. She'd said to him, 'You have other wives, but when we die we will be together.' She knew! Mum is the first child from her father, she had all that knowledge, so she had to be buried back in her home and is laid to rest at Gurrumiya near Dhanaya, across the bay from Bawaka. One of Gaymala's names is Gurrumiya. Her name was on that land, Gurrumiya, a land of the great chiefs, the ancestral Gumatj chiefs. The four chiefs, the four leaders of that area, the ancestors of modern-day Gumatj: Gätjiŋ, Daymbawi, Garrandhalu, Gurrmulŋa. This shows her specialness, because one of her names was that land. It meant respect and honour to bury her back in that place of chiefs, the ancestors of all Gumatj people.

CHAPTER 4

Becoming together

Nhinana ŋarra Rrawuḻwuḻwuyun mala maypa.
Aa'a—Dhuḻuḻŋura Balwarri, Balwarri,
Nepaway, Baway'yu miyaman ŋunha marrtji
  Dhaŋgala.

I sit comfortably, feed comfortably as part of a big
  pod, filtering food, sifting the water through my
  mouth, one among many whales.
Oh, dear whales, whales, the open sea, between
  sunrise and sunset, singing of that place over there,
  eastward, always to the horizon.
I sing towards Dhaŋgala, I see myself, standing tall
  and straight like the mast of my boat, a flag, my
  journey, Dhaŋgala.

Mum keens the Whale sitting comfortably, feeding comfortably as part of a pod. Mum keens the paddler and also the ancient Macassan boat. The paddler is the tail of the whale, paddling beneath the sea. These are the deep layers. As she evokes the mast of the boat, she becomes someone standing as she travels through the rough seas and calm waters, her journey. She controls the water, the boat, she becomes a captain for herself to navigate the sea.

It all comes back to the language, songspiral language. The language must be right, as the songspiral must be on the right track, everything must be right, you must do what our ancestors have learnt and taught. Our mother singing, she is so knowledgeable, a doctor with the deep and complex meanings. She can sing through the tears of milkarri, with one thousand meanings in one. There are so many layers. She is singing about the boat, she is singing about the whale beneath the boat, she is singing the places, she is singing about herself on the boat, navigating the sea, catching them, all in one. It is like a picture, a puzzle, she is putting everything in the right place—the right smell, the right sound; nothing wrong can go there. She has been there and then she comes back and tells us.

Mum is telling her journey, she is talking about her deep feelings. She knows where to go. She knows the songspirals. She knows all the areas. Some words of the songspirals are too deep. Only the old ones know, or the ones who have had a near-death experience, they know. In the hospital, Mum had gone on a journey. She knew she wanted to come back. She had to hear the songspiral.

Our songspirals are not written songs. The names we cry in the songspirals are not written names. We share here not to capture the knowledge or to try to set it in stone. The songspirals, the words of the milkarri, mean lots of things. The beings within them created the land, created the people that are creating that land. And they created the songspirals, the words of the milkarri, the paintings and designs for the people, and even created a structure for how to start the songspirals and how to end them. Yirritja clans always finish with the sunset; Dhuwa clans finish with the wind. All songspirals have their own structure and Law.

The paddler now thinks like a whale, is already a whale, one of the whales, one among many whales, observing how many there are. The paddler is sitting in the boat looking at the many whales feeding, before her, in front of him, in front of us. The paddler is the tail of the whale, like a mast on the boat but beneath the sea. It is another dimension. How you sing, that is you yourself. You are the boat. You become the boat, with that mast. You are the song.

Songspirals are maps, but they are more than maps too. They are about how a person and a clan connect and relate with and as Country, how people and Country are always emerging in relationship with each other. Everything within Country is alive and sentient and people are part of this vibrance. So the songspirals, which bring Country into existence, are deeply connected to people. It is a profoundly deep connection, much more than a lifestyle.

That is why women sing milkarri. People and Country express each other. Yolŋu keep Country alive with language. As Merrkiyawuy's husband Will says, the land grew a tongue and that tongue is the Yolŋu people. As we dance, we make sounds to make Country alive, so it has a tongue, ŋänarr. And not just the sound but the actions of the dance too, the deep meaning of the names, the soul of people and the land.

Gaymala Yunupiŋu, *Nyuŋula* (1996). *(The Buku-Larrŋgay Mulka Art Centre archives)*

Why did the earth put human beings on the land? It is to do with communication. Yolŋu communicate with the birds and the whales and everything else. Everything communicates and comes through the songspirals. The sounds that human beings make in the songspirals are the sounds that animals make. The names of the animals are the sounds they make. The wallaby is dhum'thum', as their tail and feet hit the ground, the dove is gukuk, the koel bird is guwak—each name is the sound that the animal makes. Their sound is them singing.

The sound of the waves through the songs is whaaa—hear the waves? This is what we are hearing now. When the song is of that particular animal, that is the sound that we make. We express the sound of the animal. Shark people, that's us sisters. Sharks are dangerous, so are crocodiles. So when we're singing sharks or crocodiles, the tempo, the mood, the action of the dance, it changes. The sound of the singing changes depending on the animal.

This communication between animals, between land, animals and people, between the tide, the sun and the moon, is about giving and receiving messages, about the seasons, about the weather, about people's and Country's safety and wellbeing. April is time for harvesting—fruits and ganguri, yams. The season tells us when we should be hunting something, gathering something, eating something. It is the sweat we feel in a hot season that links us to the fruits that ripen on the tree and the sand that burns the soles of our feet. Knowledge is created in that burning and it speaks to us as we walk quickly to the shade. It is the things we do in each season and the different things that all beings do, the warmth and coolness, and the memories of seasons past and still to come. Women keen milkarri for this. Sometimes women keen milkarri for the beginning of the new day, the birds that sing. They keen milkarri for the first rays of the sun coming out to greet the day. Every season is greeted with a song. Women keen milkarri when it is close to Christmas and we hear the thunder. We think about the loved ones who have gone before us.

We hear the napalawal, the pigeon, calling now. Napalawal talks to people. If napalawal is by the river, it tells us the tides are going in or out. If napalawal is in the bush, it tells us where the ganguri is. Napalawal talks to the people.

41

That is the communication between people and animals, the signals. Country, whales, everything that they do has meaning. Sometimes when someone passes away an animal might come and tell people what has happened by their actions. If we see a shark or a dolphin jumping, we know someone has passed away. It is a message the land itself gives to people. The dolphin or shark just know.

Our daughter Djawundil remembers when she got stuck on an island and couldn't use her left arm because of a recent operation. She was on the island in the middle of Port Bradshaw, a place called Djulpan. Bawi, our eldest son's son, and the boys were on a boat and they saw Djawundil but they couldn't get the engine working to go and get her. Luckily the tide was going out. So Djawundil sat down, thinking, 'What am I going to do?' With the tide going out she decided she could swim across to the boat and started going into the water. But Bawi said, 'You stop right there. I'll try and throw the anchor to you and pull you in.' But bäyŋu, nothing, the rope couldn't reach Djawundil. So Djawundil decided to swim and as she was getting down into the water she could see three rocks, like steps . . . one, two, three. In her left hand she had a packet of ŋarali' (smokes), in her right hand a sharp knife. But before she tried to swim to the boat, a little hawksbill turtle, malarrka, came towards her. The tide was all smooth with a slimy brown foam on top of the water. The mayawutjiri (foam), comes from the coral with a barrpa (rotten smell)—that's what the water was like. And on top of the water there was a turtle swimming towards Djawundil. Djawundil saw the turtle coming towards her and she picked it up and showed it to Bawi. She then let it go, and although there are sharks and crocodiles and everything in the water, she said, 'Okay, I'm going to swim while you throw the anchor to me.' Holding up her left arm and swimming with her other arm she nearly drowned halfway to the boat. But Bawi jumped out of the boat to get her and Djawundil threw the ŋarali' into the boat and Bawi got her.

The turtle swam towards Djawundil to say, 'It's going to be okay.' Things like that happen. The brown, slimy foam on the ocean is the totem, significant being, for the Warramirri clan, seafarers from the Wessel Islands. Djawundil's great-grand-mother's mother, Bamatja, was Warramirri, and mayawutjiri represents her clan. It comes out from the coral and it represents where the Warramirri come from, from the ocean, from underneath the water. Bamatja said the Warramirri knew the oceans, they used to paddle as far as they could. Mum told us that when they arrived on the mainland they used to have long beards and long hair because they were from the Wessel Islands. Bamatja came and married a mainland man and that's why we exist now. Otherwise we'd be out in the islands still.

When we see mayawutjiri we think about the whales down in the ocean. So when Djawundil saw the mayawutjiri and saw the turtle, she thought, 'That's my sister clan looking after me.' Because Bamatja is Djawundil's great-great-grandmother's mother, through the cyclical patterns of gurruṯu, this makes her Djawundil's sister. Afterwards Djawundil rested and then, because the sun was setting, walked all the way back to Bawaka.

Humans are deeply connected to songspirals but songspirals are beyond humans too. The whale, the guwak (koel bird), they have songspirals. So do the wind and the sand. It is all in Country, the songspirals, more than we can know. Animals, plants and other beings have understandings through each other, such as from whales to turtles to birds, to anything that makes a sound; any living thing that makes a sound communicates with each other. They have that knowledge, their own laws.

They sing to us too. Animals, plants, trees—in the morning they give the wake-up call. When you hear that bird, they are singing the songspirals into existence. And in our songspirals we sing with the bird, about that bird, we sing it. We sing mists, we sing spiders, making their web. Humans sing the spiders and birds sing along with each. Birds sing early in the morning, *gork gork gork*, the napalawal sitting on a branch, gathering food. Napalawal eating fruits, gathering fruits for their children. The winds too. They sing and we sing the winds; the songs talk about how soft the wind is, where it's coming from, what time of year it is, what food we can collect. Yes, the trees they sing too. That is in the songs too. We listen to the djomula trees, the casuarina. Songspirals make things live.

When we sing or dance a particular animal, the animal and the person become one. The feeling is to become one. It's powerful.

We can feel mädirriny now, the breeze, the south wind blowing. It is May. It is nearly the cold season, the weather is starting to change. It is halfway round the cycle. We dance mädirriny, move our arms across so it is the wind. Soon it will be cold. We sing milkarri for the seasons, we cry milkarri for the weather. Mädirriny blows, bringing rain, putting the grass to sleep. This wind, mädirriny, makes Country ready for burning off.

The whale heads east, to where the sun rises. The whales always come back eventually, whether they are alive or dead. If the tail is chopped off, they float here. That is what the current tells them to do. They float back to this land.

CHAPTER 5

Harmonising

Ŋuruku ŋarra miyaman Ŋulpurrwuyŋu,
Dhululwuyŋu, Balwarriwuyŋu, ŋeee—mitji maypa
   Balwarri.

For that I am singing Ŋulpurrwuyŋu;
I sing of the body of water.
Dhululwuyŋu, Balwarriwuyŋu, a place of many
   whales;
Yes, a clan, a pod of many whales.

Songspirals are about a person, but you can only understand
that person through Country, as Country. Songspirals bring
Country into existence, songspirals bring people into existence. We can only understand people through Country, as
Country. Songspirals are not just about hunting and looking
at the water, they are about walking, feeling the sand, feeling

the heat. Songspirals describe that person in a different way. That person is sitting down, looking, seeing dolphins jumping out of the water, seeing the tide coming in and out. We keen milkarri for the smell of the water, the salt spray on their body, we sing that too. And we dance it. When we dance the rain, we are the hands of the rain, we pat our hands down in a particular way, singing about how it is raining, how we are walking through the bush looking for a shelter. As we talk about and write this, the rain comes. We have to move our notebooks, we have to talk about mädirriny (the south wind) and the season. The songspirals, the rain, being wet, us, we become one.

That is what the songspirals are about, telling a story of that person. It might be about honouring someone who is still alive, someone who is sick or has gone away, or someone who has passed. When we sing milkarri, it is mixed with emotions, memories, all the things of that land, at that place. We cry milkarri touching the water, smelling the season, feeling the wind, doing things, hearing the laughter. To sing and keen, you have to know that place in your head and heart. You must sing about that place. When we are keening, we are travelling there, in our soul, our spirit. We are thinking about where that person has been. We know that person was a good hunter, a good gatherer, a good mother, a good grandmother.

Songspirals are who a person is, who the land is. They are describing the person and the land as one. Instead of mentioning the name of the person, we sing milkarri for animals, clouds, rocks, trees. We do this instead of using someone's name. The person is there, looking at those things. We evoke the person. Yolŋu people are named after a particular rock or a tree or soil, a place, a current, a sound, every element that we know.

If we know where we stand and belong, we have the roots to support ourselves and we have the pride of who we are and where we come from. The songspirals are the root, the people are the tree. The songspirals are our backbone, our grandmother clan. That's why when we have funerals, people come from all over, from Ramingining in the west, from Elcho Island in the north. It's because we have these connections.

Our connections are to the land and to the sea too. Sea is part of Country. We call this Sea Country. We belong to the sea and the sea belong to us, just as with the land. We don't see any clear distinction between land and sea, rivers and mangroves, earth and sky; they are all connected through relationships. That is the basis of our authority, our land rights and sea rights. One time we sat down and mapped our connections through the songspirals right into and through the Arafura Sea. We wanted to tell ŋäpaki about this, and that became the basis of our Sea Country native title case, which we won in 2008. We sat down and did the djäma, the work. So the whales and the knowledge are linked to Sea Country rights.

Mum sings of the body of water. She sings of the places, of the clans, of the whales. She is singing her grandmother clan, her märi-pulu, the Warramirri of the Wessel Islands. The language of her märi-pulu is Djaŋu. Dharrpawuy, our granddaughter, who Banbapuy is bringing up, she has a grandmother who is Warramirri too.

Merrkiyawuy, the third sister of us four, took two of her children, our children, her son Bambuŋ and daughter Mayutu, to the Wessel Islands to show them where they came from, so they could know their sister clan area. It was an adventure like in the movies. It was the land of the whales, whales everywhere in the water. It's a long way and isolated from the mainland.

You go into the islands through a gap between two cliffs, through a hole, a channel. Yolŋu went to the islands during the Second World War after Milingimbi in central Arnhem Land was bombed. Because the invasive and poisonous cane toads aren't on the islands, they also moved quolls, small carnivorous marsupials, there to protect the quolls from the toads. The Warramirri aren't living on the Wessel Islands anymore. When the old man, Burrumarra, Djamu's father, passed away and there was no leader, they broke away and are living on the mainland now.

In the songspirals about the Wessel Islands they sing a tree, and Merrkiyawuy, Bambuŋ and Mayutu saw the tree! A big giant shade tree in the field. So massive, it's been standing there for thousands of years. And when you arrive on the island, the first thing you see is the big shade tree standing there on its own. That is where the Warramirri used to sit. When you sit under that tree the wind comes, the wind comes from the tree.

The whales head towards the depths of the ocean, east towards Djayba (the islands of Saibai), to the people from where the rain comes. The whales breathe, they spout, with the misty water vapour spraying up, fanning out. The waterspout turns into a cloud and it rises above the horizon and becomes the cloud Wulpundu.

The whales head out to the Arafura Sea and the Pacific Ocean. The whales don't have a limit. They are whales. We have limits. When two waters meet, that is our boundary. But the whales, they go. Everywhere in Melanesia, in Polynesia, throughout the Pacific, the people have whales too, as a totem. The whales are important even if the names are different. We respect that.

When Mum is singing Wuymirri, she is on the boat, on the sea, in the sea. She sees the pod of whales. She is there. She surfaces, she repressurises. She releases vapour from her waterspout. She makes the little clouds above the water's edge. The vapour is released and it is a meeting of heaven and earth.

She sings what she sees on the journey, what a person would see as they look back to Country. She is singing her grandson who has passed away. And she is singing Country, because songspirals are about a person but you can only understand that person through Country, as Country.

Every Yolŋu is a singer, a painter. We need to find it within ourself. It is there. A dancer, a song maker, a teacher, a peacemaker. Everything has to be about peace and harmony. We have to find it by practising with our heart, our soul, our mind. We don't learn or acquire the song from outside but we find it within ourself so that our thoughts reflect and harmonise with Country. Our knowledge harmonises with our song, it resonates. It resonates with Country.

Yolŋu can start to sing at any age. There was a boy at the Buku Art Centre, he was singing at three years of age. We have to find it in ourself. Yolŋu are encouraged to find it. We know our own melody. We can do it if we want to. We join in the ceremonies. We sit down in the ceremony. We start dancing.

There is so much to remember, we pick one or two words each time and learn that way. Sometimes we ask older people. Then the songspiral comes around again and we learn it again. So we collect it, like collecting a word from a dictionary. Sometimes we can ask a person what it means. As a baby we listen, then we ask, building up our vocabulary, picking up the tunes. We know which is our mothers' tune, our grandmothers', which is our backbone, which our great-grandmothers'. Our daughters are starting to learn through listening. It builds up, the words and the tune.

We keep doing milkarri and it's like singing in tears. Singing their part of the manikay, sometimes the men shed tears, sometimes they may even start to milkarri for a short time, but they pull themselves back. We use deep language in milkarri and when we hear a young woman trying to do milkarri we say, 'Wow, you were doing milkarri. Good, you are giving something back.' It is respect and honour, respecting and honouring that person and respecting and honouring the land. This is your harmony.

It's a good thing but it is hard to do in public. It's very hard if you want to do milkarri correctly. Liya-manikaymirri is the Gumatj term for 'knowledge of the song'. You are displaying your knowledge in a public place. Nowadays, younger women don't want to be shamed. The words are so powerful and they are worried they will get them wrong. One name has many meanings. One name can be used for many concepts. Even though it is very hard, it's very important for women and young women to do milkarri. We want to support the younger women.

Mum was a single mum, growing up five, six, seven, eight children, and lots of other children would come over. She raised many people, very talented people. She would look after her children, her grandchildren, making sure there was food in the house, making sure they were sleeping, making sure that they were safe. Mum was very strict, there were clear routines. To be a good mother and grandmother, you have to do things that way.

We used to live in a tin shack when we were little. All we had for lighting was kerosene and candles. Every month, at the full moon, we would get new sand for the floor to make it smell better. We didn't have mattresses, just sand and blankets. We would make a pillow from sand. Inside, there was a fire. Mum taught Banbapuy Yolŋu matha here, with a kerosene light, writing it on the sand. Saying it, putting it into sentences. So Banbapuy's first language was her mother tongue, Gumatj, before English.

Mum cleaned houses for the missionaries. She made us dive into the river to get the pound coins Yolŋu would throw in there as they didn't know it was money. On Sundays we would go to the Sunday school and she would go to church. To help Mum relax, we would make her a cup of tea.

Mum was pregnant when she left Rorruwuy, and Banbapuy was born in Yirrkala. Banbapuy's dad never saw her as a baby and she didn't know her father until she graduated from the first year of her teaching qualification from Batchelor College. He came to Yirrkala and they slowly rebuilt the relationship that was lost to them.

We sisters, including Banbapuy, the youngest, were raised by Roy Marika MBE, a Rirratjiŋu leader, the clan of the land on which Yirrkala sits. He is known as the father of land rights due to his leadership in the struggle against mining and the land rights movement that followed. Banbapuy spent a lot of days sitting down with Roy Marika, in his office, listening when he had meetings. One time, a ŋäpaki man who worked with

Roy said, 'Your daughter has to be at school.' And Roy said, 'She is at school. She is sitting down, listening to the future.'

Another time, Banbapuy and a friend were speaking Yolŋu matha in the classroom, which was not allowed. The teacher made them stay behind and write lines saying, 'We are not allowed to speak Yolŋu matha.' Roy came and knocked on the door. The sun was going down. He said, 'Where is my daughter? Why is she kept back?' He went over, took away the pencil, took Banbapuy by the hand and said, 'She is allowed to speak her own language.'

In the 1970s, the first legal case for land rights in Australia was heard when Roy and his brothers led the land rights case against the mining company Nabalco. This laid the ground work for future land rights cases and became part of the broader land rights struggle. It also led to the birth of the homelands movement, in which Aboriginal people moved away from missions and towns back to their Country. We moved out of Yirrkala to the homeland at Guluruŋa, where Dad's, Roy Marika's, homeland was. That is where we all grew up. Our grandfather moved with us, as well as our grandfather's cousin from Groote Eylandt, Nanuŋutu. We went to school in Yirrkala once in a while, when there was a ceremony or we went shopping. We loved those days in a way. It was a challenge, it showed us what to do. Life was a challenge.

As Mum nears her final destination, crossing the calm, mercurial waters towards the horizon, she travels with her grandmother clan, her märi-pulu, her backbone. To Banbapuy in hospital, she says that she paddles with her grandmother, following the sea breeze to finish her journey.

The whale will pass by, this is her path. As she travels and plays, she breathes, sprays air and water from her spout. The water vapour forms a cloud on the horizon. Many can see the cloud. The people from where the rain comes from will see it. The spirits will see it. The hunters will see it too. The cloud on the horizon, formed by the waterspout of the whale.

The hunter will make the harpoon straight and ready. The hunter has seen the cloud rising on the horizon, the cloud called Marawalkarra. The hunters see it and then they push their canoe, prepare their djambatj (harpoon). They know the whale, they know the signs.

And when Wuymuyu, the hunter, has speared the whale, he takes her back to the land, the islands, home, where she will be cut. The whale is cut open, prepared in careful sections and then they dance and then they celebrate, they shout for happiness. And they share her with others, other groups, because this is our Rom, our Law. When Yolŋu get something big, we share.

When the hunters come and cut her up, that is the end of the journey for Mum. That is her, that is the whale. When the hunters come, they will cut her up, together with her grandmother. That part is very sacred to Mum and to her grandmother, to us. The story is not only about the human, but the whale as well. Mum becoming the whale is the end of her life, the end of the whale.

After Mum sang the song to Banbapuy in the hospital, she left the hospital and we took her to the beach. She wanted to go to the beach, to go to the salt water. When she was down at the beach, a rainbow suddenly appeared. Laklak was there;

we saw them and thought, ahhh, the eldest daughter of the eldest daughter, mother and child together.

Mum wanted to feel the water and the sand. This was her last day. We put her in the water. She wanted to go down to the water, to feel it, to drink the salt water as the whale. Like when you see the whale open its mouth, she did the same.

The water around her, it went smooth, glassy, gunbilk. You could see the effect on the water, making it smooth around where she stood. And then the smoothness spread out, just like the smoothness left in their wake as the turtle, the dugong and the whale move through the water. You could see that calm, glassy patch growing, extending, ranging. It sent the message out. The whale was there. That is why she wanted to go to the water, so she could feel it. She was expressing the whale. From the beach we took her to Ritjilili's place.

After, back in the house, Mum got up to crawl out of bed to the kitchen. Rrawun and Bambuŋ, two of our sons, found her just in time and they lifted her up and put her in the bed. They were crawling on the floor, like an octopus together. By her actions she told our sons she was going. She was dancing, crawling, like the octopus does.

Mum was becoming the octopus, ŋarrpiya. She was going back to the cave, underneath, the deeper level, the foundation. When someone passes away, when they are taken to the mortuary or buried, always the märi-pulu sings the octopus. They sing the octopus as she goes back into the cave, back into the djoru warrpididi (the home of the octopus), their foundation.

Rrawu<u>n</u> and Bambuŋ wrote a song for their märi, their grandmother, and her märi-pulu, Warramirri, as she travels to the ocean. They were thinking about the ocean floor and how the mud can really hide the octopus. And even though the octopus is hidden by the mud, it still has its colours. We know what the octopus are like when they come out, who they are, their beauty, their true colours. That is what we were taught; it's not the outside of what we do that is important, but the inside, what a person can do. Rrawu<u>n</u> and Bambuŋ sing it with their rock band, East Journey. Their song is called 'Ŋarrpiya (Octopus)'.

Ŋarrpiya (Octopus)

Written by Bambuŋ and Rrawu<u>n</u>

My home so far away
Follow me to the deep blue sea
Follow me to the deep blue sea
I can see the sunset changing colours like ŋarrpiya
I can see the sunset changing colours

Deep ocean floor where the foundation lays, home of ŋarrpiya
Changing colours beneath the sea, home of ŋarrpiya

Datj datj [ŋarrpiya crawling]
Datj datj

My heart goes on to the deep blue sea
My heart goes on to the deep blue sea
I can see her face, smiling at me
I can feel her embrace, lifting me

Deep ocean floor where the foundation lays, home of ŋarrpiya
Changing colours beneath the sea lies ŋarrpiya

Dhawattjun ŋarrpiya djoruŋa [Octopus coming out of its home/
   cave]
Warrpididiŋa miny'tjim djambi [Out from the corals with its
   colours changing]
Nyalanyalayŋa garrumara Bangararri [Out of the clay bed
   of the ocean, from the depths of the ocean floor]
Marpululmi diwarrmi djapana. [With its colour it comes out,
   it stands out because of the colour like the sunset.]

Deep ocean floor where the foundation lays, home of ŋarrpiya
Changing colours beneath the sea, lies ŋarrpiya
Deep ocean floor where the foundation lays, home of ŋarrpiya
Changing colours beneath the sea, lies ŋarrpiya

Ooooooh.

Changing colours.

We didn't want to let Mum go. She said to Banbapuy, 'You have to let me go.' She was waiting for Banbapuy to say yes. When she went into the water and it turned gunbilk she was telling us, in a different way, what was happening. When the turtle is cut up the water goes gunbilk. Mum was telling us, giving us the message, the time had come for her and the whale to be cut up. On the morning of 10 March, she went.

Understanding this has made us stronger, understanding the past.

Often we cry. We keen milkarri. Her memories are still here.

Gumatj and Warramirri versions

Mum's younger sister Djerrkŋu also shared with us the whale songspiral. She keened milkarri in Gumatj and Warramirri. There is not just one Yolŋu matha but different clan languages. Our clan languages are part of our heritage, our diversity. Language is not one piece. Language is who you are. It has its own place. It belongs to that place. It is not muddled. It belongs in its place, not all over the area.

Our own language is in the songspirals, the clan language, the real language. The songs keep the real language alive. Songs are very, very important as they hold the key to each clan language.

As Wuymirri is Yirritja, the Gumatj clan sings it and the Warramirri clan sings it. It has the same beginning in both versions. The songspiral stays the same but the language is different. Some words are different but the songspiral never changes; the places are the same, the passage of the whale, how it journeys to the islands and from which area, all stay the same. It is the same journey towards the same ending.

Wuymirri (Gumatj version)

Durryuna nhina Mirrinyu Makuma, Gandariya,
   Bilali.
The whales surfacing at Makuma, Gandariya, Bilali.

Yeee durryun nhina wutthun bilayu dhäwuykthun,
*Yes, surfacing and hitting the water with their tail,
   coming up with their mouth open;*

Nhina durryun Mirrinyu bayma Bilali, Makuma,
   Gandariya.
*Surfacing, playing, circling, spraying water from her
   spout, right here at Bilali, Makuma, Gandariya.*

Dhäwuykthurrana Miyapunu yeee Mirrinyu ŋunha
   marrtji.
*I can see the whales, Mirrinyu, with their mouth
   open, over there.*

Yeee Mirrinyu ŋunha marrtji durryuna dhawuykthuna
   dhäwulwulyun, yeeee,
*Yes, the whales are surfacing, coming up to the surface
   and spraying, with mouths open, scooping along
   the surface, yes,*

Durryun ŋunha marrtji yäää, Miyapunu, dhäwulwulyun Bilali wutthurruna Makuma, Gandariya,
*Surfacing over there, yaaa, the whales are scooping
   along the surface of the water at Bilali with their
   mouths open, hitting the surface of the ocean water
   at Makuma, Gandariya,*

Yeee l̲iyanydja l̲urryun dhäwul̲wul̲yun yolkala
    Matjinydjiwala L̲iya-bal̲kurrkgala.
Yes, the head, the mouth open, going deep into the
    ocean towards the island where the rain comes
    from, to the turtle hunter who hunts even when
    it rains and the sea is rough.

L̲iyayu miyamara runurunu Bandawiŋu, Bandayŋaŋu,
    Dhakalŋa.
With this knowledge, this harmony, I sing towards the
    islands Bandawiŋu, Bandayŋaŋu, Dhakalŋa.

Yeee mirrara ŋunha marrtji Mirrinyu dhäwul̲wul̲yun.
The whale, she is diving, mouth open, sinking down
    into the depths of the ocean, we can only see her
    back, her tail.

Maŋan nherrara ga̲nawirra dhäwuyunydja ga̲nawirra
    maŋana; Wul̲punduna, Balalŋuna.
The clouds stand there, the spray of the whale creates
    the clouds;
The whale thinks, I have made those clouds, I have
    created the Wul̲punduna, Balalŋuna, the clouds
    sitting on the water in the far distance, on the
    horizon.

Dhäwuykthun ŋunha marrtji d̲urryun, gaŋgatjin
    mikantha.
The whales breathe, they spout, spray as they rise to
    the surface;
She breaches, lifting her heavy body out of the water
    with her power.

Miyapunu Mirrinyu, Mirrinyu, Burarrwaŋa,
  Burarrwutwutthun.
The whale, the powerful whale Burarrwaŋa, Mirrinyu,
  lifts herself out of the water, her body hits the
  surface of the ocean.

Ŋunha marrtji yolnha Matjitjina Liya-balkurrnha
  nhäŋala maŋan durryunara yolthu Liya-balkurrkthu
  Matjitjiyu, Djambatjŋuyu Mirrinyu ŋunha marrtji
  durryun dhawulwulyun.
She hits the surface of the ocean with her tail at
  Matjitjina, the big water, a long way out in the
  deep ocean, next to the turtle hunters, Matjitji,
  Djambatjŋu; the turtle hunters see the cloud from
  far away. The cloud rises up to the horizon. There,
  the whales rise up to the surface and come with
  their mouths open, then sink down again.

Ganarrana wäŋa Makuma, Gandariyaŋu yolpa, mala
  Wulmurrkpa, Binyalinypa, yeee gilitjinana dhawal
  yolkala Bandawi, Banbayŋa, Dhakalŋa Liya-
  balkurrna Matjinytjina Wurrumila.
I, the whale, am leaving the place Makuma,
  Gandariyaŋu, behind, the land of the clan
  Wulmurrkpa, Binyalinypa, yes. I know I am
  getting close to the islands of Bandawi, Banbayŋa,
  Dhakalŋa, where the rain comes from, and to the
  hunter.

Liya-balkurrna, Djambatjŋunha Birrnyali wa nhäŋala
  dhärrana maŋanha yakarrmara lany'tjun ŋunha
  yukarra mokuy Rranyirranyi, Newunba, Marrwala

Melkuŋala Muthiḻa Marrwala Melkuŋala ḻiyanydja
Maŋanmirri Wuḻpundumirri.

I see the hunter, there he stands; with his arms
outstretched he holds the paddle and in his mind
is the cloud that he saw on the horizon.

The turtle hunter, standing, being the cloud with the
paddle, Muthiḻa Marrwala, full of knowledge and
recognition.

Yarr yarr yurra gunbilk marrawuḻwuḻ, djambi dhoru
warpiḏiḏi, dhäwalnydja dhuwala marra-wurrtjara.

Go water, take your smooth self as far as you can
see, the water glistening from our being; the coral
spawns, lifting up; the sea is glassy and calm.

Nhäŋala mokuyu Rranyirranyiyu dhawuywu Bilali,
Makumaŋu, Gandariyaŋu ḏurruna ŋunha marrtji
Mirrinyu dhawuykthun Mirrinyu ḻiyanydja
Bandawiyu.

The spirit Rranyirranyi sees it from the land, the
waterspout at Bilali, Makuma, Gandariya, that
water, that ocean. The whales rise again and
surface, their heads turning around, mouths open,
moving towards, thinking of that place, travelling
towards Bandawiyu.

Dhakalŋayu, Ŋarrayarriyu, Nalkumayu ḏurryurrna
Burarrwaŋa, Burarrwuṯwuṯthun ŋunha marrtji.
Yeee, Djaybayu maŋan nherrara Djarrpiŋu, Wuḻpundu.
Maŋan nherrara Wuḻpundu.

At the islands of Dhakalŋa, Ŋarrayarri, Nalkuma
the whale is surfacing above the water;

61

she lifts and hits the ocean water with her tail,
her body.
Yes. *The clouds over there at Djayba, they come*
together (at the Saibai Islands) far to the east, the
distant unknown ocean of the Wuymu, Nyewunba,
Bäpa'yili people. I can see the cloud, it is slanting
up like someone holding up the paddle, the slanting
cloud called Djarrpiŋu, Wulpundu, the clouds on
the horizon, the Wulpundu cloud.

Balalŋu, Gaṉawirra ḻanytjurruna maŋan Mirrinyu
dhäwuyu yeee. Yolka mokuywala Matjinytji wala
Ḻiya-baḻkurrkgala.
The Balalŋu, Gaṉawirra cloud spreading up to the air,
standing upright, like a proud person, created by
the whale's spout. Yes. The cloud in the direction of
the spirit people from the east, from Matjinytji and
Ḻiya-baḻkurrkgala, from the hunter that goes out in
all weather, with the rain and the spray of water on
his face, his face dripping water; fresh and salt, rain
and sea.

Yo bilina.
Yes, finish.

Wuymirri (Warramirri version)

Yow, dhuwala ŋarra yurru Warramirri manikay
 miyaman yapamirri ŋarrakalaŋuwu gutharrawu.
*Yes, here I will sing you a Warramirri song, sister clan
 for my grandchildren.*

Walalaŋgu manikay, yapamirriŋu walalaŋgu ga
 ŋarraku marimirri Warramirri manikay, yo.
*Their sister clan and my grandmother Warramirri
 song, yes.*

Here I will sing a song, milkarri, then stop and finish.

Yeee durryun ŋunya ŋarri Mirrinyu, Burarrwaŋa.
*The whales arise and surface, the whale, its deep
 essence, Burarrwaŋa.*

Burarrwutwutthun, Mirrinyu, Nalandji, Nalwaŋa
 Manbuyŋa liyuwan.
*Her tail rises up above the surface, the whale
 Nalandji, Nalwaŋa, together with the ocean;
 her tail hits the Yirritja water.*

Bilayu liyuwan Manbuyŋa, bilanytjiyu.
*She hits the surface of the water with her tail, she hits
 the Yirritja water Manbuyŋa with her tail.*

Durryun ŋunya ŋarri maŋan nyepan nyepana maŋan
 nyepan, nyepana aaa Nalalwaŋa Nalandji durrun
 ŋunya ŋarri Nalandji Wuymirri.
*The cloud arises, the clouds layering on the horizon,
 stacking, coming together, the clouds are there, the
 whales are surfacing; clouds made by the whales.*

Nyalpiyan l̲iyuwan Manbuyŋa, Makuma, Gandariya,
  Bilali, Bilayu, Bil̲anydjiyu Bil̲anydjiyu l̲iyuwan.
*Oh, how she hits the Yirritja water. Oh, how she slaps
  down on the waters of Makuma, Gandariya, with
  her tail, its deep names, Bilali, Bilayu, Bil̲anydjiyu,
  she hits it.*

Mirrinyu, oooo, gananan ŋaya, l̲iyuwan Bilaliŋu,
  ŋunya ŋarri d̲urryuna Mirrinyu, Wuymirri.
*The whale leaves, after marking her territory with
  her tail; she leaves that territory; the whales move
  away.*

Yeee, aaa d̲urryuna ŋunya ŋarri Mirrinyu dhawuykthun dhäwuyu nyepan maŋan Wul̲pundu,
  Balalŋu, yeee, Balalŋu nyepan, Bukuyum ŋunya
  ŋarri D̲urryun Mirrinyu Djaybayu, Bandawiyu,
  Bandayŋa, Dhakalŋayu, Ŋarrayarriya, N̲alkumayu.
*Yes, the whale dives down and then surfaces, with her
  mouth open, the whale Wuymirri. The spout of the
  whale, it leaves clouds Wul̲pundu, Balalŋu. Yes,
  Balalŋu, the marking of the cloud, the whale makes
  a cloud with her head and turns towards Djayba,
  she goes down towards the islands of Bandawiyu,
  Bandayŋa, Dhakalŋayu, Ŋarrayarriya, N̲alkumayu.*

D̲urryuwan Mirrinyu, yoltha nhäma ŋarru dhawuya
  Mirrinyu djambatjŋuyum, yeeee, L̲iya-bal̲kurrthu,
  Dhakalŋa, Ŋarrayarri, Bolumi, Wärruyu.
*The whales surface; who else will see the waterspout
  coming up and forming a cloud, the cloud created
  by the whale spout? The turtle hunter will see the*

clouds; the hunter who comes from the source of
the rain, at Dhakalŋa, Ŋarrayarri, Bolumi, where
the bamboos are; the Wärruyu wind blows, the
turtle hunters feel the salty sea spray on their body;
it stays there, as they paddle.

Yeeee, durryuna ŋunya ŋarri Mirrinyu, Nalandji.
In awe, the hunters watch the whales surface, the
Mirrinyu, Nalandji, the monster of the deep
[a deep name for the whale].

Gananan ŋaya Wuymirri Burarrwutwutthun.
The whale leaves with her tail above the surface, her
tail slides down softly; the monster so graceful and
gentle.

Ŋunya ŋarri durryun, bilayu ŋaya liyuwan Makuma,
Gandariya, Bilali.
There, the whale is surfacing, hitting the surface with
her tail, hitting the waters of Makuma, Gandariya;
the place becomes her Bilali, her territory, marked
by her tail.

Yeee, gananan ŋaya bilayu liyuwan Manbuyŋa.
With a sense of awe and wonder, I am the whale,
I hit the water with my tail and leave the waters
of Manbuyŋa, my Yirritja water.

Bi ŋaya durryun Liya-balkurrkul Dhakalŋa,
Ŋarrayarriwyu, Nalkumayu.
There, I surface, my pod of whales surfaces together,
our heads facing towards the essence of the
rain, towards the hunter; when we face towards

*the hunter our minds connect with him, we
become one.*

**Yeeee, Djambatjŋuya nhäŋal maŋan nhepaynga
neparrŋarrimunyan.**
*Yes, the turtle hunter sees the layering clouds,
one behind the other.*

Mirrinyu ŋunya ŋarri ḏurryun Djayba.
The whales over there surface at the islands of Saibai.

**Dhakalŋa, Warru, Nalkuma ḏurryun ŋunya ŋarri
Mirrinyu dhäwuḻwuḻyun.**
*The whales over there, among the elements of the
winds, the water, the spray, they surface, they
swim; then the whale, she slides down deeper,
to the depths of the ocean.*

Bilina.
Finished.

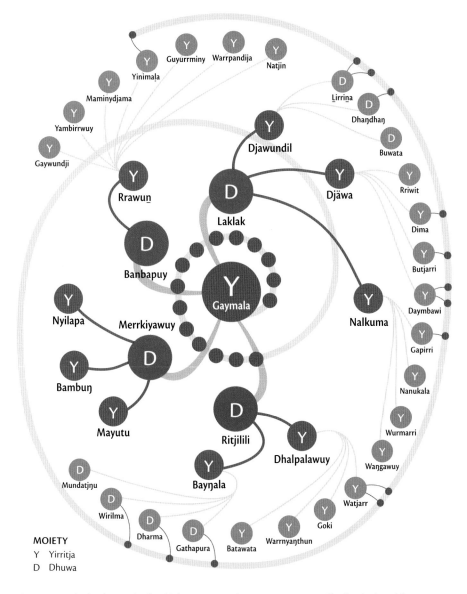

Gurruṯu spirals through the Yolŋu generations to create cyclical relationships. Gurruṯu spirals from Gaymala to her daughters, authors Laklak, Ritjilili, Merrkiyawuy and Banbapuy, from these four to their children, and from their children the generations spiral back to Gaymala, with Gaymala's great, great grandchildren becoming her sisters, brothers and cousins. This spiralling also means that Gaymala's great grandchildren are her mothers, fathers, uncles and aunties! This diagram focuses on *Songspirals*' authors. There are other important relationships. Gaymala's sons, husbands, people who have passed away and adoptive relationships are not shown.

● Gaymala's great, great grandchildren now sit next to her as sisters, brothers and cousins, and are Mawunymula, Djamuṯ Dhanaŋayala, Yumalil, Yimulurr, Lunydjuki, Aron, Yutŋin, Bulmirri, Wakunwanpuy, Nanukala 2, Ḻirriṉa 2, Djuṉbiya, Ganiŋthun and Yaŋarrtji. *(Ali Wright)*

Basket and dilly bag woven at Bawaka. *(Authors' collection)*

Laklak using gunga (pandanus) to make a handle for a basket. *(Authors' collection)*

Gathering for the final dance of the Two Sisters for Roy Marika—Garngarr,
Banbapuy, Dhuwarrwarr, Merrkiyawuy, Natati, Manybarr, Raymattja and Laklak.
(Authors' collection)

Rrakulu Marika, Witiyana Marika, Djerrkŋu Yunupiŋu and Raymattja Marika.
(The Buku-Larrŋgay Mulka Art Centre archives, courtesy of John and Trixie Rudder)

Roy D̲adayŋa
Marika with
sacred dilly bags.

*(The Buku-Larrŋgay
Mulka Art Centre
archives and courtesy
of Ian Dunlop)*

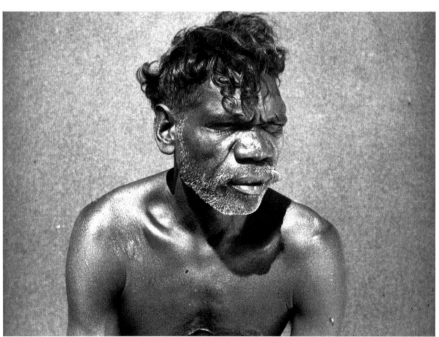

Djulwa̲nbirr Mungurrawuy Yunupiŋu, grandfather of Laklak, Ritjilili, Djal̲i,
Merrkiyawuy and Banbapuy. *(The Buku-Larrŋgay Mulka Art Centre archives and courtesy
of Charles Mountford/State Library of South Australia)*

Merrkiyawuy and Laklak working on our book. *(Authors' collection)*

Sunset at Bawaka. *(Authors' collection)*

Laklak Burarrwaŋa, *Bol'ngu* (ancestral Thunderman) (2003). *(The Buku-Larrŋgay Mulka Art Centre archives)*

Ritjilili and Yumalil eating oysters, Shady Beach. *(Authors' collection)*

Watching the sunset as we get ready for dinner, Bawaka. *(Authors' collection)*

Djawundil gathering gunga, Bawaka. *(Authors' collection)*

Laklak, Gapirri, Mawunymula and Kate walking along the beach to begin weaving, Bawaka. *(Authors' collection)*

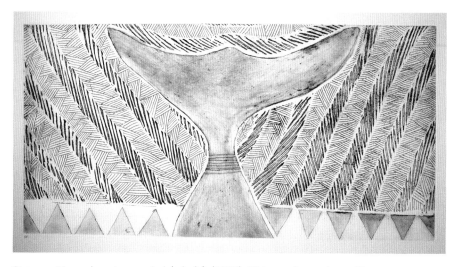

Deturru Yunupiŋu, *Lamamirri* (whale) (2009). This work consists of imagery representing the whale. The triangle designs represent clouds on the horizon.
(The Buku-Larrŋgay Mulka Art Centre archives)

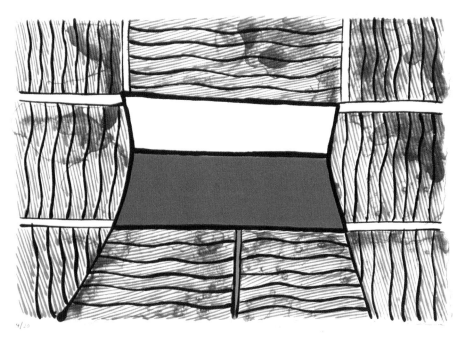

Marrnyula Mununurr, *Bawu* (2016). The white is the cloud wangupini and the blue is the gapu water at Yilpara, Madarrpa Country: Bawu is set to sail towards Mangalili Country, Djarrkapi crossing the Mungurru waters.
(The Buku-Larrŋgay Mulka Art Centre archives)

Gaymala Yunupiŋu, mother of Laklak, Ritjilili, Merrkiyawuy and Banbapuy. *(Brandi Chase)*

Gaymala Yunupiŋu, *Baybaymi* (1999). The central image is the crushing plant (alumina refinery) set up by Nabalco in 1963. Gaymala used a metaphor of a djinydjalma (crab) moving around and scooping up natha (food) and crushing it up with its lirra (teeth). *(The Buku-Larrŋgay Mulka Art Centre archives)*

Ritjilili making damper, Bawaka. *(Authors' collection)*

Banbapuy gathering ganguri (yams), Bawaka. *(Authors' collection)*

Merrkiyawuy at Martjanba, Wessel Islands. *(Authors' collection)*

Laklak stripping gunga, Bawaka. *(Authors' collection)*

Family getting ready for the ceremony and awarding of Laklak's honorary doctorate. *(Authors' collection)*

Bakamumu Marika, Laklak Burarrwaŋa and Professor Richie Howitt waiting for Laklak's cleansing ceremony to begin. *(Authors' collection)*

Mowarra Ganambarr, OAM, explaining his painting to his daughter Merrkiyawuy at Rorruwuy in 1996. *(The Buku-Larrŋgay Mulka Art Centre archives)*

Marri'marri Burarrwaŋa on the beach at Bungulu, Bawaka. *(Authors' collection)*

Siena Mayutu drawing her gurru_tu, Bawaka. *(Authors' collection)*

Sarah and Rrawu_n working on the book, Bawaka, 2017. *(Authors' collection)*

Merrkiyawuy digging for turtle eggs, Bawaka, 2016. *(Authors' collection)*

Djawundil and her granddaughters Yumalil and Mawunymula making damper, Shady Beach, 2018. *(Authors' collection)*

Gay'wu Group of Women, Bangalow, 2017. *(Authors' collection)*

The next generation—Lirrina, Dharrpawuy and Dawu visiting Scotts Head, Gumbaynggirr Country. *(Authors' collection)*

PART 2

Wukun

CHAPTER 1

Gathering of the Clouds

The Gathering of the Clouds is a Dhuwa songspiral. We are moving from Yirritja to Dhuwa now. Yirritja and Dhuwa, the two moieties, mother and child.

This songspiral sings our homeland of Rorruwuy. It is the early rain, when it is nearly time for a certain stingray, namal, to have yuṯa, new fat, before it is hunted in the harvest season. This songspiral renews life on the land. The songspiral sings the clouds coming together and the skies getting dark, ready for rain. The clouds are talking about people and about Country. A cloud comes from a particular direction and tells us about the Dhuwa clan from over there. There are clouds coming from the different clans, and in this songspiral we are acknowledging those clans, the Dhuwa clans, building up, ready for the rain.

The cloud is summoned by the Thunderman, who brings the clouds together as one. The Thunderman is an ancestral man called Djambuwal. He is the one who controls the weather, sends the clouds. When the clouds gather and it starts to rain at Rorruwuy, the two clans of Ŋaymil and Ḏäṯiwuy gather, come together as the Gapiny-mala. The two clans come together just like when the clouds assemble from two sides. The clouds gather and tell the Gapiny-mala their feelings, the happiness, sadness, heaviness. It gets dark, a storm is coming. The rain is their feeling, their expression, their ownership of that area. It is raining, on all the trees, the tracks, the plants, the bush food and the people of that land.

And when it rains, that land cools down and that is the tears; it stills our grief and sorrow and we return home. The rain makes that land new, it renews the grass and the trees grow. The trees grow tall with branches and leaves until they flower and fruits grow. The birds gather for the fruit and we, as one people, will sit in that shade.

So, this is a song of us coming together, of clouds coming together, of clans coming together. And in this part we tell the story of us coming together with our daughter Djawundil and with Kate, Sandie and Sarah to write this book. It is the story of our work together as Gay'wumirr Miyalk Mala, a dilly bag group of women. In this part, we sing us too.

We first met each other as a group at the end of 2006. That is when we started our work together. Laklak, our eldest sister, was working with Djawundil, our daughter, to start the Gay'wu dilly bag women's tours as part of our new family tourism business Bawaka Cultural Experiences. We wanted to work with some ŋäpaki to help us write information down to share with tourists. It was going to be just a booklet at first. A friend of ours, Karen Young, knew of Sandie, Kate and Sarah and introduced us to each other.

Sandie, Kate and Sarah came from down south and were starting to do their research in the Northern Territory. We invited them over. They came, they were nervous. Laklak and

Gay'wu Group of Women: Banbapuy, Sarah, Sandie, Ritjilili, Djawundil, Laklak, Kate and Merrkiyawuy. *(Authors' collection)*

Djawundil were nervous too. Now we remember that time and laugh. When we met, we were this songspiral, just the beginning of it, starting our spiral together. Our other sisters joined too, and our families. Our Elders helped us, Country guided and cared for us, children were born. We slowly gathered like clouds in the sky and things came to life for us.

Kate and Sandie had babies with them on that first visit. Sandie's daughter, Rhian, was given the Yolŋu name Laḻu, parrotfish, and we named Kate's daughter Hannah Miyapunu, turtle. Laḻu took her first steps at Bawaka that time. We did a ceremony for her, rubbing the leaves of the butjiriŋaniŋ on her legs to make them strong. We pick the butjiriŋaniŋ leaves from their tree and when we rub and crush the leaves in water

71

it goes all gooey and smooth. That's bush medicine. We all gathered around and rubbed that silky smooth liquid on Laḻu's chubby baby legs. We have done that ceremony for women's business many times before and since, including for many of our babies born since then.

Laḻu took her first steps on that visit, and it was a bit like that for Sarah, Kate and Sandie. They took their first steps there too. Together we started our gay'wu, our dilly bag. The gay'wu carries many things. Gay'wu carries the food we collect. It carries our knowledge, our stories and our culture. Anything we need, we look to our gay'wu and we can find it there. So these stories we tell you now, the milkarri we share, they come from our gay'wu.

In this part of the book we sing the rain. The rain nourishes us. It guides us. One time, early on in our relationship, when we started working together, the rain and the thunder came and sent us inside. It got us making a map about what we would share with ŋäpaki. It got us working together. We were the clouds coming together, the rain formed us.

We are going to share this songspiral with you now, just this one part of it, and share how we came together. We are sharing the songspiral as part of keeping it alive, of keeping the clouds gathering and the rains falling. If a songspiral is not practised in ceremony or in milkarri we will lose it. It will go back to sleep. Although it will still be there, people won't know how to cry or sing it. They will lose the knowledge of where to start singing, what the tune is, which clan links to that song. We will lose the dance. If we cry or sing milkarri, it will wake up, but if no one cries it or carries it on, it is going to be sleeping for hundreds of thousands of years. Other clans will know it but not from D̲ätiwuy. This is something that is very important for us women. It must not be lost. The milkarri is essential. It is part of the balance.

When we first started writing this part of the book, we called up our eldest brother's son, Gitjpurrwal̲a Ganambarr. He sang to us over the phone. We had that phone on speaker as we sat together underneath Merrkiyawuy's house on a mat on the cool concrete slab. Ritjilili joined in with milkarri. Her high, tremulous cry calling out. Laklak too began to cry milkarri and Merrkiyawuy joined in, the milkarri moving her into a beautiful dance. The south wind blew in. We sing the rain, our own song, our own tune, in our own language; a D̲ätiwuy and Ŋaymil tune. Rain, renewing life, our land.

Many people helped us with this songspiral, many brought their clouds to share, and this is an expression of their kinship and responsibility. We called Gitjpurrwal̲a from Elcho Island, and we worked with the songspirals of Manydjarri Ganambarr, Wäŋa Wat̲aŋu (custodian) of the songspiral. He is our eldest brother who walked with us and our mother right across Arnhem Land from Rorruwuy to Yirrkala. Ŋoŋu' Ganambarr, who is Manydjarri's son, sang for us too at Bawaka with our brother and sons Djal̲i, Rrawun̲ and Dhalpalawuy, and later we checked and added more understandings with Rrawun̲ back at Merrkiyawuy's house where we began. In our family, the Djungaya for this song are our daughter Djawundil and her brothers and sisters, and the Gutharra are our daughter's children.

1.

Wäŋa marrtji guyaŋa Nambatjŋu Yolŋu malawataŋu
   Dhä-malamirr.
Wan'thun marrtji Yolŋu,
Wäŋa guyaŋinan larrum Rinydjalŋu.
Rirrakay ŋarra ŋalmaraŋal wukunlil maŋanlil.

*Walking to my homeland, aching in my heart with
   love for the land, thinking about my homeland,
   this is my home, Nambatjŋu,*
*For I am Dhä-malamirr, person of the shark, my
   mouth bloody after catching prey and eating;*
*Turning my head from side to side, as a shark would,
   thinking of where I am, in my place.*
*As I am walking, everything comes to life; the sound
   of my footsteps, the laughter, the singing, the
   milkarri, the crying, the joy of being home weaves
   into the air and into the clouds.*

2.

Ŋalawurr gurrum yukurra wäŋa dhäwal mukthun
   Rinydjalŋu.
Maŋan yukurra gurrum waywayun Rinydjalŋu ŋarrak
   wäŋa Nambatjŋu bilyunmaraŋalnha.
Ŋalawurr gurruŋal dhawalŋur gurrum yukurra
   Mali-Wutjawuywa Bon waywayun yukurra bilyun-
   maraŋalnha Djarraran.
Ŋalawurr gurruŋal waywayun yukurra Rinydjalŋu.
Ŋalawurr gurruŋal Ŋamandamirr, dhäwal mukthunan
   wäŋa Rinydjalŋu Ŋalawurr gurruŋal.

Wäŋa Rinydjalŋu, wukun ŋarraku waywayun marrtji,
    Ŋalarra gurrum marrtji.

The clouds gather, the place is waiting in calmness.
    The cloud becomes a long thin line, this is my
    spear. I turn, pointing towards my homeland; the
    clouds are there at Rorruwuy for me, for I am of
    that place.
The clouds sit above me at Wutjawuy. I point towards
    Bon, the muddy waters of Rorruwuy, turning
    towards Djarraran.
The cloud points towards Rinydjalŋu, the place that
    nurtures me, the source of my life, the giver of
    Dätiwuy and Ŋaymil knowledge and philosophy.
The clouds are coming from Ŋamanda, at Yirrkala.
The clouds are now pointing towards Rinydjalŋu;
    from Ŋalarra they come together.

3.
Ŋalawurr dhäwal mukthunan wäŋaŋurnha.
Rinydjalŋuny waywayunan yukurra Bulpindi ŋuriŋiy
    bumar wukundhu.
Ŋurru djipthunanmaraŋal wukundhu.
Wukun malanynha gurrum marrtji waywayy-
    unan Ŋamanda, gurrum wukun marrtji, dhawal
    lakaraman.

The gathered clouds settle over my home Rorruwuy,
    pointing to Rinydjalŋu, Bulpindi; as the clouds
    settle, they claim the land.
The point of the cloud spear tilts downwards creating
    the waterspout.

The other clouds are still floating in, gathering,
coming together from Ŋamanda; the clouds come
from all directions, from the other Dhuwa home-
lands, declaring themselves, saying which Dhuwa
Country they come from. As they gather, they
name the places and directions they are coming
from, the places they pass through, and the places
where they are going, telling the other clouds where
to go, where to gather, where to meet.

4.

Wukun marrtji mala-wulkthuna nhaltjarr ŋanapurruŋ
bänyil bänyil muŋthunan, Yolŋunhan Mali-
Wutjawuy garŋgayarra.
Dhuwana marrtji mala-wulkthun wukun, nhaltjarr
Nyelamurru, Yurraymurru, Roniwa.
Gulkthunan ŋanapurruŋgalnha marrtji, dhuwana
marrtji mala-wulkthun wukun.

The clouds are separating. What has happened? The
cloud is over us, over me, over the person from
this land.
Here, the clouds are separating. Why? The clouds are
separating at Nyelamurru, Yurraymurru, Roniwa.
The clouds are separating here with us now, in the
future and in the past; as they always do, always
have and always will.

5.
Nhä dhuwali ganydjarr marrtjin Warŋgarrkŋaŋur.
Murray murray murray.
Garŋga marrtji dharyun, garŋga lurrmun bikulandji.
Dhukarr marrtji dharyun Yikpadi, Bunthamarr.
Wulminda dhuwali mokuywu, Namurraŋaniŋ'gu,
  Wutjawuywa.

*What is it? Look at that rain! Softly falling on our
  footprints. With its strength it comes down at
  Warŋgarrkŋa.*
*Clouds moving as they come together, the waterspout
  starts, the rain comes; the sound of the wind and
  the raindrops come together.*
*It is raining on the pathways and the water fills the
  tracks that the people and animals have made;
  filling up the depressions, the waterholes; the land
  is drinking the water, it sinks into the ground.*
It is raining on the track from Yikpadi to Bunthamarr.
*The land is drinking, it belongs to the spirit,
  Namurraŋaniŋ', to the spirits and the people from
  the past, from now and the future. When it rains,
  we walk on that wet pathway; it is the same path
  that the spirits and the people have always walked
  on. It is wet now, was wet then, will always be wet
  when the rain comes. We walk on that wet pathway
  because the pathway, the land itself, belongs to us
  and we belong to the land.*

CHAPTER 2

Singing the clouds

Wäŋa marrtji guyaŋa Nambatjŋu Yolŋu malawataŋu
    Dhä-malamirr.
Wan̲'thun marrtji Yolŋu,
Wäŋa guyaŋinan l̲arrum Rinydjalŋu.
Rirrakay ŋarra ŋalmaraŋal wukun̲lil maŋanlil.

Walking to my homeland, aching in my heart with
    love for the land, thinking about my homeland,
    this is my home, Nambatjŋu,
For I am Dhä-malamirr, person of the shark, my
    mouth bloody after catching prey and eating;
Turning my head from side to side, as a shark would,
    thinking of where I am, in my place.
As I am walking, everything comes to life; the sound
    of my footsteps, the laughter, the singing, the
    milkarri, the crying, the joy of being home weaves
    into the air and into the clouds.

Our connection to our homeland runs through us. Connections make us who we are. As we begin gathering the clouds, we walk, yearning for and thinking of our homeland. It is alive in us. It is a matter of belonging but it is more. It is our being and our longing. We yearn for our homelands, we are connected to them through gurrutu, through kinship. Gurrutu is the way we are related to one another and to everything.

Songspirals are expressions of gurrutu, they cycle out like the generations, like the family connections and kinship relationships that bind us all together, as Yolŋu and with Country. As the clouds gather and we walk together with our place, we are living our relationships.

We gathered, for this is our land, our place. We long for the land and the land longs for us. It wants to be with the person who walks. The frisson of connection, of the land and the person's co-becoming, it holds them together. It is the raki, the string. When there is no one there on the land it grows uncared for. Everything overgrows because you don't look after it, you don't burn it, you don't hunt on it to make a balance. So things get overgrown, they get out of balance.

For us, we balance as we care for Country and it cares for us. But we are not separate from it. We are in kinship with it. This kinship, gurrutu, underpins who we are. It is between us Yolŋu, with each other and the land and all its beings.

We think about our land and we think about our clan, we are Dhä-malamirr. Dhä means mouth, malamirr means blood. When we prepare namal, the stingray that is hunted, we mix the uncooked liver with the stingray meat. The body of the n̲amal is the mother and the liver is the child. We mix it and make it into fish balls and then we share with family and we eat it. It is delicious! It connects us to the stingray and with our family as we share and give and take. It is our very being, our belonging, our kinship. This is us, Dhä-malamirr, we are named for the stingray and its blood that we eat. We feel it and we know it, in our mind, in our heart, in our soul.

As we begin gathering the clouds, we first come to Rorruwuy. We walk, yearning, longing, loving, thinking of our homeland. The D̲ätiwuy and Ŋaymil people come to meet, walking along the road, following the footpath, walking towards our place and thinking about our place.

Together the D̲ätiwuy and Ŋaymil clans and their estates (smaller areas within the clan's Country: Bulkuwu, Nambatjŋu or Girriwal̲a for Ŋaymil, and Wutjawuy or Gulŋapuy for D̲ätiwuy) make the Gapiny-mala. During the Gathering of the Clouds, they are one, they are the people that represent the rain, the ones who represent the Thunderman, together. In the songspiral, when a D̲ätiwuy man or woman is dancing and singing, the estate names above are named. They use these names to tell more specifically where they come from, or where they are going. We are all part of Gapiny-mala but when we part, we go into these smaller groups, different estates.

As we walk, we turn our head from side to side, looking for and thinking of our place. We are attending to what is there, to the beings and belongings of Country, to our kin, to our land. The person walks and looks around the area, the environment, the Country, the beings there, head turning from side to side with joy.

One time, we were at Sarah's house, down south, talking about this songspiral. Banbapuy, and her gaminyarr Dharrpawuy, and Sarah, and Sarah's daughter, D̲awu, walked together to take D̲awu to school. We walked, looking at the apple trees; we noticed the blossoms coming (there will be apples this year!), and we saw the oranges were nearly finished, the cockatoos had eaten the seeds from all but the stringiest ones. We noticed the birds, the dew, the warming sun, the cycles, the land, with joy, with happiness, with a happy heart, and with respect. This is the songspiral. It is walking, head turning, looking, noticing, thinking as we watch the land, paying attention, with love. Walking in kinship.

Gurru̲tu, kinship, binds Yolŋu together with each other and the world. It is the pattern, the string, the raki, that binds us. It is so important to understand gurru̲tu, to understand songspirals and what they mean. Gurru̲tu is a fundamental mathematics, Yolŋu mathematics—a structure, a pattern— that places us in a network of relationship, of obligation and of care. It is our map. Through gurru̲tu we know how we are related. It makes the Yolŋu world. We are related as mother and daughter, as sister and aunty, as father, brother, great-uncle. This gurru̲tu is not only a blood relationship, but a place in a pattern of existence, a system of relationships. Gurru̲tu holds all to do with human beings, nature, land, sea, seasons. When it is really hot, people will say that is my waku-pulu, my child. When we see rain from the west, we know that is gurru̲tu, that is part of the pattern. We have many mothers, all of our birth mother's sisters. It cycles through the generations, everyone fits, also ŋäpaki if they are adopted, looping to infinity and back, so that our great-granddaughter is our mother. That little girl could be a mother for you. This is fundamental to our beliefs.

When Banbapuy, Sarah, Dawu and Dharrpawuy walked Dawu to school, Dawu was in year two. She was seven years old. Banbapuy is a senior teacher, a grandmother. But Dawu is her aunty. We know that. We know our relationships and we know the obligations that go with them. And this is underpinned by Yirritja and Dhuwa, our moieties.

Everyone is connected. Everyone is connected through the raki, the string that ties us together through gurrutu. And it's not just people. We are in relationship with place and with animals and all beings, including rocks and waters and winds. That's the thing with Yolŋu and culture, everything is a whole, everything is one. We do our own djäma, work, for the self. But really we are one big living thing. And that's why everyone goes through that same sorrow, crying, together.

The names given to our children can be from the salt water or the fresh water, from the rocks or the leaves, fruits, clouds, rain, animals, fish; everything that lies upon the ground, that grows upon the ground, that is in the sea, upon the sea, that is in the clouds and comes out from the clouds. A Yirritja child is named after Yirritja things, Dhuwa children are named after Dhuwa things.

Everything is sung in the songs: whether the rain is Yirritja rain or Dhuwa rain, which direction it came from, what season of the year it is. Is the rain soft and gentle, or hard and strong? Where does the water run to—does it run straight to the sea or to streams and then to the big rivers that finally lead to the ocean? Some of these names are given to a child.

Gurrutu tells us our relationship to the rock and the rain, the clouds and the homelands. It is how we know who we are, through our connections. We can't exist outside gurrutu. It wouldn't make sense. We know and can name our place through gurrutu. This is the place we hold in our mind and our heart as we walk.

We adopted Kate, Sarah and Sandie, who co-authored this book. We put them in a place. This means they are held by gurrutu now too, and their families, their children, their husbands, their parents. They have roles and they have responsibilities. We placed them in our pattern, so we would know where they fit.

When Banbapuy first met them she saw them sitting at our son Djäwa's house. She said, 'Who are those hippies?'

Djäwa turned around and said, 'I don't see any hippies. I see my family.'

We all have families, we all have children. And they are all key to making our work together happen. And why? Because one of the things is that we are all women. It can be mayhem sometimes, but in the end everyone feels good, everyone is satisfied. All our children, Yolŋu and ŋäpaki, are growing up together, knowing their gurrutu, where they fit. They all learn from each other. We are working for the universities to share our knowledge and provide something special for our Yolŋu children, so they grow up knowing about the universities, perhaps going to the university or working at the university in the future.

We are all in a journey together. We are part of a journey together. The books and all our times together form the footprints of our journey. We are family now.

We walk and it weaves the clouds. It's the walking, the joy, the sound of us moving, the thinking of our place, the love. It's in the attention too: we look around and we know what we see, we recognise and respect the beings, the feelings of Country. Everything comes to life.

Now as we walk, the sound of our walking goes up to the clouds. Our sounds, our voice, our footsteps, the sounds of our existence are woven into the clouds. We walk, we know that area. The birds start talking. It comes alive as we go. We are making sounds, the birds hear us. It is a welcoming. Our sound is called rirrakay.

We are singing the clouds and the chanting goes up, up, up, out of our mouths and up to the clouds. Like a vibration of our existence; talking to the clouds, singing to the clouds, sending our song to the clouds, because when they hear, the clouds gather.

The sound of the songspirals is the sound of the universe. We are in harmony with it, and by singing we sing our connections, our raki and our gurru_tu. The world sings all the time. We sing and the clouds sing. The planets sing, the rain sings, the birds, the plants, the rocks, the tides sing, and we sing the world. The fish, animals and different beings, they sing in different ways, at different frequencies. Some songs take a long time. The world is alive with their sound. The world is their sound, and ours. This is the music of nature. Many people have forgotten how to listen.

The sound communicates who we are, our identity, and where our homeland is. If we are sick, our singing can bring the sick back into harmony. While the women are doing milkarri, the sick person listens and takes their memories back to that place. The place and the song are one. It's soothing and healing.

We go back to our homeland through the spirit, through song. We revisit memories, living our days through song.

If a sick person is going to pass away, milkarri makes them strong for death. It encourages them not to be scared because they know that they are strong and they know who they are and who their clan is. They are strong for other people, their kin. Milkarri connects the person, the songspiral, the place. Every time we see people who are sick and we go to the hospital and the doctor says they will pass away soon, we sing the song and we see them strong, not scared of death. It helps.

When a Dhuwa person who has shark as their totem is really sick, when it gets to that deep part of the song, their head turns from side to side. Their totem is the shark and so straight away we know, through the actions they do, we know they are going to go to that place, to Rinydjalŋu. This is a peaceful going because they are connected. They are the shark, and they are telling us they are going to go. It is the right way, the strong way, the way of gurru_tu and of the songspirals.

Our sound goes to the clouds as we walk to our homeland. The clouds collect the sound, and later it will rain. In the ceremony, we sing the song, then another clan sings the song. It gathers in, and eventually it rains. Not yet, though. Now we are walking, our sound, our existence, everything comes to life; the laughter and joy of being home, coming home, it weaves up into the air, to the clouds.

CHAPTER 3

Clouds forming

Ŋalawurr gurrum yukurra wäŋa dhäwal mukthun
Rinydjalŋu.

Maŋan yukurra gurrum waywayun Rinydjalŋu ŋarrak
wäŋa Nambatjŋu bilyunmaraŋalnha.

Ŋalawurr gurruŋal dhawalŋur gurrum yukurra
Mali-Wutjawuywa Bon waywayun yukurra bilyunmaraŋalnha Djarraran.

Ŋalawurr gurruŋal waywayun yukurra Rinydjalŋu.

Ŋalawurr gurruŋal Ŋamandamirr, dhäwal mukthunan
wäŋa Rinydjalŋu Ŋalawurr gurruŋal.

Wäŋa Rinydjalŋu, wukun ŋarraku waywayun marrtji,
Ŋalarra gurrum marrtji.

*The clouds gather, the place is waiting in calmness.
The cloud becomes a long thin line, this is my
spear. I turn, pointing towards my homeland; the
clouds are there at Rorruwuy for me, for I am of
that place.*

The clouds sit above me at Wutjawuy. I point towards
   Bo<u>n</u>, the muddy waters of Rorruwuy, turning
   towards Djarraran.
The cloud points towards Rinydjalŋu, the place that
   nurtures me, the source of my life, the giver of
   <u>D</u>ä<u>t</u>iwuy and Ŋaymil knowledge and philosophy.
The clouds are coming from Ŋama<u>nd</u>a, at Yirrkala.
The clouds are now pointing towards Rinydjalŋu;
   from Ŋalarra they come together.

The clouds are gathering, they are gathering in a place, the
clouds and the people, and the place waits calmly and in anticipation. The cloud turns, pointing like a spear towards our
homeland of Rorruwuy.

When we used to go to Rorruwuy and Mum was there sitting
under the tree, she'd see us coming and she'd start doing the
milkarri of this songspiral, because we were gathering back at
the homeland. She would greet us with milkarri, sing about the
clouds, because we were returning home. That's why, when we
sing about sharks to people who are sick, they are not afraid.
They are returning to their homeland, to their backbone, their
foundation, their <u>l</u>irrwi, the layers of charcoal buried in the
sand. They are returning to the essence of the land.

Rinydjalŋu is our homeland's deep and sacred source. It is a
place we protect as the source of our life. Each clan has their
own area like this within their homeland. It's an asset for them.
It's our children's property, our property. Our Rinydjalŋu is like
a bathi, a basket, it holds everything. The <u>D</u>ä<u>t</u>iwuy and Ŋaymil
children have the authority for the Rinydjalŋu. They have the

responsibility and authority because D̲äṯiwuy or Ŋaymil gave birth to them. D̲äṯiwuy or Ŋaymil land gave birth to them as well. If they have to make a decision about that Rinydjalŋu, it has to be a consensus. If one or more disagrees then the thing doesn't happen. The children have the right to guide the Rinydjalŋu.

The rule says children of D̲äṯiwuy and Ŋaymil have to protect their Rinydjalŋu as the source of their life, their mother land. They have to speak for Rinydjalŋu. A Rinydjalŋu shelter can be built for someone if they are sick or need protection. The shelter becomes the source of protection. The children will stand and talk and protect it; protecting, defending their mother.

We are D̲äṯiwuy from Rorruwuy and we are the land.

Gathering is ḻarrpan, the long cloud, on display up high in the sky. The ḻarrpan is the spear of Djambuwal, Thunderman, and it points towards my homeland, my Rinydjalŋu, my wäŋa, my home of the shark.

When the men and boys dance this songspiral, they hold their spears over their heads, looking like the long cloud ḻarrpan, signalling the cloud with their hands and arms; slowly they turn it around, pointing to a body of water, to the stingray. It is the Thunderman who can control the weather; he can turn and move the cloud to point to each clan. The Thunderman is pointing the cloud, the spear, pointing it to the water. The action of turning to point is bilyunmaraŋalnha. That's the reason the dancers point their spears to their knees, pointing towards the stingray in the body of water.

And this land, this Rinydjalŋu, this homeland, is still. It is a quiet, calm time of day in this home of the shark, in Rorruwuy. There is a feeling of anticipation with the clouds up high in the sky.

The spear point of the cloud turns to the different areas of the land. Each place is named in turn, by its sacred names. Now it turns to point at the Bon, the muddy waters of Rorruwuy. Ritjililimirr is another name for that muddy water, the name of our second eldest sister.

The spear cloud points like a compass. In the buŋgul, when we sing, we call a direction, we call a clan and the dancers turn in that direction, where the homeland is, with a spear held above their head. We'd like to make an activity for schoolchildren based on this, make a chart like a clock, and when the schoolkids hear the songspiral, they'll know where to turn. It will point to the homelands and we can call their names out.

The spear point of the cloud is turning towards ritjililimirr. The water evaporates, the clouds gather, there is a stillness there. Waiting for the Thunderman to summon the clouds together.

This cloud is up in the sky, displayed in the sky. It is suspended there for the Dätiwuy people who live at Rorruwuy, for Dätiwuy and Ŋaymil people, two Dhuwa clans. Dätiwuy's deep name is Bulurruma. Ŋaymil's is Dharrapaŋan. Mali-Wutjawuy is the spirit of the land and the past, present and future people from that Country. Mali is a reflection or a shadow. It is also what we call a copy. So Mali-Wutjawuy is a cloud and its shadow, its reflection and its spirit. It represents the people and the land that is in the shadow of the cloud, from that place. Mali-Wutjawuy, the people from that land, that Country, Wutjawuy.

Another clan name for both Ŋaymil and Dätiwuy is Dharrapaŋan Mel'mari—both of us together, these two Dhuwa groups. Mel is the eye, mari, shark is the danger. We are the eye of the shark. It represents our clans. When you look at the shark's eye you see the power in it, the inner sense. The shark, it has the power, it protects its territory. It could be friendly but if you get close to the shark, wow, we don't know what it will do.

We have inner strength, a sense of 'Don't mess with me'. We are straight talkers, confident to talk in public. When we talk, we don't talk quickly, we explain. If you are stepping in our territory, you need to understand our point of view. There are borders. There are things that others can't step into. Always there are borders and we need to respect the limits. If you threaten us, we will tell you straight.

We are also a gentle people, we are people who help each other, we work with people. Some people will tell you we are kind, beautiful people, but others will tell you we are aggressive. Believe them both. It depends on the circumstances, what is around us.

We are Mel'mari. So the child of our clan knows how to step into that water, how to step into the muddy water to find a stingray, we know that muddy water, that Bon. We know how to hunt there. The child knows, we know. Only we know. It is all muddy. It is all ritjililimirr, muddy water.

Sometimes when other Yolŋu see us they say 'dholuwuy Yolŋu', people of the muddy water. When the water runs from our grandmother's Country, Dhälinbuy on the Cato River, to Rorruwuy, it becomes muddy. Everywhere are crabs, sharks, stingray. When we dance, we show the barb of the stingray and then we spear it. There are lots of bäru, crocodiles, so we have to know the Country to survive. Every time we go out hunting, we get a long stick and use it to feel for the stingray when we are walking.

When we dance the shark songspiral it's very dangerous because it's about how the shark owns the territory. There is spiritual danger. It's very powerful. It can be calm but it can be angry, like us. There is a dangerous part of songspirals, a good part of songspirals, an emotional part of songspirals. All these together.

The spear turns around pointing to the other groups and lands, bilyunmaraŋalnha. When we dance, we do this; the singers sing a place and the dancers know which way to turn and point to that land. Slowly, carefully, we name and map Country and the clans. We bring it to life, we respect and honour it. The cloud points to and acknowledges the other areas, the people and clans who sing cloud songs: Gälpu, Ŋaymil, Rirratjiŋu, Djapu, Djamparrpuyŋu, Dätiwuy, Dhudi-djapu.

Bon waywayun yukurra, we are the domain of the shark. Larrpan, that cloud formation in the sky, it invokes us, connects us with the land, the water and the sky. It proclaims the domain of the shark. It is the people of Rorruwuy.

When we sing this song, when we do milkarri of this song, any song, it is spiritual and the emotions come up. All the emotions come up, depending on the situation. There might be sadness, happiness, anger, joy. Emotions are so important to songspirals.

We can't be happy all the time. If something breaks, we must cry. If we are happy, we must laugh. It is the same with the land, with the wind and currents, the animals: they all have emotion. When milkarri comes, when us women cry, if something bad happens, we've got to cry, it's part of us. It's all about connecting us to the land.

We are not just crying with tears coming down, we are singing too. That is milkarri. We are healing.

After Cyclone Nathan came through Bawaka in 2015, Ritjilili was crying because the trees, the land, were hurt. That was a big cyclone that came right through here. It uprooted trees, lots of them had their tops or branches blown off, and lots of the buildings were damaged. Many homelands were badly impacted by the cyclones that year. People were sleeping in tents and some of the roads were blocked for months. The sand was gone from the beach at Bawaka, and we could see the roots of the coconuts, the tamarind and the casuarinas, all bare. Sometimes we cry in silence, between the emotion and the singing, inside the heart.

All these trees, uprooted and damaged. When our kids first arrived after the cyclone, they just came and touched them. They said, 'Marrkapmi, my dear ones, it is alright.' That's why we take the children to the homelands, so they can see. Maybe they will have a tear or two.

We came back a month later. Our eldest sister, Laklak, had been sick. We all piled in the troopie to go out there. Sarah and her family were there too. It was a time when we were sharing this songspiral. We were working on it together, the Gathering of the Clouds, and we had gathered. We needed to be out there at Bawaka.

We saw the new leaves were coming, and knowing that everything was coming back again, that the sand was coming back, we felt happy. The first thing we did when we got out of the truck and we saw the sand coming back was feel happy. The land knows this, it communicates.

The young leaves were red and fresh. Country knows how to heal. Milkarri helps that. It is a wondrous thing. If none of us came here, some of those trees would be dead. That beautiful tamarind tree that we sit under, the one that gives us shade, a big piece of iron crashed into it, wounded it, but because it knows we are here, it is starting to grow back.

In our songspirals, we do milkarri with the land, the land does milkarri with us. We have a sense of belonging, longing for the land, missing the land. We are homesick for the land, for the past. We have sadness for the state of the land, happiness for the state of the land. Sometimes it is so emotional because you haven't been to that Country for a long time. Maybe we never will get there. Yet we see it through the milkarri. We cry milkarri and we see people walking on the beach, sitting there looking out at the sea.

If we do milkarri without the names, without using the deep names, the emotions won't come out in the same way. If we do milkarri with the deep names, we feel better, we have given something back. It is healing for us and the land. That is why Yolŋu cry milkarri, to let out emotions in public. Keeping emotions in makes us sick. If we get it out, we feel good. It shows respect to other clans, to other people. It shows that we share the emotion too. Everyone is connected in the Yolŋu world, through kinship, through language and through songspirals.

And everyone has a role: women cry milkarri, men sing with clapsticks and yidaki. Women add harmony, balance, power, and they deepen the emotion. When men hear milkarri it makes them proud of their relatives and it gives them power as well, it helps them have that emotion. When the women are doing milkarri, it helps the men cry. They're pouring out their emotions, not hiding them. The women allow them to let their emotions out. These are the hidden tears for men. Milkarri allows the men to cry with the miyalk, the women. And when women are doing milkarri, it helps the men to be powerful.

Most ŋäpaki who write about songspirals are professors and they write about it in an academic way. It can be abstract and disconnected from life. Sometimes they don't do it well. The emotion isn't there. It's important to talk about this because we need to get the depth.

Also, when some ŋäpaki come, they see our dances as decorative, like a disco or a performance only for tourists, but it is totally different. We don't just go in and dance. It must be done by the right people, in the right way, at the right time. We have strict laws about this. And it must be done with emotion.

We all feel the emotion, as the clouds gather, as we do milkarri. The clouds point to our homelands that have nurtured us, our source of life, the givers of knowledge and philosophy. They bring us together.

That land in Yirrkala, right at the point where the cliff is, that is where Djambuwal the Thunderman lives. This cliff is Djawuluku, Dhawunyilnyil, Dhawulpaŋu, Ŋalarra. All this weather starts at Yirrkala. That power is coming from there, going to Rorruwuy, to our place, our homeland, the home of the shark. The spear cloud points, marking the land, naming the areas, bringing the clans together.

When the Thunderman points, he is labelling the areas, giving the scientific names of the clans, then he calls all the clouds to form and then the darkness comes. The rain, it isn't normal rain, it is the end-of-days rain, really dark and heavy. Maybe it's going to wash away the land, wash away the track. Whenever you are standing there watching the rain come towards you and you think, 'What am I going to do, stand here or find shelter?', that is the scene the Thunderman is creating, the clouds becoming the rain. Sometimes when we see the lightning in that direction we say, 'Ahh, it's raining at Rorruwuy.'

There are two types of rain, the heavy rain is Dhuwa and the light rain, just a sprinkle, is Yirritja. Thunderman has a plan: some tribes get the lighter rain, but at Rorruwuy Thunderman goes into the water and gives his feelings to the water, to the stingray and to the shark. When he jumps into the brackish water his feeling goes into the water. Other clans have rain, but Rorruwuy has the stingray as well as the rain. That's why the Thunderman turns his spear down to the water. He is tapping the water with his spear to see if there is danger around.

When someone passes away, the rain is milkarri. Everything is about life itself. The land that we are on, the sun we see, we are related to one another. Sometimes we don't see it, but if we look through ourselves and nature we will find it. The rain is very important for the land. It cools the land and gives energy to the plants to grow. Just imagine if there was no rain—what would happen to the trees, nature and all of us?

The clans and the clouds are one. As a writing collective we gather too. The songspirals have brought in Sarah, Kate and Sandie.

At sunrise, at Bawaka, we do milkarri for visitors, for tourists and guests. This is where Sarah, Kate and Sandie first learnt about milkarri, where they felt it, the emotion, the sounds, where they got further understandings of us, of our connection with Country and of the deep role women play through milkarri. We wanted to continue Mum's idea of doing the milkarri at Garma and bring it to Bawaka, to share this with ŋäpaki, to greet the new day. We do milkarri for the day, to remember the day, create the day.

In the hushed darkness we sit. It is not yet dawn, there is no light yet. The stars are bright above as we go and take our seats. It is cool too. We might have a rug around our shoulders. There are chairs for the Elders to sit on, blankets and mats for others. We sit quietly, just the sound of gentle movement. The sound of a light breeze.

Then we begin. There is a beautiful high keening, a long note, and those that can, join as they are ready. Kate, Sandie and Sarah, and the younger women, they sit feeling the sound in them, around them, through them. They often have their eyes closed. Sometimes they cry. It moves them, changes them. We cry milkarri and they are part of it.

In the darkness before dawn, we do milkarri for the land, the mist, the breeze, the webs of the spiders. We do milkarri for those people who have passed away and been with us before, their spirits. We do milkarri for the peewee bird, bidiwidi, and djilawurr, the scrub hen.

The pre-dawn comes, the stars fade until the morning star stands brightly there alone. We do milkarri for the first bird that sings, waking the other animals up. The birds awake. We finish and the land is alive. We cry milkarri for the new day.

We have been gathering and writing this book together for five years now. It has been a long process to decide what we wanted to share, and to try to work out a good way to share it. We have learnt a lot ourselves and we have taught Kate,

Sandie and Sarah a lot too. We used to joke that they were in their nappies. They are out of their nappies now. They know that our relationships bring responsibility, that they are part of gurru̱tu too.

We have met at our homeland Bawaka many times to work on the book. This is where we were when we decided to write it, when Laklak our eldest sister said it would be our next project. And we have been together in Yirrkala, the town where we younger sisters live. Twice we've gathered at Garma. We have been down south too, to Sydney, to Bellingen and Bangalow in northern New South Wales, to Adelaide, and to Christchurch in New Zealand. We have had many, many meetings and talks, much food gathered, cooked and shared, many baskets woven, walks taken, rides in cars and planes and 4WDs. Some of us have even travelled together to Canada. That is where we checked over some of the drafts of the book, if you can imagine.

Wherever we are, others seem to gather too—social media points friends and family far and near in the direction of the gathering, and gather we do.

We have shared with Sandie, Sarah and Kate about the meaning of the songspirals, we have called family to share with us the words and tune, to check we are doing the right thing. We have translated the words together—Banbapuy our youngest sister has done a lot of that. Together, we go through line by line, and also discuss the overall meaning. Sometimes, we will write pages and pages about a single word. There is so much depth to communicate.

In August 2016 we were at Garma talking about our work together. We found ourselves talking about märr, love, again and again. That was one word that got us talking. We ended up writing a whole article all about it. Märr, love, and the raki, string, bind us. This is milkarri too, the love of watching D̲awu and Ruwu, Sarah's and Kate's little girls, twirling and whirling in the buŋgul with Mayutu, Merrkiyawuy's daughter; the love of camping with the Art Centre gang in a big family group, sitting around the campfire at night and running off to celebrate the plethora of brilliant Yolŋu bands on show; the love of sitting on the sand of the open-air Gapan Gallery, sitting under the white ghost trees, the light reflecting off the clean soft white sand, sitting and drawing sand pictures of our relationships; the connections, the love between us and how it binds. And our love is not an individual thing. It is about connection, the way our gurrut̲u and our djalkiri, our foundations, overlap, how we work together and how we all overlap with the land.

Working on the book at the Gapan Gallery, Garma Festival 2016. *(Authors' collection)*

And in the middle is love. The connections make us whole, but we must have love in the middle. It is not a selfish love, but a sharing love. It is not a static love but one that is always emerging. It is a love for each other, for our families, for our knowledge, for sharing. It is a love for how we always bounce off each other and share our knowledges in different ways.

Love emerged and emerges, wherever we are, whatever we do. It spirals out and round, in our connections with each other and the land. As with milkarri.

CHAPTER 4

Thundercloud

Ŋalawurr dhäwal mukthunan wäŋaŋurnha.
Rinydjalŋu<u>ny</u> waywayunan yukurra Bulpi<u>nd</u>i ŋuriŋiy
    bumar wuku<u>n</u>dhu.
Ŋurru djipthunanmaraŋal wuku<u>n</u>dhu.
Wuku<u>n</u> malanynha gurrum marrtji waywayy-
    unan Ŋama<u>nd</u>a, gurrum wuku<u>n</u> marrtji, dhawal
    <u>l</u>akaraman.

The gathered clouds settle over my home Rorruwuy,
    pointing to Rinydjalŋu, Bulpi<u>nd</u>i; as the clouds
    settle, they claim the land.
The point of the cloud spear tilts downwards creating
    the waterspout.
The other clouds are still floating in, gathering,
    coming together from Ŋama<u>nd</u>a; the clouds come
    from all directions, from the other Dhuwa home-
    lands, declaring themselves, saying which Dhuwa
    Country they come from. As they gather, they

name the places and directions they are coming from, the places they pass through, and the places where they are going, telling the other clouds where to go, where to gather, where to meet.

The cloud is calm, quiet, still. The cloud is at home. The clouds are giving messages to each other, coming together, gathering, so they can rain. They're communicating, asking, helping each other. Just like people help each other in ceremonies, like we help each other in co-authoring this book, the clouds do it as well. As they come together they name the places, the individual places they come from, pass through and go to. This helps the other clouds know where to go. Each time they stop, the clouds gather some more.

Thunderman points the larrpan, the spear cloud, marking, gesturing towards the place, the land, Rorruwuy. He turns the spear towards the foundation, the land of the ancestral shark.

Pointing, targeting, focusing the larrpan, he pinpoints the homeland. The spear cloud bends down to point to that place, the muddy waters. Why are the waters muddy at Rorruwuy? Because it is the territory of the sharks and stingrays! Because it belongs to the shark, that territory. It is where the sharks roam.

The point of the larrpan targets the place where it is going to rain: 'This is where I will rain.'

When the men and boys are dancing with the spear over their head they point with the spear and they claim that area with a stamp of their foot. When we're dancing, we tip the spear, bend our arms, angle them down towards the ground in front of us, so they are pointing towards the muddy waters, to the special place.

As the point of the ḻarrpan tilts downwards, other clouds still come. The Thunderman is calling out for the clouds to come together; they see the signal and come together. Even when some clouds have reached the destination, others still come, until they form a big cloud. This big cloud becomes a big rain, but before the rain comes in we feel the cool wind. Then you know the rain is coming towards you. The same happens in the buŋgul. In the dances, the clan groups wait. They then come together.

Yolŋu people have always lived in a dynamic world of coming together. Many Yirritja songspirals talk about the coming of the Macassans. A long time ago, Macassan people used to travel down from Sulawesi in Indonesia with the northwest wind. We traded with them, mostly trepang (sea cucumber), a delicacy, for pottery, knives, material, tobacco and other things. We still have some of the pottery. Some Yolŋu travelled with the Macassans, got married, and formed different kinds of relationships with them. Some Macassan words came into Yolŋu matha too, like rrupiya (rupiah) for money. We had a good relationship with them. Our stories tell that they waited to be invited. They came, they respected us, but they did not stay.

The long and deep relationships between Macassans and Yolŋu show a different way of ŋäpaki and Yolŋu being together side by side. There are songspirals about that too. Tobacco, ŋarali', brought over by the Macassans, is in the songspirals. It says it is dangerous, it talks about death. Ŋarali' used to be dark, almost black, and square. That dark tobacco we call getju and gilurru'. We remember our grandfather using it. It used to be just the old men who used it. They'd cut it up, put it next to the fire, break it up with their fingers, then put it in the pipe. They'd smoke it, take turns sharing the pipe.

As new things and new people come into the Yolŋu world they are adopted into our kinship system. This is an adoption which says that you now have a place to belong here, and with that belonging comes responsibilities.

We sisters adopt ŋäpaki so that when other people in the community see them around they can call them kin, so everyone has a place, no one is a stranger. Everyone has a value in the community, a sense of belonging. The bäpurru, the clan and family, you are adopted into, they are the ones who guide you along and teach you. That is how Kate, Sarah and Sandie learn. That's why they aren't falling around, messing things up, because they are in the family. They are being guided in their journey, in our journey together, they see what it's like being in Yolŋu shoes. That underlies how we work together, how we are.

We try to break racism by adopting ŋäpaki as family. This way we teach ŋäpaki and show them what to do. Ŋäpaki kids don't just go anywhere—there are rules, quite strict rules about what to do, what not to do, what to touch, what not to touch. There are rules and regulations for the dangerous things, like for bäru (crocodile), and for the ways that learning means sharing, sharing our families and bringing them into the learning too. We see the kids all playing together, we know they are listening and taking it all in. The kids are building their own bridge. They have their own ideas. We are a big family.

We've experienced so much terrible racism over the years. Being told, 'You're an abo—a stupid abo.' We always say to ourselves, 'No, I am an Aboriginal, Yolŋu person. I am not stupid.' That's what we teach our children, not to be aggressive, to say things in a good way. No one understands unless they experience a thing. At university, in schools, and in messages they get through the media, for many Australians, all they know is the negative stuff, that's all they know of Aboriginal people. We get stereotyped, especially the young people. When we run Garma workshops, ŋäpaki ask us about child abuse, sniffing, drinking. We say, in any community, in every country, there are bad things. Ŋäpaki do it indoors, behind closed doors, like a cake with a bad inside.

We have an obligation to work together and achieve bala ga' lili, a balance, coming together and complementing each other. We have an obligation to acknowledge intellectual property, to respect where the knowledge we learn comes from and to give and take things graciously. If any of us don't feel comfortable, we say something. There are many ŋäpaki—academics, politicians, bureaucrats—who say, 'Tell me, tell me, you've got to tell me this', they just want our knowledge, all our different layers of knowledge. That's not right, that's not how it should be.

In our Gay'wumirr Miyalk Mala, our dilly bag group of women, we respect Yolŋu knowledge, beliefs and values, and Kate, Sarah and Sandie don't act like they're higher and we, Yolŋu, are lower. With Sarah, Kate and Sandie we sit down together, laughing, having a cup of tea, going hunting, digging for ganguri, the same things we'd do with our own family, checking that the kids are okay. We have come together in a different way, we've created our network, as a family. Kate, Sandie and Sarah have learnt that their gurruṯu responsibilities mean sharing and learning. Giving and taking, not just take, take, take. Bala ga' lili—we must have a balance.

All of us are always learning, learning together. Every day, anything can let you down. But if you have a mind that wants to learn, then you can overcome those obstacles. If you look after your mind you can solve problems and work things out to make your life the way you want it to be. There are always people who don't look at things our way. There are people who need to understand more, to be educated, to have a broad mind, to accept things as they are and to work their way around if they don't like it. A healthy person has a mind full of wonder. A mind full of wonder is wondrous and a wondrous mind learns so much more than a mind that is sick. A narrow-minded person is a sick person.

Living our responsibilities means opening ourselves up to being surprised and transformed, to changing what we do and to trying to do things that make a positive difference. Many people who come to Bawaka as visitors and tourists find they are really changed by the experience—being at Bawaka makes people look at the positive side of things. It is a good thing, we take people out and share with them, and they go home and do positive things, make a difference.

The clouds are all floating by, from Ŋamanda the clouds are coming. As they are drifting in towards Rorruwuy they mark and name all the places they pass by, calling out and naming the places. Every place is named as the clouds drift by. The clouds say, 'I am now passing this place, I am now passing this place', all Dhuwa places. The clouds are saying this. They are stopping at one place, then the next. They are gathering. The clouds are starting to gather to make rain. They are growing themselves. Amassing themselves.

Dhawal l̲akaraman marrtj, the clouds are going and we can see they're going, we know where they're going as they're telling us, attached to each other like a string.

We are all on a journey together. We are the clouds, bound together by raki, by ties of love and responsibility. This book is one of the footprints of our journey.

CHAPTER 5

Clouds separating

Wuku<u>n</u> marrtji mala-wulkthu<u>n</u>a nhaltjarr ŋanapurruŋ
bänyil bänyil muŋthunan, Yolŋunhan Mali-
Wutjawuy garŋgayarra.
Dhuwana marrtji mala-wulkthun wuku<u>n</u>, nhaltjarr
Nyelamurru, Yurraymurru, Roniwa.
Gulkthunan ŋanapurruŋgalnha marrtji, dhuwana
marrtji mala-wulkthun wuku<u>n</u>.

*The clouds are separating. What has happened? The
cloud is over us, over me, over the person from this
land.*
*Here, the clouds are separating. Why? The clouds are
separating at Nyelamurru, Yurraymurru, Roniwa.*
*The clouds are separating here with us now, in the
future and in the past; as they always do, always
have and always will.*

It is time to separate now. The clouds are separating, the people are separating—mala wulkthun. It is the quiet time; you can feel the stillness.

Don't worry, we might separate, but it won't be for long. It is part of the cycle. We are like the clouds that divide, that go their separate ways and then come back together. The Dhuwa clouds separate. Our Gay'wumirr Miyalk Mala separates too. We meet together in Bawaka, in Yirrkala, Sydney, Bellingen or Bangalow, then we separate. First some of us go, then others. But the gurruṯu, the raki, holds us together.

Knowing the cloud is there, knowing that we are always connected, that is our kinship, our gurruṯu, and our Law, our Rom. Rom is the underlying rules and connections that bind us together, that tell us what to do. It is the respect. Rom tells us that we are always connected even as we separate, even as the cloud covers the sun.

The clouds know things too, and they talk. They say, 'Here we will separate.' So that is part of Rom. The clouds know, they have knowledge, they can talk. We know this because it is in the songspirals.

The Law and the songspirals, like the clouds that gather and separate, tell us to live life to the fullest. Life is precious, and we must do what we have to do before we go so that later on, when we are gone, others will respect us. We don't have a word for thank you exactly, but we say buku-wekam or buku-wurrpan. These mean to give back, saying a type of thank you. It is a matter of honouring a person for what they have done, honouring them for looking after the land or for how they helped us in the past, in the days when they lived, when they were alive.

There are rules for everyone and they cover everywhere. Our houses are open, even if there is not enough room. If there is space on the floor, there is enough room for family to sleep. We were taught the rules by our grandmothers and grandfathers, our aunties and uncles. It is about learning the language, the culture, the dances, the Law, the discipline, the different ceremonies. It is about learning how to read Country, to listen to what it tells you. We listen to the water when it is muddy, the clouds when they reach across the sky like octopus tentacles to announce a message from home, and the birds when they send messages of welcome or warning. This is the spark of our mother clan, Gumatj. We see the spark of Gumatj when we look at the fire.

We part but remain connected. We are a whole big cloud and much of that cloud is going, separating. Then others go. Until we are left alone.

We sing of where the clouds are separating and going to, to Nyelamurru, to Yurraymurru, to Roniwa. Here are the clouds separating. We know where they go, their place.

This tells us that we can only speak from our place. It tells us that place is always important. When we do milkarri or sing the songspirals, we are singing from our own place. The words are not always sung in the exact same way. The order is what is important, the order of what happens in the songspiral, of what we sing through the tears of milkarri.

If the little boy is playing on the beach, we can say, 'Beach, little boy playing.' There is overlap too, not everyone is saying the exact same words. We are drawing a picture, collaboratively.

Perhaps someone else comes in, saying, 'On the beach the little boy is playing, the sand, he throws the sand in the air', and someone else does milkarri: 'The sea is calm, the little boy has tears in his eyes, on the beach.' So, we sing the boy and the beach and together we make it come alive. We all bring our resonance, our heart, our love and sorrow, our vibrations. When we do milkarri, it is to make something exist, that land in all its beauty and pain and connections.

And the land in its beauty is never one big mass. There are always boundaries within Country. The sea, land, sky, earth, rivers and underground rivers, sometimes these are boundaries where we cannot go and have to stop. Or it might be rocks or a rainforest. These tell us the land there belongs to someone else. The boundary is something that has been there for a long time.

It is not the songspiral that makes the boundary. We can go back to other Countries and start from there, with their clouds coming in. In the songspirals we can go over the person's boundary and sing from there, whether Yirritja or Dhuwa, spirit or person or landmark, as long as it is in the songspirals. Like the Yirritja hunter hunting Dhuwa kangaroo. Songspirals are open and connected.

The cloud cuts off, disperses. It goes in different ways. There is space and stillness. Our milkarri is quieter now. The cloud is getting pulled apart, like you might do with playdough, pulling it off, separating it out. Here, right now, it is doing that. In the area of Rorruwuy, our homeland, it's quiet, the clouds move off to rain on other Countries.

Cutting off, drifting aside. There is a feeling of love and of sorrow. Stillness. Waiting, maybe.

Love and sorrow connect you to Country. They help make Country part of you. And if you listen to that you will learn about limits too. We all need to listen to Country so we are not blinded by our own desires. It is time to stop and listen, to learn about the land and what nature is saying.

There are many of us breathing the same air. The clouds are above us all, with their messages and their Rom. You don't need to look somewhere else for answers, to go away and explore or build a new house or make a fortune. Life itself is important.

We need to tell those who are blinded by their own desires. It's something we don't want to hide. We want to tell the truth to the greedy people about climate change, building, building, never replanting, digging, killing. If it's something we don't want to tell the ŋäpaki, then who are we going to tell, the spirits? Many don't want to listen to us. But perhaps you can listen. Remember the limits. Those clouds are separating here, with us, with you.

It is about learning from the land, listening to the stillness, learning from the clouds as they separate. If you believe in what you believe, later you may find it. It depends on your own path and belief. That is your last destiny, your heaven. Just like an ancestor said to Yolŋu people. They said to us, 'This is your land, these are your songs, this is your strength. Through those strengths, through the dance and stories, you are going to find another world that is already there and waiting for you.'

When we sing, do milkarri, feel pain or happiness or sadness, it comes from the land and from the ancestors. It is the sadness of the clouds separating. It is the happiness, joy and longing of walking to your homeland. When we walk and practise our culture, when we dance and sing, go to ceremony, teach kids, hunt, collect food, we do these things because the ancestors said, 'You must sing the song the right way, while you are alive and still walking, so that you can make your spiritual journey after death, the right way to the heavens. Do not steal from others, do not tell lies. Stay with your foundation.' The ancestors gave us a foundation on which to stand.

Rrawun, our son, he says, 'My foundation is the rock beneath the sea, Maymuru', that's his foundation from the Mangalili clan through his father. He said, 'Ancestors gave me the marawili tree, the shade tree, where I sit and rest. Ancestors gave me the burial ground. They said, when your people die you will bury them in this particular land. Ancestors gave me the water in the land. Ancestors gave me the secrets and sacred knowledge that is my identity. They gave me my clan name. Ancestors knew that I won't float on the surface of the water, that I would stand beneath the water and on the land, that I would understand the land and the sea. I would survive in that particular area and where the land meets the sea.'

All this we share, links from one Country to the next Country, from west to east, north to south. This is the link that the ancestors have given us, through the totems, whether they are shark, crocodile, emu. We know where we are going and what we are going to sing in our milkarri. We know how we are going to present ourselves to other clans. We know our limits and our responsibilities.

CHAPTER 6

Raining

Nhä dhuwali ganydjarr marrtjin Warŋgarrkŋaŋur.
Murray murray murray.
Garŋga marrtji dharyun, garŋga lurrmun bikulandji.
Dhukarr marrtji dharyun Yikpadi, Bunthamarr.
Wulminda dhuwali mokuywu, Namurraŋaniŋ'gu,
    Wutjawuywa.

What is it? Look at that rain! Softly falling on our
    footprints. With its strength it comes down at
    Warŋgarrkŋa.
Clouds moving as they come together, the waterspout
    starts, the rain comes; the sound of the wind and
    the raindrops come together.
It is raining on the pathways and the water fills the
    tracks that the people and animals have made;
    filling up the depressions, the waterholes; the land
    is drinking the water, it sinks into the ground.
It is raining on the track from Yikpadi to Bunthamarr.

The land is drinking, it belongs to the spirit,
 Namurraŋaniŋ', to the spirits and the people from
 the past, from now and the future. When it rains,
 we walk on that wet pathway; it is the same path
 that the spirits and the people have always walked
 on. It is wet now, was wet then, will always be wet
 when the rain comes. We walk on that wet pathway
 because the pathway, the land itself, belongs to us
 and we belong to the land.

Look at that rain! Softly, softly it rains, raining at Warŋgarrkŋaŋur. As we become part of Wukun, part of the Gathering of the Clouds, we write these words. We write as nurturing rain falls, a nourishing rain.

For after the stillness comes the rain. We have separated, we have gone our different ways and the rain falls. There is power in that. We are walking, following other people's footprints.

It rains the trees. It is raining the grass, the mangroves, gunga, termite mounds, everything, anything you can think of. The land, really, it rains. When we sing through the tears of milkarri, we keen milkarri for the hands of the rain, raining on animals, trees, grass, stones, rocks and tides. The pigeon calls, telling that the tide is coming in.

The land cries milkarri too and that is the rain. Our milkarri, our keening, is the crying. Through this book you read, you become part of our milkarri.

We call that rain waltjan or goŋ-waltjan, the hands of the rain. It is getting the yams to grow, the trees to grow and have

114

fruits, the stringybark trees to bloom, the bush foods to grow, it is water for the animals to drink.

This strength, this power, ganydjarr, comes from the place Warŋgarrkŋaŋur. The power, the force, the energy of the rain is coming from Warŋgarrkŋaŋur, close by Rorruwuy. You see the rain coming in, coming with its power and force.

Murruy murruy murruy, rain softly falling on our footprints. In the buŋgul we put our hands above our heads, fingers moving as the rain.

It is raining on the pathways and tracks. It is filling up the ditches and waterholes. It's raining on the guluwu tree, on the road, in those places. It's all wet, all the Dhuwa places of Rorruwuy.

People are named after those roads, those places. Garŋga or Garŋgawuy is a name of one of our sisters. That is where we get our names. We get our names from our homelands. So mädirriny, the south wind, the name we gave Sarah, is from the songspirals from the homeland she is linked to, same for Dharrpawuy, same for everyone.

Sometimes, somewhere along the songspirals, we are given a name from our mother Country. Yothu–yindi, child and mother. So there can be some Yirritja in with the Dhuwa as they overlap. This happens with the waters of Dhälinbuy—our grandmother Country, mother Country to Rorruwuy. When it is raining, the water overlaps with the other waters. The Dhuwa waters meet the Yirritja waters, they flow past each other. The rain makes the rivers that flow through other lands. This is like the borders: you can sing across to the mother land, the children's land.

When we walk, it rains. It is raining on Yikpa<u>d</u>i Bunthamarr. The dhukarr, the road, is called Yikpa<u>d</u>i Bunthamarr and it is raining. It is not raining on just any road, but a particular road, in a particular named place. We must make sure we use the right words in the songspiral, the right names for the right places, otherwise it doesn't mean a thing. It could be raining anywhere. For us the names we use come from Rorruwuy, our homeland. Ritjilili also has the name Manybarr. Both names are from Rorruwuy; these are names of muddy waters, where the sharks and the stingrays roam.

Nhä? What is that rain we see? It is the power. Nhä means it is there for them, there, it belongs to them. The cloud is coming in, and when it rains at Rorruwuy, the cloud belongs to that land. And the spirit being Ŋamurraŋaniŋ who we keen in this songspiral belongs to that land, as do the trees and everything from that area.

We walk on that wet pathway because the pathway, the land itself, belongs to us and we belong to the land.

Our milkarri is the women's part of the songspirals that make the rain, the clouds, the land. Women's milkarri is another kind of celebrating. Here we cry milkarri for the rain. Rain has power, rain makes an impact. This is as real as the words we write together to make this book. We cry milkarri to make and remake the rain.

Raining, calling, nurturing, becoming together. The new shoots come out on the plants and the trees. When the big rain comes, sometimes it breaks the trees on the road and sometimes it grows a new life, a new beginning. New trees are born, the tree shoots come out like the fresh red leaves after the cyclone. It is a renewal and we feel happiness inside.

And through that rain and the path, there is new food growing. We will collect the new food and share it following the clouds that gathered and parted.

The falling rain is also the tears: our tears and the tears of the spirits of the land. Mum, when she was sick in that hospital bed, said that she wanted to share her knowledge with other women. One of the reasons for this is because every time she travelled to other places she found that crying connects women—crying for joy, crying for anger, for loss, different crying. This is the rain, this is the tears, this is part of the message of our milkarri.

We meet each other, our collective; we come together and we separate.

We rain. New shoots grow.

And, when the time is right, we come together again.

This is the cycle, like the cycles of evaporation and falling rain that hold us all. We are mothers and daughters and grand-daughters, we are the rain falling, the waters meeting, mixing, clashing, the moisture going up to the clouds. We are our tears and our tears are this book, this book that we have written together and that now we share.

On the pathways we listen to the pigeon calling. We call out as the pigeons do after the rain. As Merrkiyawuy wrote in her poem:

Pigeons

Starting to rain
The pigeons come
My namesake, the pigeons
After the rain stops, the pigeon calls out.

And the songs spiral on, because they always do. There is always more, connecting to other clans, spiralling out across Arnhem Land and across Australia as they are passed from one clan to the next. Wukun spirals out to talk of the tides coming fast after the rain, of the brackish murky water flooding in through the mangroves, of the coming of the ancestral shark and the pigeon that calls to announce that the rain comes.

Wukun spirals on to sing of the power and anger of that dirty water coming into the mangroves on the big rushing tide. The ancestral shark is nearby in that water, the boundary is occupied by the mother shark. And when the shark arrives, the water parts and stops, it calms, like our clan does, peaceful again. It is here in its territory now.

The song spirals on to name the different waters, following the water back out to the bay, the driftwood that has been dislodged by the fierce tide, the mangrove sticks floating and bobbing on the water, floating across Arnhem Bay, the next clan, the mother–child relationship. Onwards it spirals. And the sooty oystercatcher that rests on the stick, calling out to the clouds, naming, then taking flight, dipping its wings in the water, riding the winds.

Songspirals are ongoing. Our sharing in this book is part of the ongoing emergence and creation of Country and life. With the end of each song comes the wind. Erasing the footprints for the next day, so it is all lovely and clean for the next song.

PART 3

Guwak

Milŋiya   Naminapu Maymuru-White   11.11.13.

CHAPTER 1

Being a messenger

We cry milkarri for Guwak at night. The milkarri starts at midnight or in the early morning, one or two o'clock, when people are sleeping. Really there is no time; in Yolŋu way we just know where to start and where to end. It is a beautiful ceremony.

Two Djungaya climb trees; one climbs up one tree, and the other another tree. One calls out, 'Guuuwaak.' It is the call of Guwak, a beautiful, high sound that rings clear through the night. The other responds, 'Guuuwaak', an echo. The Guwak calls and the echoes reach from one Country to the next, the sea and the sky, up to Milŋiyawuy, the River of Stars.

The call of the nightbird wakes us up. You can hear the sound of Guwak resonant in the darkness.

The women start keening as they wake with the sound of the call, remembering the passing of their loved ones, maybe ten years earlier. In this way we respect those who have passed. It doesn't matter if someone passed away twenty years ago. When we remember and keep alive our connection with loved ones, it is like a happy ending. Our tears are for those already there, those waiting for us, those who have finally seen the heavens.

The Guwak songspiral talks about a person who has passed away. The spirit waits until Guwak calls out. Guwak and the person who has passed away will journey through the sky together. It's like opening the gates to the heavens, to the universe and beyond.

Then, when it is our time, we wait to come across the universe. We fly, entwined with Guwak, guided by the Milky Way.

Guwak is a Yirritja bird; in English she is known as a koel. She is all black. She's from a rocky mountain area of Arnhem Land called Latharra, away from the coastal area. That's the journey, the Guwak journey. Guwak is a Yirritja song.

Guwak is a messenger, a bird that travels around as an envoy, picking up songs from the land, taking them to the promised land. So Guwak opens the way to the promised land, to the River of Stars, the land that lies beyond the universe. There people are waiting for us.

The Guwak songspiral that we share was sung by our son, Banbapuy's son, Rrawun. He is Wäŋa Wataŋu, the custodian of the songspiral, and it is his responsibility to care for this songspiral through his father, who is from the Maŋgalili clan. Rrawun and Banbapuy worked closely to carefully write down and translate Guwak for this book. We are proud of our sons, knowing that they can carry on their responsibilities. Rrawun, in sharing this with us and you, is carrying on the work Rrawun's father's father, Narritjin Maymuru, did in the 1970s with anthropologist Howard Morphy. Narritjin Maymuru was a great leader, a ceremonial and cultural leader, and a famous artist. In 1962 he initiated and painted one of the Yirrkala church panels. This painting is another form of teaching, of understanding. The painting expresses the Law, and the same Law also exists in the Guwak songspiral.

In our family our grandchildren are Djungaya including Lirrina, Dhaŋdhaŋ, Yambirrwuy and Maminydjama. The children of our granddaughters, Mawunymula, Djamut Dhananayala and Yumalil, are Gutharra. And if our other granddaughters Yambirrwuy and Maminydjama have children, they are Gutharra too.

The Guwak songspiral is the story behind Narritjin and Rrawun's homeland, Djarrakpi, the land, the universe. Maŋalili are related to the Milky Way. And they paint that as part of their stories and part of their unknown heaven. From the land to the universe and beyond.

Rrawun says that the story of Guwak is an unknown story to ŋäpaki. It is one that needs to be told so ŋäpaki can understand that there already are spirits up there, in the sky. We must care for space. When we talk about space, we know that there are people already there. Already. We don't see this but we know this and this is passed on from generation to generation. Guwak is another way to tell people to look after the universe, everything within and beyond it.

Guwak journeys south, following the breeze. Guwak says, 'For the one last time you will hear my cry.' The sounds of Guwak will be heard in the River of Stars and on the earth.

We have Guwak in our family too. Our granddaughter and Rrawun's daughter is Maminydjama. One of Maminydjama's names is Guwak. Maminydjama is a very successful model whose modelling name is Magnolia. She travels around a lot, travelling as a messenger. She is a messenger of Yolŋu culture and strength.

The affinity Maminydjama feels as Guwak, to the Guwak songspiral and to Guwak's role as a messenger, is very strong. We have woven some of her story through this section of the book. We spoke to her on the mobile phone, two of us sisters, Banbapuy and Ritjilili, with Sarah and Sandie, sitting on a sarong on the green lawn of Sarah's home in Gumbaynggirr Country in New South Wales. Maminydjama was in Yirrkala, chatting to various people as they came past her during our conversation, but so enthusiastic and willing to share her story of being Guwak, a messenger, and living in two worlds.

'Guwak—that is my name. I like my name,' she said. 'Yes, it helps me be who I am. I send a message, give a message to the people. Describing it is a bit weird. It is just my name, my totem. My modelling helps me be a messenger. I tell a story. I send a message about my hometown, my people, about simple things, really—respect, manikay, buŋgul—similar to how Guwak does. It sends a message. It informs us of a death, or someone coming, things like that.'

Maminydjama's voice is clear through the phone. She sends her voice as a model and as an ambassador for the Wiyi Yani U Thangani (Women's Voices) project of the Australian Human Rights Commission. She says it is so important for women to gather, it has been so long since women in our communities and around the world have been able to do this but that now is the perfect time for women to do women's business, to come together.

Like Guwak, Maminydjama, her father Rrawun, and his grandfather Narritjin Maymuru have all travelled far. They have sent their message through art, painting, singing and modelling. They tell everyone that we are here.

When she reaches her destination, Guwak lands in a tree. She climbs and again calls out, chanting the names of the Yirritja places. The men calling in the night, in the dawn ceremony of the songspiral, call out, 'Guuwaak.' She is here, was here, will always be here.

We are, we were, we will always be here.

1.

Waŋa nhina burrkitjthun Yolŋu warray'ŋu.
Ŋuruku ŋamaŋamayunarawu burrkuṉgu, yaliyaliwu
ŋarakawu Waymumbawu.
Yurruna ŋarra yurru wunydjininymirriyamanydja
bulka gathandja gadanymirriyamanydja.

*The clans with their deep names Ritharrŋu, Bundurr,
Butjala, Djalimana, Ŋarrkaṉdja, we negotiate for
the preparation and the making of the possum
string.*
*For this string, burrkuṉ, I will prepare possum fur, the
fundamental backbone for Waymumba, the string.*
I will weave it and put possum fur on it.

2.

Bala ŋaraka dhunupakumana burrkuṉdja.
Bili ŋarrakunydja burrkuṉ marr weyin ga
Ritharrŋuwunydja marr dhumbul.

*The string is admired and measured, put in
a perfect position.*
My string is established and completed.

3.

Beŋurunydja ŋayi yurru Guwaknha waŋa.
Waŋanydja ŋayi yurru dhawalnha ŋupan wanhaka
  wäŋa, yurru ŋayinydja Guwakdja ŋathili yana
  marŋgi nhälili ŋayi yurru butthun.

Guwak, she speaks, her cries, her call is heard, from
  far away, across the sky, through Country.
Guwak speaks and her echoes reach the lands and the
  sea of Muŋurru, and from there go up to the skies;
  she already knows to where she will fly.

4.

Bala ŋayi Guwakthu dhakay ŋäkulana watana
  guyŋarrnha.
Bala ŋarra yurru ŋurrungunydja marrtji ŋunha wata
  ŋupan watamirri rirrakay dupthurruna ŋäthili
  Milŋiyalili, ga Muŋurrulili.
Ŋunhili yukurrana nhina miyalk Nyapililŋu.

Guwak feels the cold wind, the south wind,
  mädirriny.
From here I will first go to the place from where the
  cold wind blows, to the stony Country, and speak
  where my voice will reach space, the River of Stars,
  Milŋiyawuy, and the sea of Muŋurru.
There lives a spirit woman, Nyapililŋu.

5.

Guwak waŋana dhuwala ŋarra yurru marr ganana
  Dhithi, Gunbalka Rakila.

Ŋunha ŋupan guyaŋirri watamirri Wurrtjinmirri,
   Dharrpayina.
Bala buṯthurrunana warryurrunana burrkuṉdja.

I will leave this place, the essence of my people, with
   the deep name Dhithi, leave the stony Country,
   Gunbalka Rakila, from where the string came.
I will chase and remember and fly to the Country
   from where the wind blows, to where it directs
   me to Maŋalili Country, nation of Wurrtjinmirri,
   Dharrpayina, deep clan names for Maŋalili.
I take and pull the string and together we will fly;
   entwined, we start the journey, guided, directed
   by the Milky Way, we fly the universe.

6.

Ŋunhiyi ŋayi mulkana wäŋanydja nhäŋala ŋayi dharpa
   bathala yäku Marawil, ŋayi yukurrana dharrana
   waṉawilyurruna.
Ŋal'yurruna ŋayi Guwakdja bala beŋurunydja
   bulu waŋana dhä ḻakaraŋala marrtjina wäŋa
   malanyŋulili.

When Guwak got to her destination, she saw a big
   tree, called Marawili; it stood there with branches
   like arms welcoming Guwak. 'The Marawili tree
   waits for me.'
Guwak climbed onto the tree. 'I will climb onto this
   tree and again from here I will call out and chant the
   names of the Yirritja places, to tell them I am here.'

CHAPTER 2

Sky Country

Waŋa nhina burrkitjthun Yolŋu warray'ŋu.
Ŋuruku ŋamaŋamayunarawu burrkuŋgu, yaliyaliwu
ŋarakawu Waymumbawu.
Yurruna ŋarra yurru wunydjininymirriyamanydja
bulka gathandja gadanymirriyamanydja.

The clans with their deep names Ritharrŋu, Bundurr,
Butjala, Djalimana, Ŋarrkandja, we negotiate for
the preparation and the making of the possum
string.
For this string, burrkun, I will prepare possum fur, the
fundamental backbone for Waymumba, the string.
I will weave it and put possum fur on it.

Guwak is the messenger who connects. We sing from the land
to the sky up into space, from the sea and from the river that
lies beneath the path that Guwak takes. The Milky Way is the

pathway for Guwak to the spiritual world, and the possum string links land and sky and all that is underneath the sky.

To travel the pathway in the right way, we must first negotiate. We must follow the correct protocols. In the Guwak songspiral, we begin by singing the negotiation for the preparation and making of the string. This is a string that will bind us. We must always begin with negotiation. It's the start of the journey. It's the dot where you start and you need to join the dots.

In the songspiral, the negotiation is for a person who has already passed on from life. The ancestors say, if a person who has passed away travels to the next level in the universe, or on the land, we have got to have the preparation, the right tools, like a passport for that person to go.

In life and death, we always negotiate through bala ga' lili, through give and take. At the start of the Guwak songspiral, we are two clans negotiating, the Maŋgalili and the Ritharrŋu. The Ritharrŋu are the wetj, the 'giver', of the string.

We come together through bala ga' lili. It is bala ga' lili that sustains us as we live with each other and with the world. Bala ga' lili is balance, the balance where the water flows from the land and meets the salt water, where the water becomes brackish. There is balance there, between salt and fresh water, that's where the knowledge is. That is where we nourish our existence. Give and take sustains all existence, the existence of the clans, of lands, of knowledge and of relationships with others, including with ŋäpaki.

Before we begin our journey with Guwak, as Guwak, before we sing that journey, we must start with our own protocols of negotiation, the balance of give and take. This was shared during a night at Bawaka when we all sat together and talked about Guwak. We gathered there Gay'wumirr Miyalk Mala—us sisters, Laklak, Ritjilili, Merrkiyawuy, Banbapuy; our daughter Djawundil; and our adopted sister Sandie, daughter Kate and granddaughter Sarah. And we brought our families too, including Rrawun, our son.

We sit, it is night-time. A cool breeze has come up. We sit on the tarp under the edge of the verandah. It is the season of Dhaarratharramirri, one of the six seasons. That cool breeze connects us to other Dhaarratharramirris that have gone before and will come again. The cool breeze connects us to that moment.

Guwak will be sung by Rrawun, with our son Dhalpalawuy on the yidaki and with our brother Djali observing, because Maŋgalili is our father's waku-pulu (child clan). We have asked them to share this songspiral for the book. But first we do the negotiation, the negotiation that begins the songspiral, that is the first line of the songspiral. Rrawun explains the negotiation through riŋgitj. Riŋgitj is who belongs to what area and how these areas meet. Riŋgitj is like a border, but it is not a border that separates. It is a border made through relationships and connections. The borders of riŋgitj make a sacred place to clans, an embassy.

As Rrawun says, 'There is one particular land owned by the Maŋgalili clan, but in that land there is riŋgitj. The clans have their own spaces but there is always sharing. We have shared knowledge for thousands of years. Our ancestral beings are shared. It is the same in the skies. The morning star is shared by other clans, the evening star shared by others, and Guwak is shared by other clans too. But each clan sings it in their own way.'

That is riŋgitj, ancestral beings moving through Country creating interlocking responsibilities from different clans. It is not like buying property with a strict border and fence. Here we don't put up fences, we hear about it from the songspirals.

This happens when we sing milkarri too, there can be an exchange within the songspiral. Halfway through we will swap over. We use the sound of the songspiral from the other clan to show the other clan's songspiral and area. Through riŋgitj, one Country comes into another. It binds the songspiral and the sacred burrkun together. It's about full sharing. It is about respect, a deep understanding of the land, stars and the universe.

Rrawun says, 'Our ancestors said, we are giving you this. That way you can stand with your own culture, with your own song and dance, and with the land here.'

Then he sings the song which begins with, 'Waŋa nhina burrkitjthun Yolŋu warray'ŋu.' The clans, with their deep names Ritharrŋu, Bundurr, Butjala, Djalimana, Ŋarrkandja, negotiate for the preparation and the making of the possum string.

The possum string will take us, entwined, through the Sky Country. We sing and make Sky Country anew with this song. Sky Country goes beyond space. It's the heaven. We know its existence, we talk about it. This is the story in the River of Stars, Milŋiyawuy, the Milky Way.

In Sky Country, there are connections too. It is a river, not just a star or a planet with empty space between. The universe is full, full of connections and stories and beings. There are so many stories and they are in relationship with each other. When we sing the stars, we sing about which direction the morning star comes from, which direction the moon comes from, from which place they come and where they go. There are so many layers.

These layers, they are about relationships here on earth too. They are about bringing messages in the right way. They are about bala ga' lili, give and take, where the salt water and fresh water meet. That happens between Yolŋu and Western knowledges too, a mixing and merging, and a negotiation.

As Guwak, our granddaughter Maminydjama negotiates between worlds. She sends messages like the Guwak of the song-spiral. When she was little, she lived in Melbourne, Adelaide and Darwin with Banbapuy, her grandmother, and Oscar, her grandfather. She says that it was coming back home with them that made her who she is. Here in Arnhem Land she went to Yirrkala School, a bilingual school, and getting a bilingual education was life-changing. She had the chance to learn Yolŋu language, Yolŋu stories, from Yolŋu teachers.

She was in primary school then. She says, 'It made me realise who I was, where I was. It made me realise who I am, that I am Yolŋu, with connections through my mälk, through my skin name, which is another layer of connection through kinship. Also with connections through buŋgul, through everything. I love Darwin, but coming back home made me realise more of that.

'I spoke Yolŋu matha a bit but not very much. I understood sentences and stories but had trouble replying. I don't think I had a proper understanding, really comprehending it. The cultural layers—coming back to my roots was what really, really made me.'

This is her life as the salt water and fresh water meet, as they mingle, and as the knowledge that is give and take is created. She is Guwak but it is difficult to put into words what Yolŋu just know.

Maminydjama found that being home, feeling safe, being surrounded by love and family, was really good for her and kept her healthy, mentally and physically. She started playing a lot of sport with the other Yolŋu kids, her cousins, and hunting. She loves hunting and learning with Country. And we all raised her to know herself. So did Rrawun, her father.

She says, 'Rrawun was always there. Rrawun made a rule, I couldn't speak English to him ever. Always Yolŋu. Dad used to say, you are home now, you use Yolŋu. I understood Yolŋu, but I didn't speak it much because I was scared or embarrassed and didn't want to say the wrong thing.'

That was how she learnt both ways, the Yolŋu way and the Western way, and she has become a messenger. She always was a messenger. She is Guwak that speaks. She says living in both ways has given her a deeper understanding of both worlds and of life. In the Yolŋu way, she talks through the songspirals and that is where her message comes from. Guwak gives a message through flying and through her songspiral too. And that is what Maminydjama does. She talks about her people. She loves dancing and she gives a message that buŋgul and culture are important. She can't talk about it and not do it.

And this is how we live our songspirals. The songspirals are here with us, in our lives. As Rrawun sings it at Bawaka, as Maminydjama, his daughter, lives it through her messages and her life, her modelling and being an ambassador, and as we all live in many worlds.

A fashion week organiser noticed Maminydjama in Darwin when she was a young teenager. He noticed her grace and her aura and wanted her to become a model. But she said she

Magnolia: Maminydjama Maymuru. *(Courtesy of Olivia Tran)*

needed to finish school first. It was later, when she bumped into him again with a mutual friend, that she decided to do it. She had the strength to make her own decisions.

Maminydjama says, 'I feel growing up both ways has given me a very good platform and understanding. It has given me, almost given me, enough power to speak out on behalf of my people and my community from the experience I have had.'

There is power in our names, in Guwak.

We keen milkarri, 'Ŋuruku ŋamaŋamayunarawu burrkuŋu, yaliyaliwu ŋarakawu Waymumbawu.' For this string, burrku<u>n</u>, I will prepare possum fur, the fundamental backbone for Waymumba, the string.

134

We sing of preparing the possum fur using its deep names. This is the fundamental backbone for Waymumba, the string. We are calling the sacred string, we make it sacred. We call its deep names. The string is made out of possum fur. Everything is from possum fur. In the songspiral, the possum made it, the Guwak saw it and cried out.

When we see the image of what we sing, we can see it from above, looking down, flying above the earth. When we sing, sometimes we sing the surface and sometimes the stars. We sing layers. Some people, when they sing, they are looking at the land while they are singing. Some, they can feel the land and see what is happening on the land, just by singing. These are our songspirals.

We make a string, and that is our passport. We weave together our connections between space, the earth and the journey of the spirit. There is always a process, a way of going through the right process of negotiation. This is negotiating and renegotiating relationships between clans and their responsibilities as part of the songspiral. It is about respect. Other clans show respect too. It is both ways. We can't go on this journey in this life. It has to be the spirit that goes to the promised land.

Of course, we make mistakes and the relationships are not always perfect. There is the good, the bad and the ugly. There are politics in the clans, between the clans, and always there is ŋäpaki politics. Sometimes, our politics is not just conveyed by talking. Our displeasure that something hasn't been done right can be conveyed by dance, body language, by movement. Doing something can be a statement. Not doing something can be a statement too. We need to be aware. We need to watch and listen. Always there is negotiation. Always there is bala ga' lili. Always there is give and take.

The weather, the stars, the winds, they connect. There is no invisible barrier separating us. It continues through, all the way up. There is no void. The wind here is connected with the sky. When the wind blows from the north, yams are growing. We learn by when the wind blows what is edible. So, the wind from Sky Country makes life and caring for Country possible. The stars and the light shining down light the rivers here on earth.

We weave, and we put possum fur on the string, the string that binds us. And Guwak is the messenger that calls.

CHAPTER 3

This is political

Bala ŋaraka dhunupakumana burrku<u>n</u>dja.
Bili ŋarrakunydja burrku<u>n</u> marr weyin ga
  Ritharrŋuwunydja marr dhumbul.

*The string is admired and measured, put in
  a perfect position.
My string is established and completed.*

Beŋurunydja ŋayi yurru Guwaknha waŋa.
Waŋanydja ŋayi yurru dhawalnha ŋupan wanhaka
  wäŋa, yurru ŋayinydja Guwakdja ŋathili yana
  marŋgi nhälili ŋayi yurru butthun.

*Guwak, she speaks, her cries, her call is heard, from
  far away, across the sky, through Country.
Guwak speaks and her echoes reach the lands and the
  sea of Muŋurru, and from there go up to the skies;
  she already knows to where she will fly.*

As the tide gently washes onto the beach at Bawaka, we sit under the djomula tree weaving the pandanus leaves, the gunga, together into a basket. Rrawun is with Kate, Sandie and Sarah explaining more about Guwak to them. We thread the long thin leaves and observe.

Rrawun says, 'Then I will make the fur into a string, the possum string. Put it into a perfect shape, a perfect string. Then we will look at how long the string is. I will check and look and admire how long it is. Like checking identification so they can travel the universe and beyond to find their promised land.'

The string and the possum fur have many meanings, and not symbolic or metaphorical meanings. The string and fur are identities, they bring the world into being, bring worlds into being. They are passports to the universe. They embody a multiplicity of things and bring them together. They are connections between clans, between Countries, between earth and sky. The string is Guwak speaking, and Guwak in turn creates the sky anew.

Yolŋu people have always worked hard to create strings which connect—connect clans, Countries, worlds and cultures. Maminydjama comes from a very, very strong family. Maminydjama's great-grandfathers were the brothers Narritjin and Nanyin Maymuru. Narritjin was the second eldest, and his brother, Nanyin, was the eldest. In 1963, in response to the coming of the mine and the excision of their Country without their permission, these two brothers, with their cousin brother Bukarra, had the idea for the Bark Petitions to proclaim Yolŋu Law through twelve clan designs framing typed English and Gumatj text. When Yolŋu people talked about writing a petition to the Australian Government, the brothers said, 'Why can't we paint? We need to let them know that this is Yolŋu Country.' The Bark Petitions were the first documents submitted by Aboriginal people to be finally recognised by the Australian parliament, and they asserted our land rights.

Narritjin, Nanyin and Bukarra were responsible for the Bark Petitions, but their names were never mentioned. They were patient and quiet, they sat back. Now Nanyin's eldest son, Baluka Maymuru, is very old. He has passed that knowledge on to his sons and Rrawun. He is very patient, sitting down with them. Like Baluka and his fathers, Rrawun and Maminydjama too are very humble and patient.

Sometimes people look at the old man, Baluka, and then they look to Maminydjama and they say here is Narritjin's great-granddaughter. And Maminydjama, she talks about them so they are remembered. When Nanyin passed away, Narritjin taught their children how to paint to carry on the line of artists. When Rrawun's dad died, Nanyin's daughter, Naminapu, taught Rrawun to paint. Her artwork frames this part of the book. Rrawun is focusing on his painting now. They are trying to get Maminydjama to paint too.

Guwak can make peace or long-term conflict by the way the songspiral is performed, by the buŋgul. This is the feeling that comes through. The dance is very strong. The songspiral talks about the deceased person, how that person lived. The songspiral celebrates their life, dances their life. It makes us strong as we are dancing on that land, in that place. The power is in each person—it is so tangible we can reach out and touch it.

It is full of the respect, emotion, memories that the deceased person will take away from this life. The spirit remains with us right up until the end of the funeral. On that night the song and the spirit will then go to the afterlife.

It is powerful because the Law says that it should be done in this place. The Law of that land says what belongs there. That is the power. What belongs in the land, stays in the land, you can't take it out. You can't change the Law. Every dance, every movement, has meaning behind it. There is a dance for hunting kangaroo that can only be done by the right clan. The animal and the person become one. If you don't do things properly, it becomes meaningless, like a show. It must come out of the land in the proper way, showing what is precious, what is valued.

It is important that other Aboriginal people also respect that the Law must stay with the land. Other Aboriginal people shouldn't take what we have. Everything is different. The language is different. People shouldn't take knowledge, songs, art or ceremonies and try to make them their own.

People ask how we know it is our land. It's because we cry milkarri, we sing, we dance. This is the evidence. This shows that we are from our land. It shows what we are made of and who we are. Everything has to be right. Through the milkarri we know how to be true and how to show the truth with power, with passion.

There is power in it and it can also be political. That is why when we speak in conferences we talk in Yolŋu matha first, as it gives us power to speak. But if songspirals are not done properly, the right process is not followed, they can cause death. People have been murdered, speared, killed. It is like stealing someone's property. This is Yolŋu life. This is the way it is.

Yet we see the wrong processes happening all around us. People hunger, governments are hungry for what they want, what they need from Yolŋu people. They are like the djilawurr, the scrub hen, a little bird that goes around scratching at the ground. People are always scratching, trying to get at things that can be of use to them. We see so many cases of ŋäpaki being like little children—greedy, they take and they never give back. Like a child who has not yet learnt to share. We want to say to the government that you are wrong, your way of working with the Yolŋu that live in their own lands is wrong. You have to sit with Yolŋu and find out what it is that they want and need. Otherwise it is going to be a sad, sad future with all the government intervention that will have a heavy impact on our lives and the lives of our lands.

One day at a health conference a doctor said, 'You know, in the ŋäpaki world, we are better than you.' Even after all our years of working with ŋäpaki, of encouraging two ways learning and sharing our knowledge systems, many ŋäpaki think we are primitives. Maybe it's because they don't understand our Law. For example, when we get paid, we need to share our money, this is our Law. We have to give and take, share.

We face struggles like these every day. We are Yolŋu but sometimes we feel like we are powerless. We have the power here, strong culture, strong language, but sometimes we feel powerless because people, whether other Aboriginal people or ŋäpaki or academics, governments—they use people like us. We are not perfect, we fight among ourselves. We know that is there but we also know what is here. The ongoing changes of governments, of Western laws, we keep up with the evolving contemporary work, we are racing, always racing to be contemporary Yolŋu as well as old Yolŋu, the cultural Yolŋu. We are keeping up with changes.

They try to make us feel poor. But we must remember and teach our children that we are not poor, we are rich. Every time we sing, we sing about the person's treasure and belonging with Country. Every individual is rich, they have their own wealth, through song, sacred objects, their land, in the sea and in the river. That is why every Yolŋu is a rich Yolŋu because he or she carries the land. And we are sacred.

When a person passes away, they are considered a king or a queen, sacred. We know the sacredness of our bones. That is why we are sharing. This culture has been here since the day humans were created on earth. Every person, man, woman, child, has sacred, scientific names given by the Elders. They have to walk with the richness of being a Yolŋu man or woman.

Maminydjama, humble and patient, is very lovely, bubbly and easy to talk to. But if someone says the wrong thing, then see her snap.

One day, a miyalk, a woman, a journalist, asked Maminydjama about problems in the community. Maminydjama said, 'You are asking me because I am community. You come in with your city goggles.'

The journalist said, 'I didn't want to upset you.'

Maminydjama replied, 'You didn't upset me. You came all this way. I am outspoken. It is about 6 pm, we drove past kids playing football, all the kids walking from school, all the kids at the Art Centre. What did you see? All you saw was rubbish, cigarettes, bottles for sniffing—you didn't see paintbrushes, the kids playing sport, our community.'

Maminydjama thought to herself, You should chill out, but then she thought, No, the journalist asked, I need to say this. The journalist just sees what's on the news reports. Everyone has a view on the community and what it is like.

Maminydjama is disappointed as she thinks about all the positive activities the journalist saw, and yet no one wants to see them. When not modelling, Maminydjama works for Sport and Recreation in Yirrkala. She is always putting photos of healthy, active people on Facebook, but people don't want to see that. They are not ready to accept that as a people Yolŋu are rising.

When the missionaries moved us from our homelands to establish Yirrkala, the people had no idea what would happen here. The taste of the Western world came in, divided all the clans, divided their thoughts, their family, kinship. It was like a poison, they brought many poisons to destroy our Yolŋu world.

They have tried to wipe Aboriginal people out of Australia, or to say the land is empty, sea and space and all our Country is empty. Learn and remember the term *terra nullius*. They said in the past that Aboriginal people, that Yolŋu did not exist because they were not agriculturalists. They did not see rows and rows of manmuŋa (long yams), they did not see orchards of larrani (bush apples) and munydjutj (plum trees) and dingu (cycad palms), they did not see a plantation of baladay (yam) and balkpalk and wuŋapu (types of fruit), they did not see a field of räkay (edible water reed) and dhatam (waterlily), and therefore, they said, the land was empty. They didn't see our songspirals, our clan designs, they ignored our milkarri, our relationships and connections with Country.

Aboriginal history has not been told in the schools throughout Australia. People have not been told that the land they've come to call their own was the land created by mystery, taboo, sacred and holy, created by the creature spirit beings, some sights never to be looked upon by the eyes of women and children, some by the eyes of men. Then the invaders came with iron chains and they raped and plundered, murdered and forced landowners off their lands. Oh yes, we know this history, even though it is not written in the history books. But it should be taught in schools throughout Australia, must be taught. And what have the invaders done or said to the Yolŋu people of the land? At least some Aboriginal groups are now reviving their languages, their Laws, and claiming their lands back.

And it is true that in this time, Yolŋu are still strong in their culture and Law, despite the ever-changing environment around us. We still practise rituals where only women are allowed to be present, and rituals where only men are present. And there are others that are done every day, in communities throughout North East Arnhem Land, that celebrate birth or death or renewal of a person and land. It's something we don't want to hide. We want to tell the truth.

And it's the same for Sky Country. It is not empty, it is not waiting for colonisation.

Beŋurunydja ŋayi yurru Guwaknha waŋa. Guwak, she speaks, her cries, her call is heard, from far away, across the sky, through Country. Guwak speaks and her echoes reach the lands and the sea of Muŋurru, and from there go up to the skies; she already knows to where she will fly.

144

The reason Guwak does a circular journey is because of the possum fur, to circle the land and bind the people together. Guwak was a smart bird. Every time we sing Guwak, we think about our journey.

The songspiral goes to other clans too; different clans will pass on the songspiral until the day breaks. We have one ancestor, Guwak, but different ways. So if Maŋgalili are singing and there is another clan, then the other clan will sing from their side and use a different tune. When the Maŋgalili finish, the Gupapuyŋu will sing Guwak in their different tune to the day break, as their homeland, Yathalamara, is to the west, in Central Arnhem Land. The Gupapuyŋu say bil-bil-bil-Guwak, meaning looking towards the day break. This is the way that the Guwak spirals. Guwak passes onwards.

Guwak travelled and now the songspiral goes round and round and round. Guwak has a plan to bind everything up; we live under her name.

The spirits share the same journey from life to death and beyond to the afterlife. This is Guwak's journey, through life, through death, through other lives.

Guwak knows where she is going. She has repeated, and will repeat, this journey through Sky Country too many times to count. Space is intimately known, inhabited and cared for. Current efforts to colonise space are jumping ahead. Business people and governments seem to lack any sense of responsibility, or any respect. Rrawun wonders if they are scared, scared of listening.

It seems as if, having killed this planet, having damaged it with problems like global warming, scientists, business people and governments are now looking for another earth. They want to find another planet. People need to recognise their limitations. They are hoping they'll find another earth, but if they pause and meditate they might realise it's already here. They might find what they're searching for right here on earth. They are dreaming about a new house, getting away to wherever to build their new house, make a fortune. Will that keep the family happy? For those people who think about life, who recognise that life itself is important, you have to be aware of your pathway. You have to be aware of your kids and also teach them where to go, what to do. They are the important things, what your father and mother did for you.

Those that search for another planet, they won't find it. They can only find that planet when they die, only the spirit can go there.

✹ ✹ ✹

That's why we are writing this book. It's about the rights of people, of the Yolŋu people of North East Arnhem Land. We need to keep things in their place. We want this to assert our rights, to say to all mainstream Australia, 'This is Yolŋu, it belongs here. It is not yours to take away. We have songspirals, they are strong, our culture is strong, everything is strong.'

And we are writing this book, us strong Yolŋu sisters, because we are always reading about this from ŋäpaki. Non-Yolŋu think they know but they don't know. The context, the feeling, the word is wrong. We can feel that emotion, carry you beyond the word, beyond the singing.

This is political because we must protect our land, our land has its own politics, its own rights. The ancestors gave Yolŋu our borders, our understanding not to go onto other land. Land and people are connected. And we are connected through language. Communities like ours must have language. Without language, there can be no songspirals. Language, Yolŋu languages, are power. They tell the story through singing, speaking, milkarri. Language identifies who we are, where our homeland is.

CHAPTER 4

The spirits are in everything

Bala ŋayi Guwakthu dhakay ŋäkulana watana
    guyŋarrnha.
Bala ŋarra yurru ŋurrungunydja marrtji ŋunha wata
    ŋupan watamirri rirrakay dupthurruna ŋäthili
    Milŋiyalili, ga Muŋurrulili.
Ŋunhili yukurrana nhina miyalk Nyapililŋu.

Guwak feels the cold wind, the south wind, mädirriny.
From here I will first go to the place from where the
    cold wind blows, to the stony Country, and speak
    where my voice will reach space, the River of Stars,
    Milŋiyawuy, and the sea of Muŋurru.
There lives a spirit woman, Nyapililŋu.

Guwak is spiritual. When mädirriny, the south wind, blows,
it is a message from the spirits and from the ancestors to the
person who has passed away announcing their passport to the
stars, the afterlife.

Our verses, melodies, songspirals and language are ours, given to us by the spirits, the Djan'kawu Sisters, the Waterspout being, the ancient giant Shark in the timeless past beyond knowing. The water, rocks, the stream, that tree, they all have a spirit.

For Yolŋu, spirits and spirituality are not about religion, they are not about believing in this or that. We are part of the ecosystem, of everything. It is all connected. For us, spirituality is about being, about culture, about love. The spiritual world is here, it is waiting for us. We find it through dance and stories and songs.

Some people have a god; we have life force. It's like the oxygen in the water that forms little bubbles, the life force is inside. We hate the word dreaming. We are not asleep. We are here and have all this knowledge, this life force, collective thought, a soul that is created by the water.

We don't have an identity without Country. We are all connected. Every contour on the land, every rock, every water, is connected to us. They are bigger than us, we are just a little thing. There is another big thing under us. We are small in ourselves but become who we are through milkarri. It is what we cry. We are connected through songspirals.

So, when we keen milkarri, feel pain, happiness or sadness, it comes from the land and from the ancestors. Listening to the spirits and to our ancestors and learning from the land defines our spiritual affiliations to the land.

Guwak comes from a rocky place away from the coast, a rocky mountain area called Latharra Warkawarka. When Guwak felt the cold wind she said, 'I will fly over there to wurrtjin watamirri, the place where that breeze is coming from.'

When Guwak speaks, her cries are heard not only on earth but also in Sky Country. Guwak calls when the spirit arrives at its destination in the River of Stars. She is heard in the stars and her echo is heard where the river flows into the ocean, the deep ocean. This is the sea of stars on earth, where the Yaŋarrtji meets the Muŋurru.

The songspiral tells us that Guwak and Sky Country communicate and are heard by one another. The beings that inhabit Sky Country are kin with us and with Guwak. There are spirit beings up there. There are many things up there.

Guwak is someone's spirit when they pass away. The spirit waits until Guwak calls out. Guwak takes the spirit back to join the ancestors in the River of Stars. As the spirit reaches their destination the call is heard. It is heard in the Milŋiyawuy, the River of Stars, its echo is heard in Yaŋarrtji, the Sea of Stars that lives on earth. The sound goes up to the river and the echoes are heard in the sea. The echo bounces from the river to the sea, resonating between them.

The call is telling the people, giving a message, calling the names of the places, calling them into being. This is deeper than just calling out; there is a deeper level of language than there is in English. It's like opening the gates to the heavens, to the universe, for the spirit who is carrying the string. We don't see, but if we call with our true heart, our true understanding, the songspiral will be passed on and Country will continue to be kept alive.

In the ceremony, when we hear the call, a mother will keen milkarri for her children and grandchildren. All the mothers will cry and also name the ancestral Guwak, now sending the spirit. We call this Dhukarr ḻakarama—straightening the pathway, naming the road. We say, 'Tonight is the night we are going to Dhukarr ḻakarama.' We don't say we will cry Guwak.

Guwak circles around the dead, finding the soul, the sacred thread. When we dance we have the string with us, we dance around the body. We are being Guwak with her thread. We are entwining our soul, Guwak's soul, together with the soul of the person. We call it entwining because we are wrapping, circling it, with that string. It says in the songspiral, 'With that string I am going back to Milŋiyawuy, the Milky Way, the River of Stars.'

There is no big boundary between the River of Stars and the land. They are connected. When the stars are above, they shine down on the rivers of the earth. The islands of Nalkuma, Murrmurrnga, Wakuwala and Gaywndji, to which the deceased travel, exist in Sky Country and Sea Country, on earth and in the sky.

When you are alive, you can paddle to the island in the ocean; when you die you go to the island in Sky Country. Before

Naminapu Maymuru-White, *Milŋiyawuy No. 4* (2017).
(*The Buku-Larrŋgay Mulka Art Centre archives*)

Laklak's husband, Batjaŋ, died, he went to the island Nalkuma. When he was sick, Laklak contacted Binmila, another of Mungurrawuy's granddaughters, who arranged to take Batjaŋ there in a helicopter. He lay down there with the palm trees, they had lunch. It was peaceful, beautiful. Then he went back home and passed away. The islands are in both Sea Country and Sky Country, so we can visit one by visiting the other.

When Yolŋu people die, the boat, a djulpan, goes on a journey to the River of Stars. The spirits wait; when the boat comes, they jump in and together they paddle in the boat. The Dhuwa go to Dhuwa place, and the Yirritja go to Yirritja place. But there is a certain place where they go together. We know it's there because people sing, dance and keen it. Yirritja people sing, paddling, they go to their destination and they go to meet their loved ones. That song connects to when we hear the thunder, the women keen because they think about their loved ones.

In that place, up there in Sky Country, the spirit woman Nyapililŋu lives. It is a sacred place, untouched. In the quiet of the night we hear the call that signals the start of the ceremony and then it is time for the soul to join the others in the River of Stars. It's like a meditation to take that soul to the promised land.

When someone passes they will go to that place, beyond the universe, then they will come back again. Sometimes we will come back as a mammal, fish or a reptile. It could be any of the animals that are in the songs. That is Yolŋu philosophy. Sometimes when we see an animal or listen to a person singing we will remember that person who has passed away. The old person will remember someone who has passed away seventy years ago—the same creature spirit being, the same singing voice.

'Ahh, that person has come back,' they will say. To find their way back, they use the same path. They do it perfectly because it is the path given by the ancestors who knew that the person was coming back.

There is always communication between spirits and people who are living now. You see all the animals coming closer? They will come closer to you, they will not harm you, that is how you know this person has come back. At Bawaka, a monitor lizard has been coming around. We sit and talk about song-spirals and it comes to us. It walks past the fire. It comes to the house. We call that beautiful big green lizard Gali Gali. That is a skin name, a mälk. That way we know who the lizard is related to. It has the same mälk as us sisters.

All Yolŋu of North East Arnhem Land were given their totem, whether it be animal or spirit from time immemorial, by the animal or spirit being that created Yolŋu land, the oceans and the currents, the contours of our world. We received those totems, the people of the land, from those first ancient Yolŋu people to the Yolŋu of today. The dances, the ceremonies, the belief of you and your totem are one and the same, so that the power of the spirit being is manifested in the dances we do. Our body parts have the same name as the body parts of our animal or our spirit being.

The animals, the spirit beings, the stars and space, everything has its knowledge and Law. The morning star has its own understanding, and the evening star has its own understanding.

As Rrawu<u>n</u> says, we are so busy that we forget to listen to the land, to the spirits, to our ancestors. We have to stop and think what we are doing and try to listen. The spirit will tell us, the land will tell us. Everyone has their own pathway.

CHAPTER 5

Living in today's world

Guwak waŋana dhuwala ŋarra yurru marr ganana
    Dhithi, Gunbalka Rakila.
Ŋunha ŋupan guyaŋirri watamirri Wurrtjinmirri,
    Dharrpayina.
Bala butthurrunana warryurrunana burrkundja.

*I will leave this place, the essence of my people, with
    the deep name Dhithi, leave the stony Country,
    Gunbalka Rakila, from where the string came.*
*I will chase and remember and fly to the Country
    from where the wind blows, to where it directs
    me to Maŋalili Country, nation of Wurrtjinmirri,
    Dharrpayina, deep clan names for Maŋalili.*
*I take and pull the string and together we will fly;
    entwined, we start the journey, guided, directed
    by the Milky Way, we fly the universe.*

Ŋunhiyi ŋayi mulkana wäŋanydja nhäŋala ŋayi dharpa
   bathala yäku Marawil, ŋayi yukurrana dharrana
   wa<u>n</u>awilyurruna.
Ŋal'yurruna ŋayi Guwakdja bala beŋurunydja
   bulu waŋana dhä <u>l</u>akaraŋala marrtjina wäŋa
   malanyŋulili.

*When Guwak got to her destination, she saw a big
   tree, called Marawili; it stood there with branches
   like arms welcoming Guwak. 'The Marawili tree
   waits for me.'*
*Guwak climbed onto the tree. 'I will climb onto this
   tree and again from here I will call out and chant
   the names of the Yirritja places, to tell them
   I am here.'*

Yolŋu live in the contemporary world now, maintaining culture
while finding new ways to keep the Law and be true to the Law.
We keep the songspirals healthy. We live in the mainstream now.
We talk about and live contemporary lives. Through our music
we put the old into the new. We translate the old language into
English. But we can't change the deep names into new names,
as there is no such language for those words in English. The
language has to be held strong and true.

   When people hear Yolŋu sung in contemporary music, such
as the famous rock band of the 1980s and 90s Yothu Yindi, they
don't realise that the songs are manikay, they have meanings.
This is also true of East Journey, the band our sons Rrawu<u>n</u>
and Bambuŋ are in. The songs East Journey write and sing
link to everything we're talking about in this book. The songs

are part of the songspirals, the music *is* the songspirals. They have the same meaning. They are singing from the heart, with emotion. They are giving the message to the world.

These are the words of East Journey's beautiful Guwak song.

Guwak

Look up at the Milky Way,
Stars shining bright, up in the dark sky.
A story's been told,
That ancestral bird Walkuli Guwak. [Walkuli is another name
    for Guwak]
Black as the night
Guwak cry through the lonely sky,
Lonely sky.

From gumurr rakila oh gurrumtjum, gurrumtjum [Guwak took
the string and flew in front of the chest of the rocky ridge to
find a place where there is a breeze]

Where the journey begins
For the one last time
The sound of the cry,
Bird is heard as it flies.

Burrkun warryurruna wo gathanara [The guidance that gives me
    the strength]
Waraka waraka ŋuru [The string was pulled that was given to us]
Ŋarrakunydja Marrwirrny [I have this string that they have given
    me]
Burrkun yaliyali [The possum string]
Bundurrwa dharrpayinawa [It guides them back when they die,
    using the deep name of the clan]

157

With this burrkun, I'm going back to the River of Stars, to my
spiritual land.

The journey of Walkuli Guwak,
Sending message through,
Calling through the cold night,
'Where is my promised land?'

Rirrakay yurrunana Walkuli [Guwak cries]
Liyamunha ŋaraka nhina dhunupayama [At night we are sitting
down making the string, the backbone, preparing it]
Burrkun yaḻiyaḻi waymamba dilimdilim Guwak [The deep names
of the string are named]

By the sound of the cry we will reach the destination
And the echoes will be heard
By the spirit of mine.
Ŋayindja Napililŋu [The spirit woman]
The answer is her,
To rejoin her
In a cycle of life
Together in spiritual land.

Rirrakaynydja buywuyun walkuli ḻiyamunha [Echoing through,
crying in the night]
Burrkuṉdja marrtji dhunupayama yaḻiyaḻi waymamba dilimdilim
[Marawili tree is the grandchild for Maŋgalili so will be there
to welcome the maternal grandmother]
Nhenydja ŋarraku ŋathili dharpa dharri marawili djanpi-
lila wuluŋguttji [Making it, preparing it, making the string
straight, putting possum fur on it].

Guwak is our ancestral spiritual bird that carries our spirit through the night until the day break and into our spiritual world forever.

Living in two worlds is so hard. Through all these struggles and changes, we are determined to keep the old as strong as possible. We do this for the next generation, but we are also worried about the next generation—who will keep the culture strong, learn it and keep it alive? Who in the next generation? Will it crumble and die or will it not?

We change and adapt. There are new things in the songs now, in the Yirritja songs. There are things like foreigners, guns, sugar, alcohol and flags, some of which were brought by the Macassans. In the future, who knows? Maybe people will be singing of computers. Dhuwa don't sing of new things, they sing of what is already here. We are careful as we bring things in, bring people into relationship with us, like through the adoption of ŋäpaki. The order must be right, things must be in their place.

Part of learning is following the right structure, the right process. Without structure, our kids will go the wrong way, and then they'll find themselves in trouble. The bad things, the drinking, drugs that are starting to come in, and with kids experimenting. It is a struggle to tell the young, yes, you are young, you experiment, but these are the kind of things that can make you lose the foundation, the djalkiri. You will float. You will float away. And then people will come in and take what is yours. They will rip the land apart and rip you apart. You will die with nothing.

If you are a very clever Yolŋu person you should be able to use your land, find a business, that can be good for yourself in the contemporary world and the old. We try to live in a new way where we can keep to the Law, the true form, the form of the old.

We worry about our young ones and we are proud of them too. Rrawun wants his daughters Maminydjama and Yambirrwuy to go to Yilpara, about half a day's drive south on Blue Mud Bay, and see their grandmothers, stay there a while and do some artworks, and sit with them, painting, learning the Yolŋu knowledge that they will hold. He wants to make sure they know what they're doing, by going back to Country, culture. This is how it's possible to have two worlds.

We also recognise the strength in our children and grand-children. We see Maminydjama as very strong. People respect her. Maybe it is the way she is. She is humble, not arrogant. When she is walking around in the community, she wears long skirts like the rest of us, she doesn't wear makeup, she looks like herself. She sits down and talks to Elders, people that she knows.

She knows that in the community she will be the same as everyone else. When she travels, of course, she has to dress up because it is a different world. One day, she came out of the car, she came out with a short, tight skirt on. And Banbapuy said, 'Oh my god, I can see your thighs', and Maminydjama said, 'Yes, because I am going to Melbourne, Grandma.' She can be in the cultural world and the ŋäpaki world.

Maminydjama uses her position as Guwak the best way she can. She says, 'When I am in the communities travelling as an ambassador for the Women's Voices project, I see some women who are very vulnerable. Then I like to use my knowledge that I have learnt from my community. I pay attention to things like body language, eye contact, respect, personal space. But if I am working in Sydney with schoolgirls, they like touching my hair and I am comfortable with that. I use what I have learnt the best way I can, for the different communities. I am very comfortable in both worlds. I know how to organise myself, use the right language and body language, how to approach people, culturally. I feel I am a person for the younger generation and I give the message that buŋgul and manikay are important. I see myself as an ambassador and an advocate for my family, community, people. I think that is why people really respect me, because I don't have time to waste. If I feel like I have something to say to someone, I say it.'

You see white sand, white sand on a particular stretch of coastline in Maŋgalili Country. It is the possum fur coming down to wrap the tree, coming from Ritharrŋu. Guwak has come, bringing the possum string. We come together when we have that ceremony, then we fly together, take the string together. Through the riŋgitj, other people can come and join the ceremony.

Now when we see the Milky Way, that is the journey. Because it was the night-time when Guwak flew pulling the string. When we are looking for this songspiral, it is already there, where the Milky Way turns through Sky Country. That is the journey, that is the pathway.

Through Guwak we are connected. Guwak is a messenger that connects us. We are linked, one person to another, one clan to another. We are linked to the land and the sky and to space. Guwak connects us through our songspirals, through its call, and through the ways it lives in us. And it lives in our young people, as Maminydjama models and is an ambassador, and Rrawun and Bambuŋ's band sings and re-sings the ceremony in a contemporary way. They are messengers too. Guwak is a messenger that calls out and chants the names of the Yirritja places. Chanting the names of the places creates them again. It is all made anew.

When we sing the land, we sing space. When we sing about the land, we sing about space. That is Sky Country. Guwak picks up songs from the land, travelling around and taking them and opening the way to the promised land, the River of Stars. The songspiral is the pathway; Guwak gives the pathway for the people and the community to get prepared.

In the ceremony, we are in the stillness of the night. The people in trees call out. Through the night's stillness you will hear them. Guuuuuuwak, the call of Guwak. Another Guwak hears and picks it up. Guuuuuuwak. Then some may start to do milkarri, for people who have passed away, maybe a long time ago, but we hold them in our heart. It is the burial day.

Songspirals spiral to the sky through Guwak. We keen the night, during the night, as part of the night. The beauty of the night, the special and sacred time.

When we dance, there is a fig tree, a ḏawu tree, and the dancers spin the threads and put possum fur all around it. The Djungaya, our children, dance and roll the string and place it on the coffin. This says, 'It's time to be buried.' It is the pathway.

Now we come to the end of our songspiral and Guwak gets to the destination, after a long journey. Guwak sees a big tree called Marawili. That tree stands there with branches like arms welcoming Guwak. The tree waits and welcomes. The Marawili tree represents all the clans, all the yothu and yindi. It can bind and unite all the Yirritja and Dhuwa clans together under the Marawili shade.

It is here that Guwak chants, as we chant, the deep names.

Like all our songspirals, there are different levels for Guwak. Some we have shared and some we cannot. Guwak is for funerals, to help the one who died find their way. Guwak guides them through their path. And at funerals, Guwak gives us the message that it is time to get prepared for tomorrow, tomorrow is the big day, the last day, the burial. And the pathway of Guwak is for other things too; for the night, to link us to the sky. She is a messenger that calls out clearly. The pathway is for always. It is the Guwak calling out.

Maminydjama is that Guwak bird. She is a messenger and she educates people. She has the strength to become a model, she is calling out like that bird, with that power, and she tells ŋäpaki we are not just what you think. And Rrawu<u>n</u> too with his band East Journey. We are open, keeping ourselves strong, connecting out. We are entwined.

We are multilingual, multicultural. We hold different knowledges and live in different worlds. Just as the Marawili tree stands there with branches like arms welcoming Guwak, we are held.

We invite you to meet us, to learn too, to be open to your wondrous minds.

PART 4
Wititj

CHAPTER 1

Settling of the Serpent

It is dark in the rainforest, under the trees, and her body looks black. But when she lies in the sun, we see the rainbows. She shines like a rainbow in the sun. She is the Rainbow Serpent, she is Wititj. The travels of the Rainbow Serpent created the land, the people. Wititj gave birth to the Dhuwa clans in Arnhem Land and all across Australia too. She created Country as she wove her sinuous passage. This songspiral, the Settling of the Serpent, is the end of her journey.

As she travels, the Rainbow Serpent—also known as Ralinymana, Nyukumana and Gunbirrŋu—sways, sashaying like a model making her way down the catwalk. She is sensing, smelling her way, putting her smell on the land. Knowing that land, making those boundaries, naming them one after another. Threading her way. As she moves, she clears the area with her body, flattening the grass, creating a track through the bush. These are the boundaries she creates and claims. If another totem comes to that area, they can smell that she has been there and they will turn away. That is why she puts a smell on her children as she blesses them. She does this as she passes. It is part of the marking of the children, making the boundaries. Everything she touches becomes sacred, has a name, because the serpent claimed it.

But Wititj is exhausted. It has been a long journey, so much singing of the sacred places, so much giving knowledge, giving life to the land, to the animals, and so much making of boundaries. Wititj is so very tired. So she settles down, curled in a spiral with her head in the centre. She rests her weary head at the centre of her coiled body, marking a boundary of the sacred territory she has worked so hard to create and claim. When women keen milkarri and men sing, they sing the boundary. Singing and keening the land, crying the land, marking the land. They are signing the land by being there. Every Yolŋu territory is marked by that Law.

Laklak, our eldest sister and leader of the Gay'wu Group of Women, the collective, is Wititj. Some of her names come from the serpent. Laklak has the names Ŋuliny, Warraday, Djärri'mi—they all mean the Rainbow Serpent and they were given to her by our Gälpu grandmother.

Before Laklak was born, before she had grown big in Mum's tummy, she visited as a spirit. It was at Gutjitj, a freshwater waterhole in the mangroves, where Mum had gone. Mum hadn't told anyone yet she was pregnant. There was a big snake, a bäpi, named Wulara. It was the spirit of Laklak. The land there belongs to the Ŋaymil clan and the waterhole is called Milŋurr. It is a special place where fresh water bubbles up. This bubbling water is knowledge. It was in that waterhole with the rainbow water that Bilin, our yapa who was also raised by our dad, saw the snake. The snake was sitting up watching Bilin with kindness.

That happens when someone is coming in: the child gives something to the family, their spirit visits them, a message is sent or something unusual happens like getting a very big catch of fish. That is why the men honour Laklak, because she had come before she was born. Both the Dätiwuy and Ŋaymil clans taught her milkarri, and likun, the deep names, because she is Wititj. This is very special. And later, through this songspiral, we will tell you more about how Laklak was honoured, by the men, by the community, and with the giving of a sacred digging stick, a Wapitja.

Laklak was given the name Wititj from her grandmother's clan, Gälpu, whose totem is Wititj. She holds the knowledge. She is Gutharra. She has a special place as the eldest daughter of the eldest daughter in our family, as mother, grandmother, sister, Elder, teacher, leader. She has a special responsibility to care for Country and care for family, to hold the songspirals together, to cry milkarri for them and so re-create and sing the land.

As a child, she was taught by the clans. She was buku dhäwu, having a mind full of stories. She loved being around the stories. She was always sitting there, listening. She learnt from the old people, from the grandmothers and all the mothers. She would listen, go with them hunting and getting food. As the eldest, she was taught and she learnt as much as she could.

We, her sisters, as well as her daughters, granddaughters and great-granddaughters, all of us in the Gay'wu Group of Women learn from Laklak. We learn about milkarri from her. She knows everything: milkarri, the roots of the songs, knowledge of the land, the bush, Yirritja and Dhuwa songs, any songs, any clan songs. It was Laklak who decided to help ŋäpaki to better understand Yolŋu culture. She has always been a school teacher, and now continues to teach visitors through our cultural tourism business, as an Elder. Every time we saw people on the TV shouting for land rights, it was her wish to show people another way by giving a message to ŋäpaki, helping them learn. Laklak had the vision behind our Gay'wu Group of Women and she first brought Sarah, Kate and Sandie in. She started us working together and had the idea for our first book on weaving lives together at Bawaka. That book shares how to weave and the important women's knowledge that goes with that. She then led our second book, *Welcome to My Country*, which takes you deeper in to our knowledge at Bawaka, sharing stories about Bawaka and Laklak's own life. She has been key to all the academic articles written by the group as the Bawaka Collective, inspiring the group to write with Bawaka Country as the main author. Our academic articles now have Country acknowledged as the lead author, rather than just people, to show the way Country shapes, teaches and guides us. By sharing her Yolŋu knowledge in a strong way our sister has extended her teaching and made an important and challenging contribution to the university world and beyond.

Laklak also started our business Bawaka Cultural Experiences, including the Gay'wu women's tours, and was a leader in getting our family to work with tourists. People from different backgrounds have come in and are learning more about our culture, sitting on the ground with us, being equal. Even Olympian Cathy Freeman and actress Deborah Mailman, famous people who come to visit; we don't treat them as famous people, we always treat them as family.

Laklak decided that we would write this book about songspirals to share with you. She wanted to write a deep book, a book for everyone, to share and educate. She says it is important to support each other, to support milkarri, to work with people from different homelands so we can work together, as one family. And to educate ŋäpaki, open their eyes, so they realise that, yes, Yolŋu have a place to belong, Yolŋu have culture. This is why we do this.

But she started getting tired. In 2014, Laklak let us know that she would pass some of the leadership of the projects on to her younger sisters. She was not feeling well. We talked about our Gay'wu Group of Women, how we would keep working together, and we thought about Milŋurr, the fresh waterhole in the mangroves. This is because when we work together all our ideas bubble up and we have so much to share, water bubbling up from the ground, knowledge and sharing. This is Larrwaw' Larrwaw', ideas bubbling up from deep in the well, flowing out, spilling out, pouring out. That is how it is when we are together. We talked about how we all think alike, even though we live different lives in different places. We are family now.

Our work together is the Milŋurr, the Milŋurr spring where the snake came to see our mother, where Laklak's spirit came to visit when she was new in Mum's tummy.

We didn't know what would happen with Laklak, why she was tired. We didn't know if we would keep writing without her so strong. She was the one who started the writing and always led us. Now we are her arms. We didn't know she would get so sick. She started us on the sharing of songspirals. Even though she holds the knowledge deep within her, we have had to step up to learn and we share and we learn.

This Wititj songspiral comes from Waykarr Gurruwiwi. He is senior leader of the Gälpu clan, a brother for us sisters because our mothers are sisters. This songspiral is in the language of Gälpu. Our mums, Gaymala, Djerrknu, and all our mums, are the Djungaya for this songspiral, and we are the Gutharra.

There is more deep knowledge about Wititj and about this songspiral, but we can't share it with you here. It is important for ceremonies. We can't talk about how it holds the foundation. That knowledge is only appropriate for some people, the right people. It has to be the right person with the right knowledge to know it. But we are sharing what we can and what we share is special knowledge.

After her long journey, Wititj settles down in the gundirr, the anthills. She has wended her way as Country, her rainbow body slithering, sensing, smelling, threading her way, casting out with her tongue to make and remake. Now, exhausted, she rests. She finds a hole in the gundirr. She shelters herself. The temperature is really nice in there. That is her hiding place.

At the end of the songspiral, Wititj comes home.

1.
Rrepaŋu guykthuwan, Dhulunŋuru, Nyukumana,
   Ralinyŋuru, Dhulunŋuru.
Bamundurrma guykthuwan Garrimala, Yapayapa,
   Manyburrurru, Yilkiŋu, Djulalambarr.

The snake sings, she casts herself to Country, singing
  Country, blessing, naming and remaking the land.
Her head turns, she casts, claims, looks out at the
  Country, Garrimala, Yapayapa, Manyburrurru,
  Yilkiŋu, Djulalambarr.

2.

Dhulunŋuru d̲ilt̲ilyun Ralinymana, Nyukumana,
  Gunbirrŋ.
Ralinyŋuya ŋarru Djarrpiyana Wilinyguma
  ŋarruŋanan dhalawat̲pat̲tji Rrepaŋuwa, bamundurrma gurrukurru Nyukumana Ralinyŋuru.

She travels from Dhulunŋuru, swaying as she moves,
  the serpent Ralinymana, Nyukumana, Gunbirrŋu.
She settles into a spiral, resting her weary head at the
  centre of her coiled body, marking a boundary of
  the sacred territory she has created and claimed.

3.

Dhaŋurrŋun nhan dhaŋu yolŋum djal̲al̲yuwan nhan
  Ŋulupam, Dhamalkayu, Ralinyŋuyu.
Waku nhan Garinydjiŋunam guykthuwan ŋunhal
  Garrimal̲a Bawud̲uwud̲u.

To Ŋulupam, to Dhamalkayu, the Ralinyŋu, the
  serpent, made her way, with her flickering tongue,
  her powerful language.
My children, the Garinydjiŋu nation, I bless them,
  cleanse them, sing them, their sacred deep names,
  at Garrimala.

CHAPTER 2

Belonging and longing to be with Country

Rrepaŋu guykthuwan, Dhulunŋuru, Nyukumana, Ralinyŋuru, Dhulunŋuru.
Bamundurrma guykthuwan Garrimal̲a, Yapayapa, Manyburrurru, Yilkiŋu, Djulalambarr.

The snake sings, she casts herself to Country, singing
Country, blessing, naming and remaking the land.
Her head turns, she casts, claims, looks out at the
Country, Garrimala, Yapayapa, Manyburrurru,
Yilkiŋu, Djulalambarr.

Wititj, the Rainbow Serpent, claims the territory through singing. The land is sacred. There are many different territories, with many different tribes and clan lands. Wititj didn't claim it for the crown with a flag like the English. She sang that Country, made it with her body. The snake casts out by singing, claims the territory as sacred, makes that area. She sings Country.

When Laklak became tired, became sick, our daughter Djawundil, Laklak's eldest, went with her to Adelaide for a big operation. The surgeon in Darwin had met with Laklak and Djawundil and shown them a picture of a tumour in Laklak's brain the size of an orange.

The surgeon started speaking with Djawundil in English. Djawundil interrupted him and said, 'You can speak in English to Mum, she is a teacher, she can understand everything.'

The surgeon told Laklak and Djawundil that Laklak needed an operation in Adelaide to remove the tumour and release the pressure in her brain. Back in Yirrkala the family had a meeting and we all agreed Laklak needed to go to Adelaide for her operation and we didn't want anyone to go with her but Djawundil.

Laklak and Djawundil had to go far from home for this operation. Like many other Yolŋu they had to go down to Adelaide, far away from family, away from home. They didn't want to go to Adelaide. The last time they were there was with Laklak's husband, Batjaŋ, when he was sick. Going to Adelaide is associated with being sick and being away from home. Laklak didn't want to go as she was afraid she wouldn't come back. It was a big responsibility for our daughter Djawundil to be the one to go with her.

The operation was successful in removing the tumour but after the operation the neurosurgeon came to tell Djawundil that something went wrong, Laklak's brain kept bleeding, and she had a stroke. They moved Laklak into the intensive care unit and they didn't know if she would live. She went in for another operation to stop the bleeding and Djawundil called Kate, who flew to Adelaide to be with her. They sat in that waiting room a long, long time. The surgeon told them he had managed to stop the bleeding but that he didn't know how this would affect Laklak. He didn't know if she would live. For many, many weeks Laklak was in hospital. She regained consciousness and she slowly started eating but she had lost some of her language, some of her memory. She lost her ability to speak English. She would only talk Yolŋu matha and Djawundil had to translate to the nurses and hospital staff.

Although she lost some of her memory she could use her hands, they were always busy, always trying to pull out the tubes that were helping her to breathe and take off the helmet that was protecting her head as it healed from the operation. To keep her hands busy, Djawundil and Kate would give her nuts from the gum trees outside the hospital and she would try to peel them. It was important for her to go home, she wanted to go home, to be healed by Country, listening to language and being with family. The sense of belonging is important, it is a feeling, a connection with Country, with home.

Being with Country is of fundamental importance to Yolŋu. In the Yolŋu world, wherever we are in Arnhem Land, wherever we are, we are connected in some way to people, to plants. It is about always being in relationship, intertwined and connected. The Law is ancient. Old, old, old. If we dig down, we will find ashes, charcoal, lirrwi, from a long time ago. That is what songspirals are all about.

Sometimes, when people are sick and away from home, they sing, or listen to music from home, maybe East Journey, Gurrumul, maybe Yothu Yindi. It's like taking them back to their Country, seeing everything in song because they can't be there. The songs have their own language. Just imagine if we lose our language, there wouldn't be songspirals. Then the land would be silent, it wouldn't be alive.

We all start out speaking Dhuwaya as our Yolŋu matha. It's our common language between the clans, a baby language, spoken by children. That's all a lot of Yolŋu can speak, they can't speak their own clan language. So, those clan languages need us. Us sisters were all Dhuwaya speakers. That's why we started studying our clan language and why it was important. When we were younger, we went to Rorruwuy and stayed there for two weeks working with our father. Banbapuy was still too little to come with us. We came back speaking our own clan language. Banbapuy heard us. When Mum heard us, she didn't laugh at us, she talked back at us in that language. It is all there, it just needs to come out of the mouth. As we say, the tongue turns.

Doing milkarri would get the language coming back. When we sing the clan song, the words have to be in that clan language. That is the Law. This book is a drop in a pond, we hope it sets lots of ripples going out.

When we sing, everything exists. That's why when the two Djan'kawu Sisters, who created the land, when they came with the Wapitja, they penetrated the ground with the stick and they chanted, and everything came alive. And, of course, giving birth to the land they had to put systems in place to follow, to keep it going, to make it a better place. They put language as well. When we speak we are speaking from the land, from the common ground. So if you know where you belong, you are able to speak.

Language is power. It identifies the person, who you are. When a person is gone, they are guided by that songspiral, where they come from. Even if you live down south, you are guided by that song, where you belong both in life and death. The songspiral takes you back to the land, to Country.

Even though our eldest sister and our daughter were far from home, Yolŋu and ŋäpaki family and friends based in or visiting Adelaide rallied around and helped them. Some of our family who were down from the homeland of Mäpuru looking after other loved ones, spent time with Djawundil in the hospital. Martin Deadman, who had been adopted by a family from

Gaymala Yunupiŋu, *Djaykuŋ* (1992). *(The Buku-Larrŋgay Mulka Art Centre archives)*

Dhälinbuy, and his partner, neurologist Cindy Molloy, looked after Djawundil. They took her into their home for the weekends, helped her to understand the hospital system and spoke to the right people to get them to agree to let Laklak recover back home. They helped to organise a charter CareFlight to take Laklak back to Yirrkala so she could be around her family. The CareFlight jet arrived and they put the crash helmet on Laklak's head to keep her safe, to protect her head and to protect that knowledge.

It will be a long recovery, but being back on Country gives Laklak strength. It is important she is around people who speak in her language, who sing to her; language is part of belonging, her connection. It's like when we visited Bawaka after the cyclone in 2015, when all the trees at Bawaka were broken and bare. The tamarind tree would have died if none of us went to care for it. Down south, sometimes trees die as they have no one, no one to talk to them, to touch them.

It's like that with Laklak; down in Adelaide she had only Djawundil. To recover, she needs to sit under the djomula, the casuarinas, to listen, be a part of Country. To touch the sand, to peel the gunga (pandanus leaves). You remember in the hospital she took the nuts and played with them in her hands? She needs to touch the land and be part of it to recover. Sitting on the sand, feeling the sand, the coolness, everything. It is the pedagogy of Yolŋu, of everything. It is a way of learning, another way of learning. It is a real-life learning, a learning journey of another sort.

It's important that Laklak tries to sing again, to get her memory back. She can't do that without being on the land. Even if a person knows how to sing, that person has to know the map of the Country. Because when they sing, do milkarri, they think about the land, where everything is. They know. They have to know. If they don't know the area it is meaningless, it is just a song. The milkarri needs to be from the land. It is not only that we want to belong to the land, but the land longs for people too. It is giving and taking. What we give, we take, it gives, it takes.

We sisters sing with Laklak, we know the importance of her remembering her language. She has lost a bit of memory but she has it there. She was keening the other day. She keened and she cried. She started to sing, some words came back. Ritjilili started first, then Laklak heard and then they started doing milkarri together. Ritjilili learnt how to do milkarri from Laklak. Merrkiyawuy too. Another time Laklak was sitting in a chair outside Nalkuma's house in Yirrkala and she heard manikay going on for a funeral. Banbapuy said, 'Look, Laklak is crying.' Laklak said she could hear her sister clan.

Laklak needs to be on her land to rest, to heal. She needs to be able to rest her weary head as Wititj does. And she is healing. She came back to Yirrkala and to Bawaka.

After some months we decided we needed to do a cleansing ceremony for her. We do this when someone has been very sick. We needed to cleanse her. It turned out that her cleansing ceremony became deeper, a way to honour her in both Yolŋu and ŋäpaki systems. We honoured her knowledge, stories, the way she keeps the songspirals alive.

It is through the songspirals that Wititj the snake claims her territory. Through song she becomes Country.

CHAPTER 3

Wapitja

Dhulunŋuru dilṯilyun Ralinymana, Nyukumana,
    Gunbirrŋu.
Ralinyŋuya ŋarru Djarrpiyana Wilinyguma
    ŋarruŋanan dhalawaṯpaṯtji Rrepaŋuwa, bamun-
    durrma gurrukurru Nyukumana Ralinyŋuru.

*She travels from Dhulunŋuru, swaying as she moves,
    the serpent Ralinymana, Nyukumana, Gunbirrŋu.
She settles into a spiral, resting her weary head at the
    centre of her coiled body, marking a boundary of
    the sacred territory she has created and claimed.*

The men finished making the sacred object, the Wapitja, at
dawn. They had worked on it all night and they finished with
the first rays of the sun. This is the time when the women do
milkarri. The women keen milkarri when the sun rises. Dawn.

181

At first none of us sisters knew about the making of the Wapitja, the sacred digging stick. Our eldest son, Djäwa, had started organising it weeks before. He had started creating the signs and patterns on it, and then the other brothers got together with Djäwa and decided it was time that Laklak received full recognition. This is a very sacred and special thing. Guḻuwu, our brother, gave them the order to make the Wapitja in its complete form, with its deep designs, because Laklak is a philosopher in the family, because she knows so much.

Over the two weeks that the men made the sacred object, they did it in secret. We didn't know. We were organising the cleansing ceremony and a celebration of Laklak being awarded an honorary doctorate by Macquarie University in Sydney. We were organising a ceremony for her but we didn't know that the men had planned a deeper honour. Many of them had been flying into Yirrkala on charter flights from homeland communities all around North East Arnhem Land. The Wapitja is so sacred, it has to be kept secret until it is unveiled.

Wapitja is a digging stick, the digging stick used by the Djan'kawu Sisters, as they created our world. The Djan'kawu Sisters came from the sea. They emerged from the ocean and there was a deep roar. They paddled in towards the land and named everything in the sea, they created them, the fish, the waters, the plankton, the dolphins.

At the long beach near Bawaka you can see the rock that is their canoe, from where they came ashore. They rested and then journeyed, naming everything, creating everything. They carried digging sticks with them and with those sticks they created fresh water, the springs. They stuck their sticks in the ground and fresh water came out. They created trees, plants, food, animals, everything. That is the power of the Wapitja, the digging stick.

The Djan'kawu Sisters used the Wapitja to get food and dig for water. The younger sister gave birth to the Dhuwa clans. When the night came the Sisters used that Wapitja to get the paperbark to cover the children and make shelters. One day, when they were hunting, the men came and stole the Sisters' dilly bags, the bags of knowledge, and the digging sticks. They took away that power.

That's why it was going to be handed back to Laklak, because women had all that knowledge before and then the men took it away. But they didn't take away giving birth to children and so they didn't take away our power to create. A sacred object like this Wapitja has not been made for a long, long time. It is such a deep and special recognition of our sister.

The Wapitja is the knowledge and power of the Djan'kawu Sisters, the Two Sisters who created our world. Our brothers, who flew in especially from Rorruwuy and Galiwin'ku, and our male Djungaya, the children who keep our knowledge going, the keepers, Djäwa, Dhalpalawuy, Nalkuma, Bambuŋ, Botharra, Dhakaliny and Rrawun, put the feathers on the Wapitja, they made our Dätiwuy clan designs with the feathers.

Making the Wapitja had been a group effort by all these men. All day, every day, the men worked, finishing at 9 pm and starting again the next day. They had to collect the materials— the wood, the feathers. And they were not just any feathers. They had to be feathers from the lindirritj, the red-collared lorikeet.

It was Laklak's time to be honoured by the Yolŋu world and by the ŋäpaki world. We were celebrating at home, on Country, before she would travel to Sydney to receive the doctorate, and we were doing her cleansing ceremony. But we didn't know about the Wapitja or about the full depth of how she would be recognised in the Yolŋu way. We knew the men were having men's business but it was only a few days before the cleansing ceremony that they told us that they were making a sacred Wapitja. We were surprised and overwhelmed. It was a great thing, so very moving, such a thing for our eldest sister, the acknowledgement of her knowledge and her work.

A sacred object must remain hidden, under the ground as the Yolŋu say, until it is opened by the special chants, the special songs. Those deep chants are the invisible door to open so other people can see the sacred object. After the sacred Wapitja was finished, then it had to be revealed and presented to Laklak. The Wapitja would also free all the negative energy that had been with Laklak since her operation and been with those who had come into contact with her. It would connect all us sisters, we would become one.

Merrkiyawuy tasked the younger women to get the place ready. They collected the wood, made the fire, laid out the mats, the sheets and the blankets—'make sure there are some chairs too'.

The women and children started arriving. Sarah, Kate and Sandie had travelled up from down south. Many families had come in from Elcho Island and the other homelands. Laklak was ushered in to sit on one of the chairs; more people arrived. It was dusk, the sun was setting, the evening star emerged over the wind-chopped sea.

'Yapa, sister, practise your speech,' said Merrkiyawuy. Mobile phone torches lit up the words so carefully crafted by Laklak and Merrkiyawuy, but everyone had to wait until some reading glasses could be found. After a few interrupted starts, Laklak practised her speech so beautifully.

Then the men were ready to come and reveal the sacred object, to show everyone the Wapitja. Usually the women sing milkarri to welcome the Wapitja, but this time we didn't. Bäyŋu, nothing—Laklak couldn't lead us, she couldn't keen milkarri. This was a very sad moment for us all. So we have to learn! We have to learn that particular keening, from the smallest details, from the colour of the feathers. We have to learn it represents the blood of the children after the younger Djan'kawu Sister gave birth. So we were waiting for Laklak to keen milkarri, because she's got that knowledge. She didn't.

But there was joy too when the men said, 'Here it is, we made it for you. It is going back to you.'

We cried with joy.

The Wapitja was wrapped up, hidden, held by the eldest Djungaya, Dhakaliny, one of our sisters' children, and Djäwa, the eldest child of the mothers' side. They had the authority to hold it and unveil it to us.

There was no yidaki, just the clapsticks. Clapsticks and singing and chanting. Because that is how it was when the Djan'kawu Sisters came. Dhakaliny and Djäwa gave it to our daughters Djawundil and Nyilapa, who are our other Djungaya, to put it on the ground. All our children are Djungaya for the Wapitja.

They placed the wrapped up Wapitja on the ground in front of Laklak. The men started clapping on the clapsticks. Shivers went up everyone's spines. The men were chanting, singing—deep and resonant. The space was alive. Then all the men did a deep *oooom* sound, the gunbur'yun, which is Dhuwa. It is a sound you can feel right through your body. Then Nyilapa and Djawundil unwrapped the material and the Wapitja was revealed before us.

It lay on the cloth on the ground. The orange parrot feathers are layers of knowledge. The white tip is knowledge. The brown tip is the earth and soil. The two circles on the Wapitja are the fonts of knowledge, the spring of knowledge, the Milŋurr, the soft part on a baby's head, the fontanelle, the centre of the spiral of a basket. And Milŋurr is the spring where our mum saw Laklak's spirit, the snake, before she was born, the spring in the mangroves where the fresh water bubbles through the salt. That is the knowledge that has so many levels. And here it was on the Wapitja. It was recognition of Laklak's deep and sacred knowledge.

On the Wapitja were also footprints from the bird gawud-alpudal, the bird that guards and looks after the waterhole. The Wapitja is all these layers of knowledge.

'This is constitutional recognition,' said Djäwa. 'It is not an artwork. It is hurtful when people say that. It is a Yolŋu book, it is writing, it is a document, it is full of knowledge, layers and layers of knowledge. People who have that knowledge can read it by looking at it. They can read whose it is and how it can be used in different ceremonies and songs.'

Laklak has thousands of generations of knowledge, thousands of generations of teachers, thousands of generations of the land. All these were there that night. Laklak is a professor and doctor, a teacher, looking after her children, all children. The Wapitja links Yolŋu recognition of Laklak's wisdom and knowledge with the honorary doctorate that would be bestowed on Laklak by Macquarie University. The Wapitja is like a staff of office symbolising authority in the Western world. This is a doctorate Wapitja, made especially for Laklak by the men. It is a sign of recognition of higher knowledge.

Laklak was given that doctorate Wapitja because of the knowledge that she has, because she is highly respected by Elders, both male and female. She was also given it because she had that operation. It was so amazing—we had the ceremony one whole year after the operation, and most of us did not expect to still have Laklak with us. Many of us were preparing ourselves to lose her. But we didn't.

It is a terrible, tragic thing for someone as knowledgeable as Laklak to have her memories taken away by the tumour. But people know that she is so knowledgeable and they still regard her as that. All that knowledge is still there. We still come and sit with her and ask her and she can talk. That memory is there, it just cannot sometimes be shared in words, only in tears. That is the knowledge, memory, that we, as younger sisters, want to learn and share.

Anything to do with an accident, damage, loss of blood, needs renewal to get better, needs a cleansing, and cleansing can involve a sacred object. Those who have shared food, cups, utensils with someone who was sick also need to be cleansed. The Wapitja, sacred objects, sacred dilly bags, all help a person heal faster. The power in the dilly bag heals the person. Us clans, Dätiwuy, Rirratjiŋu, Dhudi-Djapu, Liya-gawumirri Djarrwark, Djambarrpuyŋu, Djapu, Bararrŋu, Ŋaymil, Gabu and Gamalaŋa, have ceremonies for the Wapitja. Everything on the Wapitja specifically comes from the Milŋurr—the life force where the Djan'kawu Sisters put that Wapitja, struck it into the ground and made the water come out. That's our land. Milŋurr.

The next day, after the sacred Wapitja had been revealed, opened by the special chants, we held the ceremony of the Djan'kawu Sisters. It was a short ceremony, but a very powerful one, that brought the deep knowledge recognised by the Wapitja and the cleansing together. It was the dance of the Djan'kawu Sisters, the story of their travels to the sites of the mala-buŋunbuŋun mala-mätjarra, the children of the Djan'kawu Sisters. It was led by our ŋathi-walkur, our märi's son, from Ramingining, performed by the Garrawurra of the Liya-Gawumirr clan from the Crocodile Islands, Muruŋga Country. Three charter flights came in for the ceremony, and people stayed at four different houses, the houses were all overflowing.

The women gathered at Laklak's house, watched her hair being done carefully and neatly. We then moved to the hill overlooking the ocean and the east.

The ceremony starts with sunrise, even if it is not the actual time the sun rises. It ends with sunset down by the Art Centre. Laklak is ushered into the house so her body can be painted up; she is getting her Yolŋu 'cloak' put on, a sign of great knowledge and respect for an Elder in the Dhuwa moiety. It is a gorgeous and powerful pattern painted onto the top half of her body. Djäwa starts the painting, another family member from Elcho Island helps, Djäwa finishes. Laklak's cloak is intricate and magnificent. So much power in the painting.

After a while the men, painted up with gapan, white clay, on their faces and in their hair, start gathering on the deck. The clapsticks come out and they start chanting.

Yulula Marika, Witiyana's little brother's daughter, and Menyalwuy Ganambarr, Djali's daughter, both our gathu (niece), are standing with their arms out for the gapan to dry; they are the Djan'kawu Sisters being painted in browns and whites. Djawundil helps to dry the gapan by fanning some paper at them. The Wapitja is lying casually on the bed. There are kids on phones and iPads, being painted up as they play games. The women paint each other. All our collective is there and the children. It is a very special day.

Everyone looks after Laklak, rubbing her back, bringing her a chair, keeping her involved and mentally active, prompting her and her knowledge, drawing her out. When we are all painted with white gapan—on our faces, in our hair—Djawundil and Djäwa put the sacred armbands and headband on, and the dilly bag over Laklak's head. The women start gathering on one side of the room, the men start filing in, and Laklak is ushered into the place of honour. The deep resonant chanting enables the invisible doors to open and the Wapitja is given to Laklak to hold.

The procession moves to overlook the ocean. Laklak sits next to Professor Richie Howitt, who is there on behalf of Macquarie University to present the honorary doctorate to Laklak. Richie is adorned with gapan and cloaked up in his academic dress—its maroon shade complements the Dätiwuy clan colours.

There is more than one clan there to bring Laklak out, to present her. All the clans that sing about the Sisters are here, our songs interweave with each other. They clap their clapsticks together, one song. But all in different ways. The Rirratjiŋu, L̲iya-Gawumirr, Dhud̲i-Djapu, D̲ät̲iwuy mala. Garrawurra of the L̲iya-Gawumirr clan is one of the keepers, beside us and beside the Rirratjiŋu who are the keepers of the knowledge of the Djan'kawu Sisters. It is a Rirratjiŋu song that is sung, they are one of the few keepers of this songspiral. The Garrawurra lead the song, as that is where the Djan'kawu Sisters travelled first. Then the others come, the children of those clans.

From the hilltop the procession makes its way down the hill to where the sun sets at the Art Centre. Laklak sits in the passenger seat of Merrkiyawuy's car, accompanied by Richie who walks next to her window. Leading the procession are the men, singing life into being, through the road, through the air. The women following, swaying, dancing and becoming life. The procession winds its way down, past the gathered friends and family sitting under the trees on the sandy mounds which form an amphitheatre around the Art Centre stage with its stunning cut-art aluminium framing.

As we walk down the hill towards the Art Centre we can hear a sound, a *brr, brr*—that's the wave, the swaying, that's the Djan'kawu Sisters walking, carrying dilly bags, sacred objects. When the Sisters put their Wapitja into the ground, the water spread out from the ground. So water is knowledge and with that knowledge we think, sing, talk, make decisions. We live with that knowledge, it is our wisdom.

We make our way onto the Art Centre stage and Richie places the university stole over Laklak's shoulders and the bonnet on her head, carefully placed next to the headband.

After a short speech by Richie, Laklak gives her reply. She begins: 'Some of you know me, some of you don't know me. I am Barbara Laklak, Biwud̲alŋu, Ŋuliny, Warrad̲ay, Dhatam',

Procession down to the Buku-Larrŋgay Mulka Art Centre, Yirrkala. *(Authors' collection)*

Djäri Burarrwaŋa. The core of my life, my spiritual being, is Djurtjurŋa Galirriŋbuŋ Berrwaŋa, and then the Ŋaymil Dhar'miny Gamburrtji. It is nothing new, they are closely connected in this longstanding Yolŋu kinship structure, it is everlasting. Like the honey, our knowledge and our Law flows, since that time of long ago.'

Laklak introduces herself as one of the Elders in the community, in her family of Rirratjinu and Dätiwuy. She explains how she began her work and research ten years earlier with the book *Weaving Lives Together at Bawaka*, and the other books that followed: 'These books tell the story of people and family coming together and living in harmony.'

Laklak thanks Sarah, Kate and Sandie for the work they have done with us. She thanks Macquarie University for their support and direction, and for their belief, recognition and respect for Yolŋu knowledge.

Then she thanks her family and shares: 'We argue, we go hunting, we laugh, we cry, we come together again, we are a close-knit family.'

She thanks Leon White for his work with Yolŋu teachers, academics and Elders, and she thanks friends from Nhulunbuy and wider Australia.

Laklak finishes: 'Our verses, melodies, songspirals and languages are ours, given to us by the Djan'kawu Sisters. We write these books to tell everyone that the Yolŋu are still here and we are here to stay.

'I dedicate this award to all my Gumatj mothers and to my fathers both Rirratjiŋu and D̲ätiwuy. To you Roy D̲aday̲ŋa Marika MBE, whose deep name is Malpitjiŋu. To you

Laklak delivering her speech at the Buku-Larrŋgay Mulka Art Centre. *(Authors' collection)*

Daypurryun' Ganambarr, whose deep name is Bonyinya. To you Mowarra Ganambarr OAM, whose deep name is Bulurruma.'

When Laklak thinks back to this ceremony she remembers feeling anxious, some doubt and nerves. It was the first time she had received such an honour. But she also felt happy because all her family was there. She felt very emotional, also, thinking about her husband. She emphasises that she wants the younger generation to 'work wide, so that people will see. I want them to do the same that I did. Like write a book. Djäma—work, run a business, I want them to write.'

She wants them to dig and eat ganguri, yams. Nowadays, the ganguri is often hanging, coloured—from green to yellow to brown—the vines are withering, because no one is digging the yams up.

The Wapitja holds in it everything that happened, the songs, the stories, the knowledge. Now it also has that special day, the cleansing ceremony and the presentation at Yirrkala. The Wapitja has the honorary doctorate woven into it; it is a sacred object, an heirloom. It is something important that will be passed down through the generations, to the children, to Bambuŋ, Rrawun, Djäwa. Our grandson Gathapura has those märi-pulu skills, so he has the Wapitja now. He is the one with the knowledge to look after it.

CHAPTER 4

Women's knowledge and wisdom

Dhaŋurrŋun nhan dhaŋu yolŋum djalalyuwan nhan
Ŋulupam, Dhamalkayu, Ralinyŋuyu.
Waku nhan Garinydjiŋunam guykthuwan ŋunhal
Garrimala Bawuduwudu.

*To Ŋulupam, to Dhamalkayu, the Ralinyŋu, the
serpent, made her way, with her flickering tongue,
her powerful language.*
*My children, the Garinydjiŋu nation, I bless them,
cleanse them, sing them, their sacred deep names,
at Garrimala.*

Wititj, the Rainbow Serpent, travelled, slithered, to Ŋulupam,
Dhamalkayu, Ralinyŋu, to give birth to those clans, to the

Yirritja clans, to her children, her kin, the Garinydjiŋu clan, at Garrimala. The younger Djan'kawu Sister gave birth to the Dhuwa clans. The Wititj to the Yirritja. Always there is balance. Always there is Yirritja and Dhuwa.

Wititj sensed with her tongue, using it to cast out, spelling out the language. When she spoke, she created, blessed. She blessed the children, the clans, the Country, cleansed them, sang them, created them. Wititj sanctified them with her blessing spray, a special act, like giving birth, or cleaning the child.

When we sing this songspiral this is what is happening. The songspirals sing us, giving birth to us, singing where we were born, every mother, whether Dhuwa or Yirritja, giving us our sacred, deep names.

Wititj, the Rainbow Serpent, went to Garrimala because that is her place. Wititj's homeland is Garrimala and she gave birth to Garinydjiŋu people there. We sing Wititj travelling to Garrimala, and blessing the Garinydjiŋu clan. Garrimala is a Garden of Eden, the grass is cut, we don't know how, there are so many different kinds of flowers. Everything is paradise. Garrimala, which is Gälpu Country, and Garinydjiŋu are linked together, through yothu–yindi, child and mother.

Through Laklak and her sharing of knowledge, as a mother, grandmother, teacher, messenger, Bawaka and Yirrkala are now linked to Macquarie University and the University of Newcastle. Recognising Laklak's knowledge and contribution to academia, Macquarie University awarded Laklak's honorary doctorate during a graduation ceremony in September 2016, two months after her cleansing. Initially Merrkiyawuy and Banbapuy were going to travel to Sydney on Laklak's behalf, but just a month before the ceremony the doctors gave Laklak the go-ahead to travel to Sydney. Everyone was so delighted that Laklak herself could be in Sydney to receive her honorary doctorate.

The Vice-Chancellor, S. Bruce Dowton, wheeled Laklak's wheelchair onto the stage, and everyone was spellbound while she read her speech. Chris Tobin, a Darug custodian, spoke movingly of the connections between Yolŋu and Darug during a celebration following the ceremony. The university's recognition of Laklak's work is a big shift for academia. It expands understandings of what knowledge should be valued and is a long-overdue acknowledgement of women's wisdom.

For Yolŋu, the Djan'kawu Sisters created everything in the world. Women are the givers of life, they sing life. When babies are born, whether male or female, women teach them first, the mothers teach them. The mothers know the sound of their cry. The Djan'kawu Sisters made the knowledge. Women are the givers of wisdom.

Manikay are our ceremonial songs and milkarri is the women's aspect of the manikay. We can sing our milkarri with the full ceremony, or in small groups, or keen by ourselves, where we might be moved to keen to heal the land, or for our sorrow as we think of those who have passed away. Women do milkarri of both Dhuwa and Yirritja songs. Dhuwa men sing Dhuwa songs, and Yirritja men sing Yirritja songs, but women do milkarri of both moieties' songspirals. While we each have our roles, it is not just about men doing their own business, women doing their own business, it is about women and men together. That's how the Yolŋu world operates. The recognition and respect given to a person depends on how deep a person's knowledge is and their connection to the song rather than whether they are a woman or a man. So when women are doing milkarri, men listen and learn one word, or two or three words, and use them in their songs too. And like in the process of writing this book, us women have listened and learnt from men. Yolŋu knowledge doesn't end halfway; you've got to have everything to understand.

Somehow, maybe because there is sexism in ŋäpaki culture, there has been more attention to the men's side. There are more recordings of men, and books about and by men. We need to bring back the balance. Women's part of songspirals is vital. Without women's milkarri the songspirals, life itself, won't be whole.

Sadly, a lot of women are not doing milkarri now. A lot of the older women are getting frustrated that the younger women don't join in. The voices are getting less and less. We are frightened it will stop, there will be no voices. Sometimes we think we'll go to our graves not explaining lots of things—it will be lost. Already, there have been some songspirals destroyed. There are only a few people who know how to sing milkarri. The worry is the women of our age, the middle-aged ladies, not joining in. Maybe they are shy. This book is a way of waking them up, waking us up. We have milkarri. This is our Law. This must be strengthened.

We see how the songspirals can be destroyed. If Yolŋu all die, then the land dies with us.

There has been mining up in North East Arnhem Land. The land here has been dying through that mine. And people too. Merrkiyawuy says she has never seen so many people die with it, in her life.

Things need to be done right. The mine, it destroys things. Even when they are planting trees there can be problems. The company running the mine were putting the wrong trees back in through their regeneration. The trees they put in were from the coast. The songspirals tell us that those trees shouldn't be there. The songspirals tell us where everything grows. Every tree, every rock, has its place. Now Yolŋu do the regeneration, they get the right seeds and put them in the right places. We have our system of rangers, too, who care for the land in the right way and make sure the miners don't go where they shouldn't. They try to make sure that the miners respect our Country properly.

Laklak has lost a bit of memory, but she has it there, in her head, in her body. As Ritjilili says, 'One word, three words, is enough for a start. All the other words start coming in when you are doing it. It is there in the memory. All Yolŋu have it. I don't know why or how. Is it because we are young when we hear the songs? When we are still in the tummy we hear it and from birth on it is there, already imprinted in our memory. If we don't use it, practise it, or if Yolŋu are taken away, songspirals will die.'

Milkarri is there in our memory; we have to open our mouths and sing.

Seeing Laklak on stage receiving the honorary doctorate at the university was wonderful. She was right in the front with her stole, surrounded by the other academics. Macquarie University acknowledged Laklak's contribution to research and leadership, recognising the incredible role Laklak plays in leading the award-winning Bawaka Collective. As the citation reads in part:

> Laklak Burarrwaŋa is an inspiring Yolŋu Elder from North East Arnhem Land . . . with a distinguished record of contributing to research, higher education and the wider community . . . She is the eldest child in her family and has a special responsibility to care for her family, her Country and to educate non-Indigenous people about Yolŋu knowledge. She has deep and profound knowledge of Yolŋu culture, ceremony and Yolŋu worldviews and is an important senior knowledge holder. She has worked to educate non-Indigenous people about the existence and complexity of Yolŋu knowledge, providing rich understandings of some of the patterns and relationships connecting human-ecological systems and underpinning ways of being and belonging at her Indigenous homeland of Bawaka . . . Her work has also explored the complex historical, cultural and political challenges Yolŋu have faced while bringing to life the strength and pride of the Yolŋu people. Her work is not only an invitation to learn but also an invitation for non-Indigenous and Indigenous people to reconcile and envisage a shared future . . .
>
> This honorary doctorate is a profound way of recognising an important Indigenous knowledge holder, her sustained links with Macquarie University *and* her distinguished contribution to the academic community, to Indigenous Australia, and to

the community generally through her work in reconciliation and the sharing of Indigenous knowledges.

We feel proud that her work has been recognised by the university. We are proud that she is recognised as Wititj here at home. She sings her Country, has sung it, keened it, and it keens her. She has made her way and keeps making her way, with her powerful language, her knowledge of the sacred deep names that she holds and will always hold.

After her long journey, after all the healing and creating, after all the work, this is the Settling of the Serpent. This is complete.

Yet, while the serpent settles, the flame keeps burning.

Part 5

Gon-gurtha

CHAPTER 1

Keepers of the flame

The flames keep burning and there is one who holds the fire, Goŋ-gurtha.

We turn around and we see a fire from a long way away. We say, 'Aaaah, there is fire. Someone has lit fire.'

Goŋ is the hand, gurtha is the fire. So, Goŋ-gurtha is someone who lights the fire. Goŋ-gurtha is keeper of the flame, the holder of knowledge. Long time ago, the Goŋ-gurtha carried the tools for the fire. They were the ones responsible for lighting the fire with the wood from the duṯtji, pandanus trunk, that burns slow. The Goŋ-gurtha could swim across rivers holding onto the duṯtji like a torch, holding it above their head.

The fire clears and cleanses the land. It is looking after the land, making sure that everything is right for the turning of the seasons when the wind blows and dries Country.

One of our other mothers, Marri'marri Burarrwaŋa, shared the songspiral of Goŋ-gurtha with us at Bawaka. She keened, cried milkarri for the gurtha, fire. Marri'marri comes from the

Marri'marri Burarrwaŋa, mother of Laklak, Ritjilili, Merrkiyawuy and Banbapuy.
(Authors' collection)

eldest grandfather and our mother comes from the youngest grandfather. She is a grandmother for Djawundil and Kate, a niece for Sarah. Marri'marri was Banbapuy's nurse when she was born. Banbapuy, like all of us, was born in the bush.

Marri'marri has the name Goŋ-gurtha. That name is a Yirritja name. Goŋ-gurtha is of our mother clan, Gumatj, and Marri'marri is the Wäŋa Wataŋu for this songspiral.

Goŋ-gurtha is the keeper of the flame, the one who lights the fire and the one who sends a message with fire. When we are in a boat or in a canoe, paddling, and we turn around and see a fire burning, we connect with the Goŋ-gurtha who lit that fire. The Goŋ-gurtha is also the hunter who goes out to hunt and then lights a fire to signal that the hunt has been successful. They light the grass, sending out a message. These are the songspirals that bring us and the land to life, that connect us across space and through time and to each other, now.

Our children and grandchildren are Goŋ-gurtha too, keepers of the flame. They are keepers of tomorrow's knowledge. This is our next generation.

So this is a story for all the children. They are the caretakers of the land and the keepers of the fire. We need them to look after the Law and the knowledge of the land, to lead the dances of their mother clan. Our children are keepers of the flame; they are Gutharra of and for the Goŋ-gurtha songspiral. Yolŋu children learn from the songspirals. They are the songspirals. They learn from Country as they are part of Country.

Our children know where they come from, and they all know how to live now. It's true that this world that they live in is the new world, not the world of our ancestors, of living in shelters, lean-tos and caves, although that was not so long ago. That was the time of owning no material things but decorating ourselves with woven strings, beads and shells.

We are in the twenty-first century now, and even if we have our own Yolŋu Law we also have to live by the ŋäpaki law. This is where we all are at this very moment. So, this story is for our children whom we encourage to stand firm, to stand strong, to learn the sacred designs of our paintings, the songs, the dances, the stories, the contours of our lands. Keep it safe in your hearts, our children.

And the children take this message to their hearts, as they do the sacred designs, stories and contours of the land. They do this in different ways, in learning and in being. Mayutu, Merrkiyawuy's youngest daughter, felt that she needed to honour what her mothers, grandmothers, her ancestors had done. She wanted to make sure everything they had done was worth it, was carried on, because she is young and she is proud. Mayutu helped create a cultural group at her high school. Merrkiyawuy chose the name for the group: Goŋ-gurtha. For they are keeping the fire alight. The flame is in their hands.

In this last part of the book, we will share two aspects of Goŋ-gurtha. One is the milkarri of our mum Marri'marri. The other is the singing of Wurrumila, the hunter, by some of our sons—Djäwa, who is Laklak's eldest son; Galimara, who is Gärŋarr's son; Rrawun, Banbapuy's son; and Dhalpalawuy, who is Ritjilili's youngest son. Our brother Djali, a Djungaya, is with them. They are all painted up with gapan, very special white clay. We have asked them to sing Wurrumila, the great hunter, the keeper of the flame, and we have asked Rrawun to explain it. Rrawun was raised at Bawaka and taught by Laklak and her husband, Batjaŋ, who taught him Law and songspirals. He has learnt and he now shares. We have asked them as we are their mothers and Djungaya for this song.

Where Marri'marri keens the flames on the horizon, the awareness and care of the Goŋ-gurtha who sets the fire and keeps the flame, Rrawun explains that Wurrumila is the hunter and he shares the hunter's journey that comes before the flame is lit. While the men sing the hunt, it is the fire at the end that is the depth of the songspiral, the fire that announces that the hunter has been successful. This is the fire of Goŋ-gurtha, the keeper of the flame, which becomes again the milkarri that Marri'marri keens. After our mum Marri'marri has cried the milkarri of her Goŋ-gurtha, our sons will take a turn. We want to share both aspects with you. You will see how they connect. We hope you will see the balance.

The Goŋ-gurtha sees Wurrumila's ŋara', the fire, sees the cloud from the smoke of the hunter. They see each other.

They are the same person. This is the balance, the balance between women and men, between here and there, between then and now.

Sometimes the Goŋ-gurtha sees Wurrumila, the hunter, and she makes the gurtha, the fire. He has a turtle and is eating it. Or he sees her fire and knows she has been successful in the hunt. They are communicating with each other. And as we listen to the men sing the hunter, we, as Goŋ-gurtha, look back, we look from afar at a distant fire, knowing that there, someone has been successful in their hunt, in their journey. If we are successful, we too will light the fire to show others.

This songspiral that we share, the story of Wurrumila and of Goŋ-gurtha, the keeper of the flame, is the story of our children, the girls and the boys, the men and the women. It is the story of us as we spiral through the generations. The generations of our ancestors, those who have come before, as well as the generations yet to come. When we cry milkarri or sing at a funeral, it is the deceased person who is alive. They are seeing, they are looking, feeling, walking, breathing and smelling. All senses are there and all things, the talking, doing, hunting, in the songspiral. We go together with that person, guiding them, with their spirit. We are taking them back to where they started, back to that same spot where they were conceived. It is the journey back, guiding them back to that place.

You see already there are many layers. Goŋ-gurtha is the one who holds the knowledge of fire, the one who starts the fire. Goŋ-gurtha is Marri'marri's name. Goŋ-gurtha is Mayutu's cultural group that she started at school and their holding of tomorrow's fire. Goŋ-gurtha is the one who connects us through the generations and connects us across space as we see the flame on the horizon. Goŋ-gurtha cares for Country and cleanses it, cares for us and provides for us. Goŋ-gurtha is the one who has passed away and whose memory lives in our milkarri, the sounds, smells, the time they were here, they are here. And Goŋ-gurtha is the journey of the hunter who, if successful, will light the fire. It is the flames that hold us, connect us, reach out, across to the horizon, back to our ancestors and on to our ancestors who are still to come.

Marri'marri cried this milkarri of Goŋ-gurtha.

The fire burns. The smoke billows. The flames rise.

1.

Gurtha nharana Goŋ-gurthawuŋu,
Djambatjŋuwuŋu, Wuymuwuŋuna.
Gurtha nharana.

The fire is burning from Goŋ-gurtha,
From the Djambatjŋuwuŋu and the Wuymuwuŋuna,
   the expert hunter, the determined hunter we
   depend on.
The fire burns.

2.

D̲urryuna ŋunha marrtji Maywalkarra,
Goŋ-gurthawuŋu, Goŋ-yakaywuŋu.
Nyewun̲ba, Gulthana, Rranyirranyi.

The fire rises on the horizon at that place
   Maywalkarra,
From Goŋ-gurtha, the person who starts the fire
   that burns the land,

From Goŋ-yakaywuŋu, the person who starts
*   the fire with great care and great awareness.*
The fire rises on the horizon in Yirritja Country,
*   at Nyewunba, Gulthana, Rranyirranyi.*

3.

Goŋ-gurtha nharana, Djilayŋaŋu, Batumbil,
    dhakalnydja durryunara nhäŋala Maywalkarra.

The Goŋ-gurtha lights the fire at Djilayŋaŋu and
*   Batumbil; the fire is burning along the coastline.*
The smoke billows and the flames rise; it is burning
*   along the coastline.*
I can see it burning at Maywalkarra.

4.

Wuymuwuŋu nharana gurtha Rranyirranyiwuyŋu
    Gulthanawuyŋu.

The Wuymu, the hunter, lit the fire. The fire is burning
*   from Wuymuwuŋu, from Rranyirranyiwuyŋu, from*
*   Gulthanawuyŋu and from Nyewunbuwuyŋu.*

5.

Nyewunbuwuyŋu yeeee.
Wulpunduna nhäŋaya durryunara Goŋ-gurthawuŋu.

From these Yirritja people, the fire burns. We see the
*   smoke clouds rising up high from Goŋ-gurtha.*
From there, the smoke's mist rises up and becomes
*   the cloud Wulpundu, a big cloud stretching*
*   forward into the sky.*

6.

Yeeee, runurunu Djilayŋaŋu, Batumbil dhakalnydja
  durryun ŋunha marrtji.
Yeeee, Goŋ-gurthawuŋu.

*Yes, those islands Djilayŋaŋu and Batumbil, I can
  see the jawline of the coastline through my crying.
  I can see those islands very clearly as the smoke
  rises up.*
Yes, from Goŋ-gurtha.

7.

Ŋunha Nyewunba, Rranyirranyiwuŋu,
  Gulthanawuyŋu,
Goŋ-gurtha Mätjitji.

*There, that one now, the fire is from Nyewunba,
  Rranyirranyi, Gulthana, from the people who hold
  that Country, keepers of the land.*
*From Goŋ-gurtha Mätjitji, the keeper of the fire,
  the one who starts the fire.*

8.

Djambatjŋuwuyŋu gurtha nharana Bolumi,
  Djilayŋaŋu, Batumbil.

*From Djambatj, the hunter, the fire burns. From the
  place Bolumi, a distant place where the bamboo,
  bolu, grows. From the islands of Yolŋu Country,
  Djilayŋaŋu and Batumbil.*

9.

D̲urryunara nhäŋala Maywalkarra.
Ŋunha Djilayŋa Batumbil Goŋ-gurthawuyŋu,
D̲urryunara nhäŋala Nyewu̲nba, Rranyirranyi,
    Goŋ-gurtha.

*The smoke rises high from far away, from islands
    a long way away. See the smoke rising high at
    Maywalkarra.*
*There at Djilayŋa and Batumbil from Goŋ-gurtha,
    the flames are rising up high. See the hunters
    Nyewu̲nba, Rranyirranyi, Goŋ-gurtha.*

Passing it on to the kids

Gurtha nharana Goŋ-gurthawuŋu,
Djambatjŋuwuŋu, Wuymuwuŋuna.
Gurtha nharana.

The fire is burning from Goŋ-gurtha,
From the Djambatjŋuwuŋu and the Wuymuwuŋuna,
the expert hunter, the determined hunter we
depend on.
The fire burns.

The fire is burning from Goŋ-gurtha. The fire burns from the expert hunter. It burns over there. A journey has been completed. Marri'marri keened milkarri for the fire on the horizon. And here? Here we are beginning.

Rrawu<u>n</u> describes the singing of the hunter, the hunter who is beginning a journey. Marri'marri keened, we have seen and smelled and felt the smoke rising. Now we begin from a different beginning. The men begin with the hunter. The hunter has many names: Wurramala, Wurrumila, Wuymu, Bäpa'yili, Goŋ-gurtha and more. Here Rrawun uses the name Wurrumila. Wurrumila is the name from the songspirals, the name of the Gumatj hunter.

First they must sing the shelter that the hunter is building there on the beach. This is where he begins. He's building a shelter from a local tree, maybe it is a coconut tree, maybe a bamboo tree. When the shelter is finished he says, 'This is my barrum barru.'

Every Gumatj person who passes away, if they're living in a coastal area, there's a special shelter for their body, and that's called the barrum barru. The iron shelter we sit under at Bawaka, where we have shared many of the songspirals for this book, where we listen and watch and talk, that place had been the barrum barru for Laklak's husband's funeral.

The hunter starts in his mind. He is thinking where to go, where's the best place to go to get dugong or whale. He is thinking of the area, gamata, the place of the sea grass, a place of dugong and whales, the big sea animals. That's why the hunter, Wurrumila, is the man who provides the food. He feeds the family. He starts by sitting down and thinking, thinking where to go, planning the hunt.

The Goŋ-gurtha could be the hunter. It would be someone who knows the sea, knows the land, knows the places, the map of the country, the map of the sea. It's a person who knows the area really, really well, someone really intelligent for the place. Even when it rains they know where to hide, what to do, how to make a shelter. They know the reef, where it ends, where the dugong are hunted. They're like pirates, pirates of the sea. Seafarers.

In the songspiral, we use different names for the hunter. We sing Djambatjŋu, the one who spears the dugong or whale. Djambatj means the person we can rely on to get something for us. They are experts in getting food, they are determined. We can rely on them. Even if the sea is rough, muddy, or it's raining, the Djambatj knows where to get something. We can count on that person. Djambatj also means harpoon.

That's why we named Bambuŋ, Merrkiyawuy's son, Djambatj, because he always gets something. Even if it's raining, high tide, he brings something home. He has the stubbornness —'I'm the hunter, I have to get something.' It's determination. Even if the Djambatj doesn't bring back something big, they can bring back crabs, or a rock of oysters, something for the women.

Before the missionaries came, women and men had to provide for their family and children so the family wouldn't starve— hunting, fishing and gathering yams, oysters, clams and other bush foods. That is why we have so many names for hunter. If you were Djambatj you were given another wife, because you were motivated and not lazy. A woman can't marry a lazy man or they would both be dead. Djambatj knows the tide, knows the turtle, the dugong. This is not new, it's been done for a long, long, long time. It's very, very old Law. It's been done a long time and it's there in the new generations' blood. The hunters know where the dugongs gather, where their territory is, their gamata.

We don't catch a big animal like dugong or turtle to waste, we catch to share and eat. We are hunting for the family, hunting for the songspirals. Every part of the animal is labelled.

All the parts on the dugong's body are sung in the manikay. Each part has a name, even the juice of the dugong has a name. The position of the hunters in the canoe goes with the name of the parts of the animal. The captain gets the tail; the Djungaya, the caretaker of the ceremony, who is in the middle, gets the middle part; the person who steers gets the shoulders. The Djambatj only gets a tiny bit.

The people who go out with the hunter share. Part of what we are talking about here is sharing the dugong or the whale, but underneath is the importance of sharing as part of the Law. Sharing is not only dugong or whale, but it is what it means to be Yolŋu, how to look after Yolŋu, how to look after the homeland. With the Law we were taught to respect other people, to be honourable, to talk straight and to despise greed and envy. It's been like that since the Law was laid down, passed down through the generations, and exactly the same things happen today.

In Goŋ-gurtha, we sing about the canoe. The canoe is on the land, beside the beach. Resting, waiting. The canoe is resting in the shade or somewhere, away from the water. Before the canoe can be put in the water, the hunter has to check it, to see if there are any holes or cracks. Checking it out. You can see it in the dance, hear it in the song. He is checking everything about that canoe.

After the hunter has checked the canoe, we sing about him making his harpoon, cutting the harpoon, the djambatj. Cutting a special tree. Sometimes they talk about bamboo in the songspiral.

Then we sing about the marrwala, the paddles. Wurrumila is a very knowledgeable and wise hunter so sometimes he puts ŋara' on the paddles, a particular cloud pattern made by the smoke. The cloud pattern represents the cloud far beyond the surface of the sea. That cloud communicates, it is like a GPS.

When the cloud rises in the distance, it's from the fire. It rises from a place where people are burning the land. Yes, a Goŋ-gurtha. When we see the fire we go, 'Yaaah, the fire's started from the Goŋ-gurtha, the hunter.' When we see it, we know the Goŋ-gurtha has started the fire. The fire burns.

When we do that, we are also looking back at our mum Marri'marri who keens the fire. The two songspirals connect. They are one. And after Wurrumila has hunted, he will make a fire too, and then when others see the fire, they see someone has caught a dugong or whale there.

The hunter can read anything from the sea to the land. He owns the sea, the reef, this is his. It owns him too. Sometimes he makes the marrwala with a carving of dugong or jungle fowl. That is very sacred. For this songspiral, here in this book, it's just a normal paddle, marrwala.

After the marrwala are finished we sing about the water, about the tide coming in and the tide going out. By the timing of the tides coming in and going out, the gunbilk marrawulwul, the calm glassy water, the hunter knows he is ready. He also knows from his feeling, gatjbu'yun, as he has sat and hoped.

Sometimes we sit and hope, gatjbu'yun, because we have run out of food and the wind is so big. There are waves, the water is murky, and sometimes we think, 'Aaaah, I hope we're going to get something for the family.' And when we go hunting we always feel like we're going to get something, and sometimes we get it.

Back in the early 1990s a category 2 cyclone came to this area from Groote Eylandt. Laklak, Merrkiyawuy, Rrawun, the old man, Batjaŋ, little Bawi and Nalkuma were staying at our house at Bawaka. We couldn't get back to Yirrkala because of all the rain that comes before a cyclone. So we stayed there for maybe a week and we ran out of food. We only had rice, no milk, no tea, no anything. So the old man and Laklak said to Rrawun, Bawi and Nalkuma, 'Okay, we want you boys to hunt and get turtle for us.'

It was all murky and rough. Rrawun remembers, 'So we went to the other side of the bay and while we were there I was hoping, gatjbu'yun, and suddenly we saw a big turtle and we got him. We came back and that night, with the cyclone about to hit, we had that miyapunu. We cooked the miyapunu and put it inside out of the weather and that night and that morning the cyclone passed north of Bawaka.'

That miyapunu lasted maybe nine days. It was all cooked and safe to eat.

That cyclone reminded us of Wurrumila. We try to re-enact that Wurrumila. Our hunters learn from a young age, like that time with the cyclone. Wurrumila is an idol for our people, for everyone who lives in Arnhem Land. If you are like him you have his hope, his ability to hunt and act and feed the family. When we are growing up we have to learn how to catch everything to feed our family. We learn where to get water, where to get kangaroo, emu, oysters, bush foods, whatever.

It is so important that our children and our grandchildren learn. As they are growing up they listen, and then, when they are older, they learn, so they have knowledge that they will use. When they go hunting, they know what to get. So songspirals connect us through the generations, to our knowledge, to those that have come before and those yet to emerge. Our children are also keepers of the flame.

Djawundil remembers Laklak sitting down with Djawundil's granddaughter, our little mother, Mawunymula. She was only six or seven. Laklak said, 'What will happen if I die? Will you sing for me?'

'Yes, waku, child, I will,' said Mawunymula.

'Show me.'

So Mawunymula sang Laklak going to get ganguri, yams, maypal, oysters. Straight away Mawunymula sang.

That's how the children learn, sitting down with their mothers and their fathers, the grandparents, listening, talking about that Country. If there's a story, there's meaning behind that story. If there's a song, there's meaning behind the song. We don't sing meaningless songs! Country, whales, everything that they do, have meanings. If the kids are all sitting down looking out to sea, then someone tells them the story, like how when they travel they will see whales.

It's to do with the nurturing of oneself, one's children, one's parents. All our children—they are our wonder. We nurture them to take their wondrous minds even further. We nurture them to explore, touch, smell, taste. We take them outside, in the mud, get them to feel what's in the mud, to go through the mangroves, walk on that beach of coral so their feet can feel what it's like to walk on the earth. This is them learning, this is preparing them for university, for leadership, for business.

They are all Goŋ-gurtha, keepers of the flame. Like with Mayutu's cultural group. After Merrkiyawuy gave them the name, Mayutu explained to the other students something about what Goŋ-gurtha means. She said, 'Goŋ-gurtha meant literally, first, the flame in our hands. Then in the songlines, a lady holds the fire, up in the stars, in the galaxy, our galaxy, the Milky Way. It is the spiral. Up there are the Yirritja Gumatj sisters, Naynay and Guthaykuthay who light fires. They are the keepers and they light the fire. They keep the fire glowing all the time. Then I explained in the olden days there was only one person who was the keeper of the flame. When they moved, that person had to grab the stick from the embers and make the fire from the pandanus trunk, dry one, light it up and carry it to the next wäŋa, camp, and then from there, again.'

Her cultural group is made up of students from different backgrounds: Yolŋu, ŋäpaki, Māori, all the other cultures in the area at the high school in town. They started out doing a play that was written by two teachers at the school, Juran and Cameron, a couple from New Zealand and the Cook Islands, who feel passionate about the sharing of culture.

The play was about a Māori boy, Tama, and a Yolŋu girl, Dhayka, who didn't have any respect for their culture. So the spirits made them travel. The spirits put them in Samoa. They were confused, disoriented. The boy and the girl, who was played by Mayutu, travelled and they watched the Samoan cultural dance and then they were dancing, they were singing. They walked off and went back onto the stage and they found themselves in a totally new culture. They learnt about this culture and they joined in: they went to Samoa, Papua New Guinea and many other places. They were so confused as to why they were made to go to these places. But through this journey they learnt a love for culture.

So, in this play, they start wondering. The boy wonders, what is my culture? I don't know my culture. I know that I am Māori, but what is it? The music starts and his family comes in. They sing one of their songs to him. They say at the end, 'Welcome home, Tama,' and he remembers who he is. Then he says, 'I must help Dhayka to find her culture.' So in the end they come back to Arnhem Land and then her family starts singing 'Dhayka', a slang word for girl in Yolŋu matha to remind her of her language. In the end, the Yolŋu family adopt Tama and the two young people have found their culture. They have respect for people, for themselves. It is all better again. They know who they are. The culture is not going to be lost.

That is why the group is Goŋ-gurtha. The students meet and they talk about their cultures, learning and sharing, learning to value themselves and where they come from. A lot of those kids feel so happy to be in this group, they feel proud again. They know that it is their job to carry their culture on. As Mayutu says, 'I make sure I will know my Country, talk about it, not hide it, open up my feelings about it. Our cultural group is like a family as well, like a big family.'

The fire burns from Goŋ-gurtha and from the determined hunter.

Wurrumila is reading the sea. The hunter can read, he can read everything, he can read nature. Like when we woke up this morning we thought about the tides and hunting. Straight away we think, 'The tide's going out, I could go hunting before the tide comes back.' But sometimes the tide coming in is the right time to get a certain animal, like dugong or turtle.

He's there, he's waiting for the tide. The canoe is a long way from the water, so he's waiting for the tide to come in. That's what we do in the song too. Sometimes the Djungaya in a ceremony might say, 'Wait, we have to sing the tides before we head off, before we go in the right direction.' It must be in the right order.

So wise women and men, old people or even middle-aged or younger, they sit there and listen. These wise people sit next to younger people when they're singing and listen and they correct them. They make sure they start and stop in the right places, correctly.

For the hunter, it is time to travel, time to go hunting.

CHAPTER 3

The fire on the horizon

Durryuna ŋunha marrtji Maywalkarra,
Goŋ-gurthawuŋu, Goŋ-yakaywuŋu.
Nyewunba, Gulthana, Rranyirranyi.

The fire rises on the horizon at that place
   Maywalkarra,
From Goŋ-gurtha, the person who starts the fire
   that burns the land,
From Goŋ-yakaywuŋu, the person who starts
   the fire with great care and great awareness.
The fire rises on the horizon in Yirritja Country,
   at Nyewunba, Gulthana, Rranyirranyi.

Goŋ-gurtha nharana, Djilayŋaŋu, Batumbil,
   dhakalnydja durryunara nhäŋala Maywalkarra.

The Goŋ-gurtha lights the fire at Djilayŋaŋu and
   Batumbil; the fire is burning along the coastline.

The smoke billows and the flames rise; it is burning along the coastline.
I can see it burning at Maywalkarra.

Wurrumila is ready to walk to the canoe. Country has told him that the time is right.

In the songspiral, we sing about walking towards the boat. Warrinda birru birru, that's the name of the canoe. He is walking with the paddle over his shoulder, on the sand down to the warrinda birru birru. As this is sung, so we dance him walking down.

'Weh, weh,' the men sing with a particular beat. They step and jump on one leg. In the dance, they walk to the boat, they are him walking to the boat, walking with his paddle. And we call out the names: the names of the boat, the names of the paddle, the names of the hunter. All this we do while Wurrumila and the dancers walk down.

Rrawun walks down at Bawaka, showing Kate, Sandie and Sarah the steps, chanting the names. His feet on the white sand, the sun, the wind blowing sand onto the tarp. All these are one: Rrawun and us, Wurrumila himself, the women and men who have been sung as Wurrumila through the generations, the ceremonies held, the milkarri keened, Goŋ-gurtha and the fire, the songspirals and the connections they bring, this time and all times.

We sisters and Marri'marri, our mum, the Goŋ-gurtha, we look on. This is our role as Djungaya. This is the balance between generations, between women and men.

And then they stop. Wurrumila is at the canoe. And now they must push the boat down to the water. First, though, they put the paddle in the boat. Because in manikay, if someone walks down and starts to push the boat without putting the paddle in it, the old people will say, 'He's still learning so we're going to put the paddle in the boat. You can't push the boat while holding a paddle.'

This is part of the learning, part of learning culture and how we pass that knowledge on through the generations, how the songs spiral out and on and on. The old ones teach the young ones. We learn from the young ones too.

When Mayutu was small, her grandmother Gaymala would come over and teach her. She can't remember it now, she was too small, but our sister Ritjilili keeps this story alive for her. And now Mayutu tells it, 'Ŋamala Ritjilili lived across the road from us with my grandmother. I don't remember but I knew it. And Ŋamala Ritjilili told me that every morning my grandmother would say, "I am coming over now to see my granddaughter. Get ready!" I have to, I am meant to carry on my culture.'

We used to hear Mayutu's high voice from a long way away, 'Here I am, Manyi.'

Mayutu has her own journey of learning culture. She went to kindergarten in New South Wales, far from Arnhem Land. As she says, 'So that is the time when you are learning how to talk, how to learn, and because I was there I lost it, I lost a bit of my culture. That is why I talk English all the time. But the last couple of years I have made an effort to talk my dialect, Dhuwalandja, and Mum has been helping me with the structure. I am talking to Yumalil, Djawundil's granddaughter, who is my little namesake. I have wanted to be there to watch her grow up, to grow her up and make sure that I am her namesake, and make sure I can talk to her in Yolŋu matha. It's important that I talk to her in Yolŋu matha. And consciously I am trying to learn. My Ŋamalas, my mothers, are keeping me close and they teach me and talk to me. I'm Yolŋu and it's my job. Mum met Dad and they had me but that doesn't change my responsibility. I've got ŋäpaki, non-Indigenous, in me and Yolŋu in me but that doesn't change the fact that I am carrying the Yolŋu culture on.'

As Mayutu learns, she also feels a responsibility to carry and share culture. She decided that she wanted to introduce more Yolŋu culture into her school, Nhulunbuy High School, in the nearby town of Nhulunbuy, when she was on the Student Representative Council. She thought, 'We are on Yolŋu land.' She taught teachers before school each day. For Mayutu, putting Yolŋu matha into the school is about respecting Yolŋu culture first and then other cultures. Mayutu explains, 'First I made a slideshow of animals and trees and things. I told the teachers the Yolŋu names for them and how to pronounce them. I showed them that each of these are split into Yirritja and Dhuwa. Then I told them about the importance of names; they're not labels, they have true meaning behind them. The teachers were good students and said, "Thank you, Mayutu. Now I understand." I told them it takes practice, like trying to perfect a trick on the skateboard. Now I don't know whether it was because of that but they decided to build a boarding house at my high school to support the Yolŋu kids from the homelands in North East Arnhem Land. I said, "I'm tired of not seeing Yolŋu kids in my school." Now they can come and stay at the school and still be on Yolŋu land and learn to live in both worlds.'

Family down at Bawaka: Galpu (Samson), Ruwu (Amelie), Gara (Cadan), Mayutu (Siena), D̲awu (Heather), Gawiya (Mikayla) and Nanukala (Grace). *(Authors' collection)*

Banbapuy adds, 'It's good to have a Western education but you're still Yolŋu. It is right to have other education too, Yolŋu education.'

Merrkiyawuy says, 'The students need people there to make them feel comfortable and make sure they're learning what they need to learn.'

Living in both worlds and keeping Yolŋu culture strong means a lot of learning. And there are lots of teachers: the mothers and grandmothers, fathers and grandfathers, the old people, aunties and uncles.

It's like that big boat that Wurrumila will hunt in as he continues his journey. We need lots of people to push the boat. In the songspiral, some push and some pull the boat, the big canoe. That is in the dance. We heave it down the sand to the water, saying, 'Oooooh weh. Oooooooooh weh.'

In the dance the dancers create that movement. With their hands they pull and push the boat together. 'Ooooooooo ooooooh, weh weh.'

Now the boat is in the water. Before Wurrumila jumps in the boat, he must sing. He stands with his arms up in a special shape. With his hands over his head, bent at the elbow, he holds his spear and stands with his power ready to go hunting.

His hands are up representing the cloud, representing the cloud beneath the sea, the reflection of the cloud on the ocean's still surface. This is the cloud you see across a far distance in the ocean; the small cloud you see reflected in the sea. He's telling himself, 'I am like that cloud that stands in the far distance in the ocean.'

Rrawun puts his hand up at Bawaka to show us and he is that cloud too. He is Wurrumila and the cloud and himself showing us, teaching you.

As he stands, Wurrumila is empowering himself for the big hunt. He might be getting whale or dugong. He is calling the names, the different names of the hunter: Bäpa'yili, Wurramala, Lanytjun Dharra, Wurrumila, standing tall and strong. In the songspiral, we always do that, call his name. Wurrumila, a great sea hunter in his time, in the beginning.

From there, we feel emotion. We feel like the spirit is ready to hop on that boat. Honest, sometimes we cry, we feel our brothers or sisters who have passed away on that boat, on that same journey. They're dancing with us. We feel the motion, their presence. We feel their help. Then we start crying milkarri. We think about that person, when they were alive, what they saw, seeing the fire. We don't keep that to ourselves, we express it through milkarri. It's healing.

Our memories are released through milkarri. We don't keep them bottled up in our bodies. It is healing and healthy. We do it in the song and in the open. People see us keening, singing. Tears may roll down the men's faces as they think about their fathers or sons as they share the feeling of being a hunter. It is driven by our feelings.

The men might sing about Djambatj, a person who provided for the family, getting fish, turtle, dugong. The women crying milkarri might go, 'Yeeeeeeeeeeeeeeeeeeeeh, djambatj-djulŋi, our dearest hunter. You provided all the meat and were a very good hunter.'

Or we might cry for the dulŋay-djulŋi, the one who is an expert at gathering bush tucker and maypal. We might sing milkarri, 'Yeeeeeeeeeeeeeeeeeeeeh, dulŋay-djulŋi. You've done well in collecting yams, gathering bush tucker, getting maypal for us.'

With the milkarri, if you see the fire, you start straight away singing the fire. We cry tears of milkarri for the fire that's started from the Goŋ-gurtha. When we see it, we feel the one who has started the fire, the Goŋ-gurtha. The fire burns from Wuymuwuŋu.

Even though you may have passed away a long time ago, for Yolŋu you are still alive. Why? When we sing we always think about that person. It doesn't matter if they passed away twenty, thirty years ago, we can still think about that person. Because the manikay, the song, tells the story of each particular person's journey.

When that person was alive, they saw the hunters go out to get dugong or whale, pulling the boat into the water, going out and paddling, that person saw the Goŋ-gurtha's fire burning and saw how the gurtha, the fire, lights up the islands along the coastline. And then we see the hunter. We stand by the fire we have lit and we see afar, another hunter on their journey. From there it goes back around and starts again. We see the hunter.

Goŋ-gurtha is a celebration of someone's life. When we see the cloud that's that person seeing the cloud. They're not there to see it, so we keen and sing to make the person and the cloud alive together. It is the same for the land too. If trees have been damaged by mining, if there is death or destruction, or if Country hasn't been visited for a time and is missed, we sing it to make it alive. We feel Country with us.

Things that happened a long time ago are with us now: people and Country. The songspirals hold us together, the songspirals and Country, the winds and the animals and all the beings that communicate with us. It happened then, it will happen in the future, and it happened now, in this season, in and with this place, through the songspirals.

Even the starting point is with us now and always. The land sang itself into existence and it still sings. At the beginning of time someone had to talk for the land, it was quiet, nothingness. And then it began with the sound from deep within the water, 'Hmmm hmmm'. That was the starting point. We know that is the water from the land; in all the songspirals, that is where it all began, life and language begin. The first language was the 'Hmmm' from the songs, the sound, the sound that we make. Without dhäruk, without language, there is bäyŋu, nothing.

Water is life, knowledge, and what came out of the water is sound. On a baby's head, the Milŋurr, the fontanelle, that is where the water came out, the knowledge, like on the Wapitja given to Laklak. So, we have water and we have fire. These things have knowledge, are knowledge.

Wurrumila, Goŋ-gurtha, they are here now. Not only Wurrumila, not only Goŋ-gurtha, but our other ancestors. They still hunt with us, look after us, show us their ways, and that is why we always announce ourselves, to let them know we are coming, because they are still around.

Merrkiyawuy remembers the time she went with Bambuŋ and Mayutu to the Wessel Islands and she felt this connection, 'We got there, and I said to the others with us, "Wait, we will go onto shore first, me and my children." We went on the boat. I got onto shore and announced us to our ancestors. I said Bamatja's name and her brother, the old man, Daymaŋu, he was like the king of that island. He was my great-grand-father but he was also my child, through gurru_t_u, the cycle of kinship.

'I called out, "Hellllloooooo, waku! Hellllloooooo, child. We are here. You don't know me but . . ." I told him who I was, and my children. I announced myself and we walked. And Mayutu looked. One of her names, Mitjparal, is the name of the Wessel Islands. There was a little cave on the beach and bigger caves up on the hills, caves with handprints all on the walls. Mayutu looked and said, "Mum, I can see something there."

'I said, "Careful, it might be something dangerous."

'She said, "No, it's fine. Look, that is a swag." She looked in and found a brand-new swag, a beautiful pink canvas bedroll used for camping.

'It was a gift from one of her yapas, her sisters, the old one there. So Mayutu is yapa to her great-great-grandmother. That is gurru_t_u. Mayutu has a link with that one.'

Even though no one lives on the island now, they are still there, all the time.

Time is co-existing. We are with them. They are in their time. You are in your time. We are in time together. We feel them. Wurrumila, a great sea hunter in his time, is here now as he was in the beginning, as he will continue to be.

We know the tide is controlled by the moon. Nowadays we look at watches, but we still look at the tide and the moon to do things, like Wurrumila does. The full moon is good for getting turtle and crayfish because the tide is really low at night-time and it is good for wäku<u>n</u>, mullet, too.

When we keen milkarri, it takes us back. We have travelled. They have travelled. Wurrumila the hunter has travelled, as have those who have passed away. We know where their land is, a person who has never been there can go there. We are thinking about those trees, that raŋi (beach), the person, when the person was born, when they grew up. It's all about life, what happens when they're alive. We are all part of the ecosystem. It's memory and actually telling a story, remembering that person, Country, what you've seen, what we hear.

Milkarri tells a story of a person or being that created life or that was there creating the land. As we tell the story of Wurrumila here, we say 'he' because this is the ancestral hunter but the Wurrumila songspiral may be for a woman too. We are all here creating and re-creating life and the land. And then is now. It all co-exists. It is all here.

For Wurrumila, now that he has walked down to the canoe, he gets in the boat. He begins to paddle. He is pointing. It is the

feelings of the ocean, the feelings of the wind and the feeling of
the floating of the boat. He knows that it is the right time. He is
getting near to the destination, pointing back to the island. He
does this with his arms. The dancers do that. We sing and do
milkarri. He is connecting to the land, pointing at the different
spots to make sure he is going to the right spot to get the meat.

He uses the harpoon to point. He sees sea grass that is eaten
in a certain way. He knows that the whale or the dugong is
travelling and which direction it heads. He sees that in the
grass and the water. So, then the hunter will know which way
to go. It's like reading the wind, holding up the marrwala, the
paddle, to make sure we are on the right path, making sure
we are going the right way. It teaches us and connects us and
makes it all again.

Wurrumila is pointing to the gamata, the sea grass sanctuary
area. Wurrumila is pointing, and behind him are the paddlers.
They have to adjust their pace and direction depending on what
Wurrumila sees. With the buŋgul, the ceremonial dance, we
re-enact Wurrumila. He is pointing, they are pointing, Rrawun
is pointing, and in their mind they are going, 'Which way to go?'

They all become as one, as the sea, thinking which way to
go, on the sea, floating. Where to get dugong.

We may come back with nothing; sometimes we come back
with something good. But the best hunter knows where to go.
Even though it's rough or murky, the best hunter will come back
with turtle or dugong. Like Wurrumila, the one in the songspiral. We are re-enacting him now. He is who we would be.

And beyond this, we can tell you, it's not just the hunter's
song. It's about all the family's journey. It is all about the flames,
lighting the fire, caring for ourselves and Country. Goŋ-gurtha.

The song is the person who goes hunting, but it is also the family going on a spiritual journey. The hunter guides the journey. The hunter is the one who is guiding the journey to get the family a feed, ŋatha. It might be a woman or man. It is not just one person's manikay. That's why it's more complicated to understand the songspirals. It's got layers of meanings inside, it is a spiritual journey.

The spiritual journey is hard, it is difficult. It takes time. We must listen and learn from Country, like Wurrumila. We must be in and with time. And the journey links with other journeys, other families and other hunters. We know this through Goŋ-gurtha, through its connections with the songspiral that Marri'marri keens. For we see the smoke on the horizon and we connect. Goŋ-gurtha is the keeper of the flame, the one who has been successful in their hunt. Goŋ-gurtha lights a fire. Goŋ-gurtha lets us know with the flames and the smoke. We see the flames on the horizon.

**Durryuna ŋunha marrtji Maywalkarra,
Goŋ-gurthawuŋu, Goŋ-yakaywuŋu.
Nyewunba, Gulthana, Rranyirranyi.**

*The fire rises on the horizon at that place
    Maywalkarra,
From Goŋ-gurtha, the person who starts the fire
    that burns the land,
From Goŋ-yakaywuŋu, the person who starts
    the fire with great care and great awareness.
The fire rises on the horizon in Yirritja Country,
    at Nyewunba, Gulthana, Rranyirranyi.*

And the women see and keen milkarri for the deceased person. The one who passed away can see the land and the fire. They are the hunter. Through our keening, that person is there, through the songspirals. It reduces the distance between the deceased person and the person singing or keening.

They have undertaken their spiritual journey. They have hunted. They lit the fire.

Oh, my dear, you saw everything with your beautiful eyes.

With your nose, you smelled the smoke.

With your ears, you heard the bird singing.

Order

Wuymuwuŋu nharana gurtha Rranyirranyiwuyŋu
Gulthanawuyŋu.

*The Wuymu, the hunter, lit the fire. The fire is burning
from Wuymuwuŋu, from Rranyirranyiwuyŋu, from
Gulthanawuyŋu and from Nyewu̱nbuwuyŋu.*

Nyewu̱nbuwuyŋu yeeee.
Wulpu̱nduna nhäŋaya durryunara Goŋ-gurthawuŋu.

*From these Yirritja people, the fire burns. We see the
smoke clouds rising up high from Goŋ-gurtha.
From there, the smoke's mist rises up and becomes
the cloud Wulpu̱ndu, a big cloud stretching
forward into the sky.*

Yeeee, runurunu Djilayŋaŋu, Batumbil dhakalnydja
ḏurryun ŋunha marrtji.

Yeeee, Goŋ-gurthawuŋu.

Yes, those islands Djilayŋaŋu and Batumbil, I can
see the jawline of the coastline through my crying.
I can see those islands very clearly as the smoke
rises up.
Yes, from Goŋ-gurtha.

Ŋunha Nyewunba, Rranyirranyiwuŋu,
  Gulthanawuyŋu,
Goŋ-gurtha Mätjitji.

There, that one now, the fire is from Nyewunba,
  Rranyirranyi, Gulthana, from the people who hold
  that Country, keepers of the land.
From Goŋ-gurtha Mätjitji, the keeper of the fire,
  the one who starts the fire.

Let's sit down on raŋi, the sand, at Bawaka, and continue with
Wurrumila, the hunter. Marri'marri will sit with us in the
shade. Kate, Sarah and Sandie are there taking notes.

Rrawun is talking about the songspiral. He says that if
someone else was telling this, they would share it in their
own way. If the old man, Batjaŋ, was here he would talk from
morning to evening every day, enough for five books. But we
are leading this, and we have asked Rrawun, our son, to share.
It's important for us to talk about this, to put it into words,
and give other people an understanding of the meaning.

Wurrumila paddles out. He stops, slows down; there's
something there, a big sea animal. It might be dugong or whale.

Wurrumila has seen something that will feed the family. He doesn't hurry. He moves very carefully, slowly now. He's trying to adjust the boat, reverse, reverse, come back, come back, go forward, forward.

He sneaks towards it with his djambatj, but oh, he has missed! The dugong gets away. He watches the dust inside the water as it swims beyond reach.

Wurrumila has followed his knowledge. He has gone the right way, sung the seas and the animals. He has thrown his harpoon, but it plunges into the sea. He misses. He must go back. We must go back.

He heads back to his camp. When he arrives at the shore he pulls the boat out of the water, gets the djambatj, and walks back.

He's walking from the boat with his paddle, calling 'weh, weh' again. He goes back with the paddle over his shoulder.

After he puts his djambatj down, he sits under a djomula, a casuarina, and sees that the waters are all calm. He relaxes. He's thinking about the day and what happened and why he didn't get that catch. He has not yet lit his fire. Then he sings all the things he saw on his journey to the hunting place: the matjala, the floating driftwood; the galuku, coconut; the minyga, garfish; yarrwarri, queenfish; and barrak barrak, the tern, a small bird with triangle wings that hangs about the sea. And he sings others, everything he sees, everything in Country. Every time a Yirritja hunter goes out hunting these are the things he sees. They're in the songspirals. This is singing Country, singing the sea. And as we sing the beings of Country, we are never alone. We are all together. The whole universe is with us through the songspirals, through our kinship. We can't just sing a hunt. We can't just sing a whale. We can't just sing a fire. We must sing it all and all the connections. We sing Country.

As he sits in the shade, Wurrumila thinks about the day, how he didn't get the dugong or the whale, and he sings Country. Rrawun thinks about the day, we sing Country. The dancers and the listeners, those that do milkarri, the one who has passed away, all that came before and will come, we all follow this journey, thinking about the dugong, singing it up, singing all that is there, dwelling with Country.

Rrawun explains that in the manikay when we come back from hunting we sing about what we have seen. He says, 'We don't say, "Wurrumila saw this and this." We sing the bird, we sing the driftwood. The way is to sing it but not to describe it. The leader of the clan will say, "Matjala gu" according to the song and we will sing the Country.'

As part of the journey, we might keen and sing other clans' parts too, because Country is connected to many people. Songspirals connect through space and time. If Wurrumila is coming back and he sings the coconut, that is a different clan, Birrkili, so we will sing that in a different language, a different tune, then we will go back to Gumatj. And that coconut might have floated in from far away. As we sing it, we sing those other places, where it has travelled, and in this way the songs, the coconut, link us with other clans and other places, near and far.

There is order in all the songspirals, it ensures that we do things for a purpose, we burn land for a purpose. Process, order and structure must be followed. It is important that songs are sung in the right place, in the right way. If you are inland, then you sing about the inland. If you are on the coast, you sing the coast.

If it's not in order it's dhawa<u>d</u>atj, mixed up. The process is not right. In songspirals and ceremonies, when things become dhawa<u>d</u>atj everyone says 'errgh' and claps to erase the mistake and start again. We have to make it right, we have to go back to ceremony, and then we give back something, something that is very, very sacred.

After Wurrumila has sung the Country, then the <u>d</u>irrmala wind comes from the north. After all that journey, the hunting and the long day, the wind makes him relax. The <u>d</u>irrmala wind is bringing in the ŋara', the cloud from the smoke of the Goŋ-gurtha, and the hunter is looking at the ŋara' and thinking maybe that lot are the lucky people who got turtle or dugong. Maybe it's a signal from another place, or a sign of people leaving that island or land and moving to another estate. And the hunter is conscious of thinking different ways. He knows what the mob is doing.

When we sing Goŋ-gurtha from the perspective of the hunter, we sing about the land, the wind touches there.

We learn this from the women when we are little. When the women cry milkarri we learn, we learn how they're describing the people and the area. When they see the smoke forming into a cloud, and it's all black, in the distance, it's ŋara'. Like our young ones, the keepers of the flame, who learn from listening to Marri'marri, to Laklak and to us.

Wurrumila watches the smoke from the fire of Goŋ-gurtha, over there, as the cloud blows towards him. He watches the smoke of the hunter far away, the Goŋ-gurtha who has lit that fire. We keen milkarri for that fire, we feel it in our heart.

The fire is burning from Wuymuwuŋu, from Rranyirranyiwuyŋu, from Gulthanawuyŋu and from Nyewu<u>n</u>buwuyŋu. From these Yirritja people the fire burns. We see the smoke clouds rising up high from Goŋ-gurtha. From there the smoke's mist rises up and becomes the cloud Wulpuṉḏu, a big cloud stretching forward into the sky.

When we sing this songspiral at a funeral, the singing goes for several days. On the first day of the funeral, we do Wurrumila but the hunter misses the whale. The Djungaya of the clan, the caretaker, will say, 'Oh, we missed it.'

For this singing of Wurrumila at Bawaka, Rrawuṉ is the Gutharra. He is the grandchild in the märi-gutharra relationship with the song. Djaḻi, our brother, is the Djungaya and has the responsibility to make the call on the timing of the ceremony. Rrawuṉ was sharing the manikay and he was also learning the process. He is a keeper of tomorrow's fire too. He will keep the songspirals alive.

This is all according to the songspirals. The way the song-spiral progresses is led by the Djungaya. The caretaker and the songspiral story tell us what is happening. For us, the hunter missed today. The hunter went back to the shore and watched the smoke from another Goŋ-gurtha, from another fire. He will try again tomorrow. One day, our journey will be complete.

There is a fire on every island. We don't know who made the fire but we can see the smoke on the horizon and we can smell the smoke. When the smoke rises it forms a cloud in the shape of a person standing, holding their arms up above their head, elbows bent, like a cloud. That is the shape we dance.

We sit at Bawaka and look out to the sea, we see a cloud forming.

As Marri'marri keens the milkarri, she cries, 'Yes, those islands Djilayŋaŋu and Batumbil, I can see the jawline of the coastline, through my crying. I can see those islands very clearly as the smoke rises. Yes, from Goŋ-gurtha.'

When Goŋ-gurtha is lighting the fire, it goes up and forms a cloud, then it rains, liya-balkurrk. Yirritja makes the clouds and Dhuwa sings the rain. Yirritja and Dhuwa, mother and child. Goŋ-gurtha, looking after the land, burning the land, as a messenger, saying, 'Hello, we're here.' And thanking the land. Burning the land so new shoots grow up for animals to eat. Marking the land, cleaning, claiming.

Wurrumila, a great sea warrior and hunter. When the clouds go up we go, 'Waaaaaah, a hunter is there.'

CHAPTER 5

Connecting generations

Djambatjŋuwuyŋu gurtha nharana Bolumi,
Djilayŋaŋu, Batumbil.

From Djambatj, the hunter, the fire burns. From the
place Bolumi, a distant place where the bamboo,
bolu, grows. From the islands of Yolŋu Country,
Djilayŋaŋu and Batumbil.

Durryunara nhäŋala Maywalkarra.
Ŋunha Djilayŋa Batumbil Goŋ-gurthawuyŋu,
Durryunara nhäŋala Nyewuṉba, Rranyirranyi,
Goŋ-gurtha.

The smoke rises high from far away, from islands
a long way away. See the smoke rising high at
Maywalkarra.

There at Djilayŋa and Batumbil from Goŋ-gurtha,
the flames are rising up high. See the hunters
Nyewuṉba, Rranyirranyi, Goŋ-gurtha.

Goŋ-gurtha tells us when it is the last day of a funeral ceremony, the day for the body to be buried. The songspiral will
have been sung on the preceding days but the hunt would have
been unsuccessful.

On the last day, everything is sung. Anything that has been
missed before has to be in the songspiral. On the last day, the
hunter is going to catch something, a dugong, turtle, whale.
This will satisfy the spiritual journey of the person's life, of
their clan and related clans. This is the final day, coming back
to the person, their family, and saying goodbye.

On this day, we will light the fire. Our fire will be seen and
keened by others. The songspirals shared by Marri'marri and
Rrawuṉ connect again. They connect, and they are one. Now
it is the hunter here that is lighting the fire. Elsewhere, another
hunter may look back and cry, 'Ahh, the fire.'

The manikay is very intense. The songspiral is giving the
person back to their family. Acknowledging the person who
passed away and their family, saying goodbye to the spirit
and taking the spirit back to the spirit world. Everyone has to
be satisfied. The clan leader has to be satisfied he's given all
his memories, all his life, all his heart to the person and the
person's family. This is the full journey of Goŋ-gurtha. The
fire will burn with the flames rising high.

When we sing, we will go deeper, deep to the octopus. The
hunter knows beneath the sea, under the corals, is the octopus

always changing colours. As the octopus changes colour under the sea, so the land changes with the sunset. This time, the songspiral will sing the sunset. The hunter brings octopus and sunset together as one.

Leading on from sunset, the song must be finished by the wind. It is time for the hunter's resting.

Every manikay has that journey from the start to the end. The funeral ceremony doesn't happen in one day, it can take one to two weeks as we sing the right songs.

Marri'marri keens many fires, fires from many hunters that are connected through Goŋ-gurtha and the way we see the smoke from the journeys of others. She keens the hunter, the hunter that comes from Bolumi, a place where bamboo grows. We don't know where this is, but it is far away, a faraway island. Maybe there are fires all across the islands and the hunter sees them from a long way away, from where the bamboo grows, like Saibai in the Torres Strait or Fiji, Vanuatu, Tonga. Wurrumila's story links to the great hunters here and across to there.

The canoes are coming back, we can see the smoke rising high.

I see the smoke. I can see the smoke rising up from Goŋ-gurtha. I see the work of the hunters.

When Marri'marri keens milkarri of Goŋ-gurtha she sings with feeling. Her voice is high because of the fire burning up. She doesn't just say the words, she has to change the tone to show the fire is burning upwards, to make it strong. When you keen a song it has to be with feeling, it is a story you are telling. But it's also more than a story, it's a way of life. It's bringing life through song and milkarri.

It is in our hearts and our emotions as we keen milkarri and as we sing. And it is also the smelling, we smell it too. The keening brings up the smell. It brings up being on the land, walking along the beach, starting the fire, what sounds we hear. It makes it alive. It is a way of keeping the memories alive in sound and song. It is revisiting that past, that event that happened, bringing it to now and making it live.

As manikay, milkarri tells the story. It is healing for everyone. In a funeral, it's a celebration too for that person's life, a celebration and saying thank you for what that person did for us and for the land, the clan and the family. It is respecting the person's knowledge, when that person was alive for the clan and for the people.

When that person was alive they have given to the family, the grandchildren, the land, the Country, and in return we have to respect that person through manikay including milkarri. Even if we don't know that person, we still go to the ceremony to sit down and be with our gurrutu, our kin relations. We are connected through kin, through the land, through the songs. So even if we're not dancing, we are sitting there, showing respect. And even if we're young or just a baby we still do that. We show respect because of likun, the deep names, or bäpurru, the clans. Maybe we cook up something, a fish, and bring something to the family.

Ensuring the babies, children and young ones are always there, always included, is really important to the songspirals. Mayutu talks about how she learnt who she is and why passing on her knowledge is so important.

'I just love my homeland Bawaka,' she says. 'I remember every weekend, going out, growing up in Bawaka. We are all here together, we are the young people, we need to pass on our message, we need to do it together as one. When my mum was young, older generations before mine, they learnt from Yolŋu, they sat around, they lived Yolŋu life and learnt the knowledge ever since they were young. It was just living and learning. And they learnt the songspirals. They learnt the meaning of it all. That's how you did it. I need to start learning it so it can't be lost. I'm going to be the one who has to tell my daughter or son. I don't want to say, "Don't ask me, because I don't know." I'm meant to know that because that's my culture.'

Whatever our children like to pursue or want to do, we are totally behind them, encouraging them, nurturing their interests, whatever they may be. Although if it is bad, we let them know right away. But if it's good, we encourage them all the way.

Songspirals, respect, connections, kinship are all about helping each other, being part of the community, being part of who you are, being Yolŋu. When we go to someone's home-land, they will say, 'Oh, you looked after us at the funeral,' and they will offer something, they will make a bed for us, we can stay over there. The same with Sarah and Sandie and Kate. They look after us when we go to their homes to work, and when they come to Yirrkala and Bawaka we look after them. This is give and take. Bala ga' lili.

You see in that songspiral how powerful the Wurrumila is, the hunter. When the young men first get a turtle we all put ochre on to celebrate. Their mum, sister, uncle, grandmother all put ochre on.

The grandmother is the boss, she says who is going to cut and eat the turtle first. When Rrawun got his first turtle, his mum and grandmother put ochre on their bodies. This is also in the songspirals.

The wataŋu, the clan leader, they always choose a person who will re-enact Wurrumila. This will be someone who has got the movement of that dance. They will choose someone from the right family. They always choose the best dancer to lead the dance. It's the same for the songs, we always follow the best singer. We always know who is the best. No, not the best, the most spiritual singer, the person who always has the spirit and songs inside them.

Milkarri comes when the hunter catches something, then the old ladies will cry. We cry about how far he went, did he travel far or not so far. We sing though the tears of our milkarri all the parts. If something bad happens, we cry that, we keen our milkarri. We've got to cry, it's part of us. It's all about connecting ourselves to the land.

This emotion, this passion, has been passed on to many of the youth. Mayutu talks about who she is and what being Yolŋu means to her, 'At my school I am the school captain. I learn about maths and English but I can't let that take my true knowledge away. It is my job to make sure I pass it on. It has been passed on by my family, for generations. I can't be the one to let it pass away, I can't be the one to lose it.

'It's not just me, it's the others, we can't let our culture be lost because of the modern way. We should use that to carry our knowledge on. What Maminydjama is doing with her modelling and other family with their dance and music.

'I need to make sure that ŋäpaki know that I am Yolŋu. I need to let other Yolŋu kids know I am Yolŋu. Some might

Siena Mayutu Wurmarri Stubbs, daughter of Merrkiyawuy, signing her book at the Buku-Larrŋgay Mulka Art Centre. *(Courtesy of Will Stubbs)*

think I am not Yolŋu because I have lighter skin. It used to be difficult but you can't tell me what I am or what I'm not. I know the knowledge, I am learning the knowledge, so I am Yolŋu. It doesn't matter what I look like. I am still Yolŋu even though there is half ŋäpaki in me. I am not favouring one side. I am making sure they are balanced.

'I do singing and dancing. I have an education, but my mothers and my ancestors had a different education. I get this opportunity so I should use that opportunity to learn, to have knowledge. I am Yolŋu and I am educated and I know about the world. I have won awards, using that motivation, that drive. I push back against stereotypes.

'Every weekend we go hunting. My mums have always been teaching me words, singing me songs and telling me about the fruits, the trees and the birds. When I was younger I don't think the knowledge they were telling me sunk in as much. But since I was twelve, I have been thinking, remembering: the tree with the long leaves and green fruit is munydjutj, the rainbow bee-eater is wirriwirri. I used the knowledge to write my book about the birds I see around me, sharing some meanings and stories. I was taking photos and learning more about the birds. Then I thought I should use the knowledge to make the book.

'I've made an effort to really learn my culture and my clan language. I hear about other Aboriginal people down south, from the stolen generation, who didn't get the chance to learn from their mothers or grandmothers or even to know who they are or where they are from. But I get to know, I am here, I am living it, so I should use that power to learn.

'Through ŋäpaki side, I go to school, I do all of that stuff. So I have to make sure I am strong with my culture, with my inner Yolŋu. That is why I am here. Because my grandfather and my grandmothers made sure they stayed strong for Yolŋu and the ancestors stayed strong and it is good.'

Mayutu didn't know Goŋ-gurtha was a songspiral until the collective were meeting with our publisher Elizabeth in Bangalow in northern New South Wales in 2017. Mayutu then suddenly realised that her culture group was part of the songspiral, part of the connection. 'Oh, that's Goŋ-gurtha, like Mum told me. Wow—I didn't know that.'

Sandie then described how Goŋ-gurtha became a songspiral for the book and how she, Kate and Sarah also slowly came to realise how everything was connected through it, how the story of the hunter and the milkarri of the fire are one, how they spiral out and in, balancing and connecting. Indeed, in September 2016, when everyone was down in Sydney staying in Sandie's house for Laklak's honorary doctorate ceremony, Sandie's daughter Lalu took it upon herself to ensure we always had a fire burning in the firepit in the back garden—a place to sit outside and keep warm during a particularly cold snap in Sydney's spring. Watching her at work, Banbapuy said she is the keeper of the fire.

Then, when we were all together in Bawaka in July 2017, Lalu had a primary school assignment about energy and where it came from. When we were talking about it, Banbapuy reminded everyone that Lalu is Goŋ-gurtha. We sat there thinking about the connections between fire and energy, between Sydney and Bawaka, and between generations as Marri'marri was there too, as Marri'marri sang Goŋ-gurtha for the book and Banbapuy explained how Marri'marri is Goŋ-gurtha 1 and Lalu is Goŋ-gurtha 2. Granddaughters always get names from their grandmothers. Marri'marri has given her name to Lalu too.

Mayutu's cultural group has a song that they wrote together, the song that led Merrkiyawuy to give them their name. It is the young people keeping the flame, lighting the fire, confident and strong in their knowledge. They are Keepers of Tomorrow's Sun. The flames rise high. They can be seen from afar. They are Goŋ-gurtha.

Keepers of Tomorrow's Sun

We are lighting a fire
We are guiding the flame
To pass on our story
To pass on our name

We're guiding the people
United as one
We are the keepers
Of tomorrow's sun.

Ending with the wind

Previous page: Manala Marika Guluruŋa (our brother's daughter), *Rulyapa* (2018).
(The Buku-Larrŋgay Mulka Art Centre archives)

Women cry milkarri to guide our loved ones, living and dead. We cry milkarri to greet the dawn, to make the new day. We remake ourselves and Country, we gather the clouds. We cry milkarri in grief, bittersweet, with love, to heal.

Milkarri's healing sound, its intensity straight from our heart, from our love and grief. Our tears.

Women keen the tears of milkarri for what is there. We keen milkarri for Country, for all our beautiful Countries, both Dhuwa and Yirritja.

If we are keening milkarri for the dawn at a Yirritja place, we cry the milkarri for the mist and through the mist, the spiders making their web. We cry milkarri for the first bird that sings at dawn, waking the other animals up.

When we do that, we are making the spider exist, helping it along, building its home, so that it can get its food and be alive, so that it can continue to be alive and survive. This is not make-believe, not something imagined. It is true, and it's the same for Dhuwa. Whatever we cry, whether it be animals, grubs, trees, sun, wind, person, anything on the earth as well as in the sea and in the sky, we bring it to life. The ecosystems exist because we do the milkarri.

And we are part of the ecosystem, that's what we are. We have lived like this since forever and beyond. Lots of things have changed since the arrival of the missionaries, but luckily lots of things have not changed. We eat off the land. We go hunt and we gather meat, fish, eggs, shellfish, honey, and food

Djulwanbirr Mungurrawuy Yunupiŋu painting.
(The Buku-Larrŋgay Mulka Art Centre archives and courtesy of Peter Wiedkuhn)

plants, including vegetables, yams, nuts and fruits. They are pleasurable activities, plus you get to eat what you find and catch.

And we haven't lost our milkarri, our crying for the land, our grief or the deep connection. That is the beauty of it.

Our milkarri, our keening, is the women's part of the spirals that make the rain, the clouds, the land. A women's cry is another way of celebrating. When we keen or cry, it's a story we are telling. It's telling a story in keening.

We keen our lives and Country. We keen a person's birth, we keen what they've seen in life, what they hear and what they feel. We cry the wind blowing, them going out and getting something, what they catch. If they're Dhuwa, then we keen milkarri and sing Dhuwa songs. If Yirritja, Yirritja songs, the same. From the day they are born to the day they die, we cry them. We sing the person, us women make the person alive by singing through the tears of our milkarri, telling a story of what that person did when they were alive.

How deep it is, the milkarri. The person becomes part of that songspiral, part of every particle, every being that we sing. So, Goŋ-gurtha is about the hunter and the fire. When we keen milkarri, we become the hunter, we become the fire.

It brings us back to the moment. It is the present, the past and the future. If we are singing about the rain coming down to the land, we become part of that water that drops to the soil, that sinks into the soil. We see the particles of the soil, those tiny pieces become huge rocks. We see them, we see them as we go down, inside the soil and then deep in, we see the roots of the trees as we pass through. We fall in between, we seep into the soil, down past the roots, past worms in the soil, the creatures and bugs, we travel down to the underground water and travel with the flood, out to the river, into the currents, down to the sea. We travel past different lands. Waters and currents speak to each other. One might be Dhuwa and one might be Yirritja. 'Don't collide with me,' we might say, 'I am just passing through.'

That is why people become so emotional. Even if we don't go back to that Country for a long time, we become so emotional we just cry. This is how Yolŋu think. This is how it has been passed on for so long. It is a whole way to be.

And it all depends on the particular Country, where we are doing it. We can't just write it down. We have shared some songspirals here, some layers, put some things in words. But it is beyond words really. Don't think what we have shared only exists here on the page. It does not. It lives. It has to be what the land tells us. What animals are there, in a particular land. The totems. The trees. The birds. The bush. The water. The rocks and all. We have thousands of songspirals. From the tiniest of things to the biggest of things, everything in the world.

And this milkarri we share with you is shared out of love, for our children, our grandchildren and for all. We are sharing our women's wisdom of Country through songlines. We ask you to respect this knowledge, to be respectful and be aware of the limits of what we are sharing.

When the court failed to recognise Yolŋu land rights, it was because they said we didn't have their kind of agriculture or fences or anything that they could see or recognise as using our land. We don't use the land, not in that way; we sing the land so that new trees grow, new plants come, animals flourish. We build our fish traps, we hunt and dig, we nourish our ganguri, our yams, and they nourish us; fire shapes Country, we light the land to renew it. It is sustainable for Yolŋu and everything

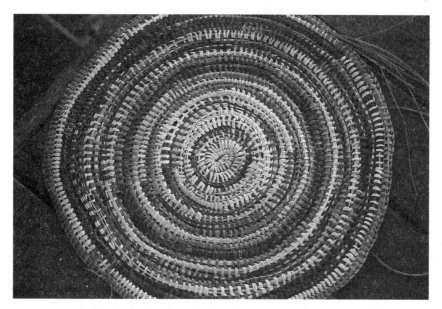

Weaving our spirals. *(Authors' collection)*

to live there together. With our songspirals the land renews itself, our songspirals are our land rights. After that land case a lot of our old people were so saddened by what the court said—that this was not their land—that it killed them. For us, for the new generations, we feel it is time that the stories we are telling in this book must be told. So ŋäpaki can start to understand why we don't want our land to be devastated by destructive mining, digging, farming, putting poison on the land. This book is dedicated to our grandfather, who was such a strong man and who worked so hard to communicate to ŋäpaki what we are explaining with this book, even though English was his fourth or fifth language. Our grandfather gave his paintings to ŋäpaki visitors but got nothing in return. 'This is my story and this is my painting, take it with you,' he said, sharing the depth of our connection with Country. He shared his story, expecting something for it in return, respect, recognition of our rights, but he got nothing. Many ŋäpaki couldn't or wouldn't understand. Now maybe they will.

Our book started with the Whale Songspiral and ended with Goŋ-gurtha. We spiral back to where we started.

Ŋarra yukurra nhäma moṉuk gapu, gäma yukurra
    ŋarranha bala ŋuylili barrku gulula,
Ŋarra yukurra Dhäwuḻwuḻyun Yiwarrnha.
Ŋupan Marrawuḻwuḻ Gunbiḻknha,
Ŋilinyu yurru marina rrambaŋina Mirrinyuna
    Marrawaṯpaṯthun.

I can see the salt water carrying me, moving together
    with the current;
Carrying me further into the depths of the ocean,
    where the foundation of my bloodline lies.
Here my grandmother and I, together we paddle,
    following the sea breeze, to finish our journey,
    across the calm, mercurial waters towards the
    horizon, our final destination.

We are carried out to the far horizon. We are Wuymirri, the Whale. The whale is our grandmother, our backbone, our present, our future, our past. We head to our final destination.

We breathe and our waterspout forms a small cloud. On the horizon it ascends and becomes the cloud Wulpuṉdu. We head eastwards, towards the deep ocean, to where the rains come from.

The hunter, he sees the clouds formed by our waterspouts. He makes his harpoon straight and ready. He knows. He travels west. He sees the clouds rising, the little clouds that float above the horizon. He gets his paddle ready and stands with it, hands above his head. We are him. He is the cloud.

Our book is a spiral, showing how we are connected. It shows how the songspirals link us through time and place, and bring those times and places together, the land and the people. The spiral is infinite, it is how kinship spirals through the generations, from before and into the future. It is all connected.

In Goŋ-gurtha, we catch the big sea creature. Our catch might be the dugong. It might be the whale, a whale that travels across the calm mercurial waters.

As Goŋ-gurtha, we are the hunter with their deep knowledge, listening to Country to know where to go, what to do. We value that knowledge. The knowledge feeds us. We light the fire and the smoke tells all that we are successful on our journey. The clouds of smoke rise to the horizon.

In Wuymirri, we are the whale. It is our mother's journey, as she passes away from us. We swim together across the mercurial ocean, to our final destination. You remember our pain when she got ready to be taken by the hunter? The pain as she passed?

The whales travel to another songspiral, connect with other clans. That's where they cut her up properly. The Warramirri, they cut Wuymirri up very, very carefully.

But did you realise, did you see? There are tears in our eyes. This is milkarri. Let loose your grief. The whale that the hunters catch, that the expert hunters worked so hard to get, the joy and pride we feel? They caught the same whale.

Our mother, her final destination.

This is the understanding we share with you. The hunter catches the whale. We are both hunter and whale. We light the fire of celebration. We cry in grief at the clouds of smoke that rise to the horizon.

The hunters go hunting because they know, they can feel it. And when the hunter spears the whale, she will be cut up carefully and she will feed many. We will share her. Many people will share, this group, that group.

We can see the salt water carrying us. We move together with the current towards the shimmering horizon. We dive deep. Deep. Our mother.

It is grief. It is pain. It is joy, love, healing.

It is songspirals.

And for now, we are done. An evening breeze rises. The song-spiral must be finished by the north wind, by dirrmala.

Wind is the one that cleanses, cleanses the footprints of the day. It smooths the sand, for a new beginning and a new song tomorrow. We can only do so much. Our book doesn't tell all, only a few of the layers. We light a fire on the beach. The heat radiant against our skin. The smoke cleansing, calling, sending those messages. Remember Goŋ-gurtha.

We always finish with the cleansing, smoking the spirits with fire. Both Yirritja and Dhuwa cleanse with smoking.

It is sunset, the day has ended. It is time to rest. The tide is coming in, dancing with the wind. When the sun sets, the north wind rises. We are the sunset. It is night-time.

And tomorrow, we cry the dawn.

Glossary

There are a range of extra letters and sounds in Yolŋu matha that don't exist as individual letters in English. These include ŋ, a soft 'ng' sound like that at the end of the word 'sing'; ä, a long 'a' sound similar to that in 'father'; the glottal stop (represented by an apostrophe, '); and the retroflex letters ḏ, ḻ, ṟ, et cetera, which are made with the tongue curled back.

B

bala ga' lili—a balance; coming together and complementing each other; give and take

balaḏay—dried yellow ganguri, yam, whose leaf is just about to fall; a vine used to make string

baḻkpaḻk—tree, yellow almond-shaped fruit, edible black nut, good for firesticks, also used as a medicine

balwarri—whale

bäpi—snake

bäpurru—clan, family group

barŋgitj—Yirritja bees

barrak barrak—tern

barrpa—rotten smell

barrum barru—special shelter

bäru—crocodile

bathi—basket

bäyŋu—nothing

bidiwidi—peewee bird

bila—the whale tail

bilma—clapsticks

bilyunmaraŋalnha—the action of turning to point

bintha—head of the whale

binydjalŋu—children of the shark; can also mean liver or fat
    of the shark

Birkarr'yun—ritual recitation of power names; when a man of
    authority is calling out the sacred, deep names he is called
    Birkarr'yun

buku dhäwu—a mind full of stories (buku means 'face' and
    dhäwu means 'story'—story-face)

buku-wekam—giving back

buku-wurrpan—to give back; to say thank you

buŋgul—dance, ceremonial dancing

burrkun—possum string

butjiriŋaniŋ—a leaf from a particular tree that is crushed and
    used for bush medicine

D

Dalkarra—leader, knowledge authority; as with Birkarr'yun,
    a man calling out the sacred names is called Dalkarramirr

dawu—fig tree

dhä-malamirr—Dhä means mouth, malamirr means blood

dhaŋbulyun—head of the whale

dhäruk—language

dhatam—waterlily

dhawadatj—mixed up, muddled up

dholuwuy Yolŋu—swamp person

dhukarr—road, path, track, footpath

Dhukarr lakarama—straightening the pathway; naming the road

dhum'thum'—wallaby

Dhuwa—one of the two Yolŋu moieties

dingu—cycad palm

dirrmala—the north wind

djalkiri—our foundation or feet

djäma—work

djambatj—hunting expert; one who spears the dugong or whale
    (also known as Djambatjŋu); also harpoon (djambati)

Djan'kawu Sisters—Dhuwa ancestral beings who create Country

djilawurr—scrub hen

djirikitj—quail

Djirrikay—leader, knowledge authority

djomula—casuarina tree, she-oak

djoru warrpididi—the home of the octopus, corals

djulŋi—our dearest

djulpan—boat

Djungaya—caretaker of the songspiral, director, child of the clan

dulŋay—female or male gathering expert

duttji—fire-making tree, pandanus trunk

G

galuku—coconut

gamata—sea grass; also called Wulu, Wuluwurrthun, the place
    that is covered with sea grass, the territory of the big sea
    animals

gaminyarr—paternal granddaughter

ganguri—yams

ganydjarr—strength, power

gapan—white clay, ochre

Gapiny-mala—the two clans of Ŋaymil and Dätiwuy coming together, gathering

gara—spear

garak—space

Garma—an open area, a place where ceremonies are held or knowledge is shared; a common ground for leaders and clans to meet

gathu—niece

gatjbu'yun—hoped for, to hope, be hopeful

gawudalpudal—a small black waterbird that guards and looks after waterhole

gay'wu—dilly bag, woven string bag

Gay'wumirr Miyalk Mala—Dilly Bag Group of Women

getju—dark tobacco

gilurru'—dark tobacco

goŋ—hand

Goŋ-gurtha—the keeper of the fire, or a person who lights the fire

gukuk—dove

guluwu—mangrove

gunbilk and gunbilk marrawulwul—calm, smooth, glassy water

gunbur'yun—chanting, calling out sacred names

gundirr—anthills

gunga—pandanus leaves

gurrutu—kinship

gurtha—fire

gutharra—grandchild through the maternal line; a daughter's child

guwak—koel bird, messenger bird

L

lalu—parrotfish; another name is yambirrku

larrani—bush apple

larrpan—spear cloud, long cloud

likun—the deep names

lindirritj—red-collared lorikeet

lirrwi—layers of buried charcoal

liya—head

liya-balkurrk—a type of rain, the hunter that goes out in all weather, with the rain and the spray of water on his face

liya-manikaymirri—has a head full of the songs, has knowledge of the songs

liya-ŋärra'mirr—has a head full of knowledge, a master of ceremony

M

mädirriny—south wind

mala—group, nation

mala wulkthun—the clouds are separating, the people are separating

malarrka—hawksbill turtle

mali—reflection or shadow

mälk—skin name

mamidal—the deep connection between the hunter and the whale

manikay—song, ceremonial singing including keening

manmuŋa—long yam

manyi—children's use of the term for maternal grandmother

manymak—it is good, fine

mari—danger

märi—grandmother, mothers' mother

märi-gutharra—maternal grandmother–granddaughter
  relationship

märi-pulu—grandmother clan, mothers' mother

märr—love, feeling of truth, strong in self

marrkapmi—my dear ones

marrwala—paddle

matjala—driftwood

maypal—oysters

mel—eye

Mel'mari—eye of the shark

milkarri—songspirals as cried and keened by women

Milŋiyawuy—the River of Stars, the Milky Way

milŋurr—fresh waterhole, water bubbling up from the ground,
  fontanelle

minyga—garfish

Miwatj—the people of the sunrise

miyalk—woman, women

miyapunu—turtle

Mungulk—clear to brackish Yirritja water that runs down
  towards the sea

munydjutj—wild plum tree

murruy—pouring rain

N

ṉamal—the black stingray

ŋamala—mother

ŋaṉarr—tongue

ŋäpaki—non-Indigenous people

ṉapaḻawaḻ—pigeon

ŋara'—the cloud that stands like a whale tail on the horizon, the cloud from the smoke of the hunter

ŋarali'—cigarettes, tobacco

ŋarrpiya—octopus

ŋatha—food

ŋathi—grandfather, mother's father

ŋathi-walkur—märi's son

R

räkay—water reed with edible roots

raki—string

raŋi—beach

Rinydjalŋu—our homeland, its deep and sacred source, our shelter

riŋgitj—place which is sacred to clans; an embassy

rirrakay—sound, noise, voice

ritjilili manybarr and ritjililimirr—muddy water at Rorruwuy

Rom—Yolŋu Law

rrupiya—money

W

waku—child

waku-pulu—child clan

wäkuṉ—mullet

waḻtjan or goŋ-waḻtjan—the hands of the rain

wäŋa—home, camp

Wäŋa Wataŋu—custodian, landowner

Wapitja—digging stick

warriwaṯpa—the whale fin and the whale paddling beneath the sea

wetj—to give, giving, the giver

wirriwirri—rainbow bee-eater bird

wititj—snake, olive python, Rainbow Serpent

Wukun—Gathering of the Clouds

Wulpundu—a big cloud stretching forward into the sky

wuŋapu—a fruit that is purple, blackish and looks like an olive

wuymirri—whale

Y

Yaŋara—the people of the sunset

yapa—sister

yarrpany—Dhuwa bees

yarrwarri—queenfish

yidaki—didgeridoo

yindi—mother

Yirritja—one of the two Yolŋu moieties

Yolŋu—people from North East Arnhem Land

Yolŋu matha—the family of languages from North East Arnhem
  Land

yothu—child

yothu–yindi—child–mother relationship

yumalil—harmony

yuta—new fat

Acknowledgements

In our language we say buku-wekam to honour those who have helped us bring *Songspirals* to life. Living, breathing, nurturing Country—thank you for shaping and enabling everything we do. We honour Country and all those who have shared with us and supported us as we have worked on this book. Allen & Unwin and Sarah Brennan, you supported us from book to book, and Elizabeth Weiss, Angela Handley and Clara Finlay—your deep respect, care and incredible attention to detail has blown us away and we can't put into words how much we appreciate it. Will Stubbs, Joseph Brady, Vanessa Spinelli, Lirrina Munungurr, Bambuŋ Pearson and Dave Wickens from Buku-Larrŋgay Mulka Yirrkala Art Centre, thank you for your fantastic assistance with the art work and images for the book. We thank all the artists who have given us permission to use their work—Deturru Yunupiŋu, Naminapu Maymuru-White and Manala Marika Guluruŋa as well as the memories of our mother, Gaymala Yunupiŋu and Dad, Roy Marika. Oscar Whitehead, thanks for your eye for detail with the Yolŋu matha spelling. Richie Howitt has always been part of our journey and his careful reading and review are so appreciated. Matalena Tofa, Jill Sweeney, Cigdem Guzel, thank you for your incredible assistance. Ali Wright, you are so patient and through your graphic design eye make what we do look so beautiful! To Macquarie University, the University of Newcastle and Yirrkala School, thank you for your unwavering support for our collective, and to the Australian Research Council for funding our work together. We especially thank a beautiful lady who shared Goŋ-gurtha with us and recently passed away. She had so much knowledge and her knowledge has been passed on to us. And to our parents, grandparents, partners, children, grandchildren, we get the knowledge, determination and courage from you and we love you all so, so much.

Notes

These notes serve two purposes. The first is to help readers to find further information about key concepts raised in the text. The second is to recognise previous research and knowledge, and to highlight connections between this book and other published works. See our Bawaka Collective website, www.bawakacollective.com, for a full version of these notes and a range of other materials and resources supporting and elaborating on this book.

Key texts which cover a range of topics discussed in more detail below include:

Keen, I. (1994). *Knowledge and Secrecy in an Aboriginal Religion.* Oxford: Oxford University Press.
Morphy, H. (1991). *Ancestral Connections: Art and an Aboriginal system of knowledge.* Chicago: University of Chicago Press.
Watson, H., with the Yolngu Community at Yirrkala, & Chambers, D.W. (1989). *Singing the Land, Signing the Land: A portfolio of exhibits.* Geelong, Vic.: Deakin University Press.
Williams, N.M. (1986). *The Yolngu and Their Land: A system of land tenure and the fight for its recognition.* Canberra: Australian Institute of Aboriginal Studies.

DJALKIRI

The term 'songline' was arguably popularised among non-Indigenous people through a 1987 novel entitled *The Songlines* by British author Bruce Chatwin. Along with such terms as 'Dreaming', 'Dreamtime' and 'song cycle', songline is now widely used to describe foundational Aboriginal Australian stories, songs, knowledges, and connections with Country. The term 'songlines' or 'songspirals' does not have a direct translation in Yolŋu matha. We use the term songspirals to recognise Yolŋu understandings of ongoing co-becoming and interweaving through song. Yolŋu songlines have been studied by non-Indigenous anthropologists and ethnographers for many years, and information about songlines has been recorded in many books and articles. For example, see:

Berndt, R.M. (1976). *Love Songs of Arnhem Land*. Melbourne: Thomas Nelson.

Berndt, R.M., & Berndt, C.H. (1954). *Arnhem Land: Its history and its people*. Melbourne: F.W. Cheshire.

Hinkson, M., & Beckett, J. (2008). *An Appreciation of Difference: WEH Stanner and Aboriginal Australia*. Canberra: Aboriginal Studies Press.

Keen, I. (2011). 'The language of property: analyses of Yolngu relations to country', in Y. Musharbash & M. Barber (eds), *Ethnography and the Production of Anthropological Knowledge: Essays in honour of Nicolas Peterson* (pp. 101–20). Canberra: Australian National University Press.

Indigenous communities around Australia have also helped non-Indigenous researchers to learn about songlines and their implications for various fields and topics. See the following publications for further information:

Bradley, J., with Yanyuwa families (2010). *Singing Saltwater Country: Journey to the songlines of Carpentaria*. Sydney: Allen & Unwin.

Ellis, C.J., & Barwick, L.M. (1987). 'Musical syntax and the problem of meaning in a central Australian songline', *Musicology Australia*, vol. 10, no. 1, pp. 41–57.

Fuller, R.S., Trudgett, M., Norris, R.P., & Anderson, M.G. (2017). 'Star maps and travelling to ceremonies: the Euahlayi people and their use of the night sky', *Journal of Astronomical History and Heritage*, vol. 17, no. 2, pp. 149–60.

Information about songspirals from around Australia has also been shared in films, exhibitions and online lectures such as the following:

Guyula, Y. (2015). 'Manikay (songline) and Milkarri', *Yolngu Studies, Charles Darwin University*. Retrieved from https://livestream.com/accounts/2047566/events/1840804/videos/88483496 on 22 November 2018.

National Indigenous Television (2016). *Learn Indigenous Australian creation stories—'Songlines on Screen' multimedia features.* Retrieved from www.sbs.com.au/nitv/songlines-on-screen/article/2016/05/25/learn-indigenous-australian-creation-stories-songlines-screen-multimedia-features on 22 November 2018.

National Museum of Australia (2018). *Songlines: Tracking the Seven Sisters*. Retrieved from www.nma.gov.au/exhibitions/songlines on 22 November 2018.

Research into songlines has sometimes been controversial, and it is important that knowledge about songlines is shared by the right people and with the right permissions. There are also important ethical issues that must be considered when recording, digitally archiving, and watching communities singing their songlines. These are discussed further in the following:

Christie, M. (2005). 'Aboriginal knowledge traditions in digital environments', *Australian Journal of Indigenous Education*, vol. 34, pp. 61–6.

Magowan, F. (2007). 'Honouring stories: performing, recording and archiving Yolngu cultural heritage', in U. Kockel & M.N. Craith (eds), *Cultural Heritages as Reflexive Traditions* (pp. 55–74). London: Palgrave Macmillan UK.

Morrison, G. (2017). 'In the footsteps of the Ancestors: oral fixations and ethical walking on the last great songline', in S. Strange & J. Webb (eds), *Creative Manoeuvres: Writing, making, being* (pp. 33–52). Melbourne: Melbourne University Publishing.

Not much research has been done into milkarri, perhaps in part because many anthropologists and ethnographers working in this field have been men. One notable exception is the research of Fiona Magowan, who worked with Yolŋu women in Galiwin'ku to learn about milkarri. Because it is difficult to describe milkarri in words alone, it is important to see and hear milkarri to gain a fuller understanding. Audio and visual footage of the songspirals presented in this book can be found on our Bawaka Collective website and further information found in:

Aboriginal Resources and Development Services (ARDS) (2016). *Bulunu Milkarri: A story of sky, sea and spirit.* Retrieved from https://ards.com.au/resources/external/bulunu-milkarri on 20 November 2018.

Magowan, F. (2001). 'Shadows of song: exploring research and perform-ance strategies in Yolngu women's crying-songs', *Oceania*, vol. 72, no. 2, pp. 89–104.

Magowan, F. (2007). *Melodies of Mourning: Music and emotion in Northern Australia.* Crawley, WA: University of Western Australia Press.

Magowan, F. (2013). 'Performing emotion, embodying Country in Australian Aboriginal ritual', in L. Wrazen (ed.), *Performing Gender, Place and Emotion in Music: Global perspectives* (pp. 63–82). Rochester: Boydell & Brewer Australia Press.

The concept of Country is explored in the following:

Bawaka Country, Suchet-Pearson, S., Wright, S., Lloyd, K., & Burarrwanga, L. (2013). 'Caring as Country: towards an onto-logy of co-becoming in natural resource management', *Asia Pacific Viewpoint*, vol. 54, no. 2, pp. 185–97.

Bawaka Country, Wright, S., Suchet-Pearson, S., Lloyd, K., Burarrwanga, L., Ganambarr, R., Ganambarr-Stubbs, M., Ganambarr, B., & Maymuru, D. (2015). 'Working with and learning from Country: decentring human author-ity', *Cultural Geographies*, vol. 22, no. 2, pp. 269–83.

Bawaka Country, Wright, S., Suchet-Pearson, S., Lloyd, K., Burarrwanga, L., Ganambarr, R., Ganambarr-Stubbs, M., Ganambarr, B., Maymuru, D., & Sweeney, J. (2016). 'Co-becoming Bawaka: towards a relational understanding of place/space', *Progress in Human Geography*, vol. 40, no. 4, pp. 455–75.

Rose, D.B. (1996). *Nourishing Terrains: Australian Aboriginal views of landscape and wilderness*. Canberra: Australian Heritage Commission.

Rose, D.B., Daiyi, N., & D'Amico, S. (2011). *Country of the Heart: An Australian Indigenous homeland*. Canberra: Aboriginal Studies Press.

The phrase 'more-than-human' refers to a way of thinking about the world that 'spans the human–non-human divide' and focuses on relationships between humans and non-humans (Greenhough, 2014, p. 95). The following explore this idea in detail:

Gibson, K., Rose, D.B., & Fincher, R. (eds) (2015). *Manifesto for Living in the Anthropocene*. New York: punctum books.

Greenhough, B. (2014). 'More-than-human geographies', in R. Lee, N. Castree, R. Kitchin, V.A. Lawson, A. Paasi, C. Philo, S.A. Radcliffe, S.M. Roberts, & C.W.J. Withers (eds), *The SAGE Handbook of Human Geography* (pp. 94–119). Los Angeles: SAGE.

Head, L. (2016). *Hope and Grief in the Anthropocene: Re-conceptualising human–nature relations*. London: Routledge.

Tsing, A. (2013). 'More-than-human sociality: a call for critical description', in K. Hastrup (ed.), *Anthropology and Nature* (pp. 27–42). New York: Routledge.

Whatmore, S. (2002). *Hybrid Geographies: Natures, cultures, spaces*. London: Thousand Oaks, California: SAGE.

Wright, S. (2015). 'More-than-human, emergent belongings: a weak theory approach', *Progress in Human Geography*, vol. 39, no. 4, pp. 391–411.

The implications of a 'more-than-human' approach for research and methodological approaches have been explored in the following:

Bawaka Country, Lloyd, K., Wright, S., Suchet-Pearson, S., Burarrwanga, L., Ganambarr-Stubbs, M., Ganambarr, B., Maymuru, D., & Hodge, P. (2018). 'Meeting across ontologies: grappling with an ethics of care in our human–more-than-human collaborative work', in J. Haladay & S. Hicks (eds), *Unsustainable Environments* (pp. 219–45). East Lansing: Michigan State University Press.

Johnson, J.T., & Larsen, S.C. (2017). *Being Together in Place: Indigenous coexistence in a more than human world*. Minnesota: University of Minnesota Press.

Panelli, R. (2010). 'More-than-human social geographies: posthuman and other possibilities', *Progress in Human Geography*, vol. 34, no. 1, pp. 79–87.

Co-becoming is an idea the Bawaka Collective has explored in our work; see above and in the following:

Bawaka Country, Burarrwanga, L., Ganambarr, R., Ganambarr-Stubbs, M., Ganambarr, B., Maymuru, D., Wright, S., Suchet-Pearson, S., Lloyd, K., & Sweeney, J. (2016). 'Co-becoming time/s: time/s-as-telling-as-time/s', in J. Thorpe, S. Rutherford, and L. Sandberg (eds), *Methodological Challenges in Nature–Culture and Environmental History Research* (pp. 81–92). New York: Routledge.

PART 1: Wuymirri

CHAPTER 1: MUM

Search our Bawaka Collective website for recordings of milkarri for the Whale Songspiral and other songspirals. In addition, see the following texts for further information about the Whale Songspiral:

Cawte, J. (1973). *The University of the Warrimirri: Art, medicine and religion in Arnhem Land*. Sydney: NSW University Press.

McIntosh, I. (1994). *The Whale and the Cross: Conversations with David Burrumarra MBE*. Darwin: Historical Society of the Northern Territory.

McIntosh, I. (2000). 'Aboriginal reconciliation and the Dreaming: Warramiri Yolngu and the quest for equality', *Cultural Survival Studies in Ethnicity and Change*, series editors David Maybury-Lewis and Theodore Mcdonald. Boston: Allyn & Bacon.

McIntosh, I. (2015). *Between Two Worlds: Essays in honour of the visionary Aboriginal Elder, David Burrumarra*. Indianapolis: Dog Ear Publishing.

Shepherdson, E. (1981). *Half a Century in Arnhem Land*. One Tree Hill, SA: Ella and Harold Shepherdson.

The Bawaka Collective has identified key ideas about intercultural communication between Indigenous and non-Indigenous peoples, drawing on our experience of working together. See our Intercultural Communication Handbook on the Bawaka Collective website. There has also been considerable work that explores Yolŋu communication styles, cross-cultural and intercultural communication. See:

Boyukarrpi, G., Gayura, J., Madawirr, P., Nunggalurr, H., & Waykingin, M. (1994). 'Yolngu ways of communicating', *Ngoonjook*, vol. 10, pp. 21–7.

Magowan, F. (2018). 'Song as gift and capital: intercultural processes of indigenisation and spiritual transvaluation in Yolngu Christian music', in M. Ingalls, M. Reigersberg and Z. Sherinian (eds), *Making Congregational Music Local in Christian Communities Worldwide* (pp. 97–116). London: Routledge.

Morphy, F. (2007). 'The language of governance in a cross-cultural cultural context: what can and can't be translated', *Ngiya: Talk the Law*, vol. 1, pp. 93–102.

CHAPTER 2: COUNTRY

Much research with Yolŋu and other Indigenous peoples highlights that water is considered part of Country and that relationships with water are crucial. This point has been especially salient to challenging Western notions of property, ownership and rights in relation to various bodies of water. For further information, see:

Buku-Larrngay Mulka Centre (1999). *Saltwater: Yirrkala bark paintings of sea country. Recognising indigenous sea rights.* Buku-Larrngay Mulka Centre in association with Jennifer Isaacs Publishing.
Jackson, S., & Barber, M. (2013). 'Recognition of indigenous water values in Australia's Northern Territory: current progress and ongoing challenges for social justice in water planning', *Planning Theory & Practice*, vol. 14, no. 4, pp. 435–54.
Jackson, S.E. (1995). 'The water is not empty: cross-cultural issues in conceptualising sea space', *Australian Geographer*, vol. 26, no. 1, pp. 87–96.
Rose, D.B. (2005). 'An indigenous philosophical ecology: situating the human', *Australian Journal of Anthropology*, vol. 16, no. 3, pp. 294–305.
Rose, D.B. (2014). 'Arts of flow: poetics of "fit" in Aboriginal Australia', *Dialectical Anthropology*, vol. 38, pp. 431–45.
Weir, J. (2009). *Murray River Country: An ecological dialogue with traditional owners.* Canberra: Aboriginal Studies Press.
Wilson, N.J., & Inkster, J. (2018). 'Respecting water: Indigenous water governance, ontologies, and the politics of kinship on the ground', *Environment and Planning E: Nature and Space*, vol. 1, no. 4.

In Yolŋu Law everything in the world is divided into two complementary moieties, Yirritja and Dhuwa. They are understood by anthropologists as a way of ordering or organising the world. The two moieties are also explained in the following:

Hutcherson, G. (1998). *Gong-wapitja: Women and art from Yirrkala, northeast Arnhem Land.* Canberra: Aboriginal Studies Press.
Yolŋu Sea Country (2008). *Living Knowledge: Indigenous knowledge in science education.* Retrieved from http://livingknowledge.anu.edu.au/learningsites/seacountry/index.htm on 22 November 2018.

The Bawaka Collective explored weaving both as a cultural activity and as a metaphor for our developing relationships and connections in our first book and in a journal article:

Burarrwanga, L., Ganambarr, R., Ganambarr-Stubbs, M., Ganambarr, B.,
    Maymuru, D., Wright, S., Suchet-Pearson, S., & Lloyd, K. (2008).
    Weaving Lives Together at Bawaka: North East Arnhem Land.
    Callaghan, NSW: Centre for Urban and Regional Studies, University
    of Newcastle.
Lloyd, K., Wright, S., Suchet-Pearson, S., Burarrwanga, L., & Hodge, P.
    (2012). 'Weaving lives together: collaborative fieldwork in North
    East Arnhem Land, Australia', *Annales de Geographie*, vol. 121,
    no. 687–8, pp. 513–24.

The Garma Festival is held annually and is organised by the
Yothu Yindi Foundation. The festival includes workshops and
forums, songs, art, and music, and is a widely recognised
Indigenous event in Australia. Further information about the
festival, and the Gapan Gallery, can be found by searching
online for the Garma Festival.

CHAPTER 3: MAPPING

Diverse ways of mapping and understanding place and space
have been explored in a number of publications:

Magowan, F. (2001). 'Syncretism or synchronicity? Remapping the
    Yolngu feel of place', *The Australian Journal of Anthropology*,
    vol. 12, no. 3, pp. 275–90.
Tamisari, F. (1998). 'Body, vision and movement: in the footprints
    of the ancestors', *Oceania*, vol. 68, pp. 249–70.
Turnbull, D., & Watson-Verran, H. (1989). 'Aboriginal-Australian
    maps', in *Maps Are Territories, Science Is an Atlas: A portfolio
    of exhibits*. Chicago: University of Chicago Press. Retrieved from
    http://territories.indigenousknowledge.org/exhibit-5.html on
    22 November 2018.

The mission at Yirrkala was established in November 1935 in
response to conflicts and tensions between Aboriginal people
and settlers. See:

Dewar, M. (1995). *The Black War in Arnhem Land: Missionaries and the Yolngu 1908–1940*. Brinkin, NT: Australian National University, North Australia Research Unit (NARU).

By the 1970s, many Yolŋu lived at mission settlements like Yirrkala for most of the year. In 1972–73, as part of a strong political homelands movement, many Yolŋu began to move to 'homelands' or 'outstations' on their own clan territories or Country. See:

Kearney, A. (2016). 'Intimacy and distance: Indigenous relationships to Country in northern Australia', *Ethnos*, pp. 1–20.

CHAPTER 4: BECOMING TOGETHER

In 2014, the state government in Western Australia announced plans to close 100–150 remote Aboriginal homeland communities on the basis that they were too expensive to maintain. Similar policies and issues were also identified in the Northern Territory. In an interview with John Pilger, the prime minister at the time, Tony Abbott, stated that 'it's not the job of the taxpayers to subsidise lifestyle choices'. This was met with outrage, which highlighted that homeland communities are not a mere 'lifestyle choice' and that closing these communities would create problems and be culturally damaging.

Pilger, J. (2015). 'Evicting Indigenous Australians from their homelands is a declaration of war', *The Guardian*, 22 April 2015.

CHAPTER 5: HARMONISING

The following publications document the extent of Yolŋu participation in military activity and various impacts of the Second World War on Yolŋu in North East Arnhem Land:

Berndt, R.M. (1962). *An Adjustment Movement in Arnhem Land, Northern Territory of Australia*. Paris: Mouton & Co.

Riseman, N. (2008). 'Colonising Yolngu defence: Arnhem Land in the Second World War and transnational uses of indigenous people in the Second World War', PhD thesis, The University of Melbourne.

Thomson, D.F. (2005). *Donald Thomson in Arnhem Land* (compiled and introduced by Nicholas Peterson). Carlton, Vic.: The Miegunyah Press.

Narritjin Maymuru shared his story about the sinking of the boat *Patricia Cam* and helping the survivors on the Wessel Islands in:

Long, J. (1992). 'The sinking of the *Patricia Cam*: Narritjin's story', *Aboriginal History*, vol. 16, no. 1, pp. 81–4.

The term 'stolen generations' refers to Aboriginal and Torres Strait Islander children who were legally removed from their families by staff working for government agencies and church missions from approximately 1905 until the 1970s. See:

National Inquiry into the Separation of Aboriginal and Torres Strait Islander Children from Their Families (Australia), Wilson, R.D., & Australian Human Rights and Equal Opportunity Commission (1997). *Bringing Them Home: Report of the National Inquiry into the Separation of Aboriginal and Torres Strait Islander Children from Their Families*. Sydney: Human Rights and Equal Opportunity Commission.

Roy Dadaŋa Marika is known as the father of the land rights movement. His contributions are described in the following:

Dunlop, I. (director) (1983). *In Memory of Mawalan* (video). National Film and Sound Archive of Australia.

Dunlop, I. (director) (1995). *Pain for this Land* (video). National Film and Sound Archive of Australia.

Dunlop, I. (director) (1996). *Singing in the Rain—Yirrkala in 1974* (video). National Film and Sound Archive of Australia.

Marika, B. (2017). *Desperate Measures: Roy Marika the father of land rights* (video). Melbourne: Informit.

Marika, W. (1995). *Wandjuk Marika: Life story (as told to Jennifer Isaacs)*. St Lucia, Qld: University of Queensland Press.

Part 2: Wukun

CHAPTER 2: SINGING THE CLOUDS

Gurruṯu is a system of kinship that underlies and creates the Yolŋu world. See:

Christie, M., & Greatorex, J. (2004). 'Yolngu life in the Northern Territory of Australia: the significance of community and social capital', *Asia Pacific Journal of Public Administration*, vol. 26, no. 1, pp. 55–69.

Djambutj, N. (1994). 'Connections through the east wind and morning star', *Ngoonjook*, no. 10, pp. 30–7.

The relationship between gurruṯu and mathematics has been explored by the Bawaka Collective and others through the concept of Yolŋu mathematics:

Bawaka Collective (producer) (2017). *Knowledge on the Land: Two-ways learning through Yolŋu mathematics*. Retrieved from www.youtube.com/watch?v=wyaOzZmAAl4 on 20 November 2018.

Burarrwanga, L., Ganambarr, R., Ganambarr-Stubbs, M., Ganambarr, B., Maymuru, D., Wright, S., Suchet-Pearson, S., & Lloyd, K. (2013). *Welcome to My Country*. Sydney: Allen & Unwin.

Cooke, M., & Batchelor College. (1991). *Seeing Yolngu, Seeing Mathematics*. Batchelor, NT: Batchelor College.

CHAPTER 4: THUNDERCLOUD

The relationships between Macassans and Yolŋu are discussed in a number of publications that highlight the extended period of cultural connection and exchange:

Bilous, R.H. (2015). 'All mucked up: sharing stories of Yolŋu–Macassan cultural heritage at Bawaka, north-east Arnhem Land', *International Journal of Heritage Studies*, vol. 21, no. 9, pp. 905–18.

Bilous, R.H. (2015). 'Making connections: hearing and sharing Macassan–Yolŋu stories', *Asia Pacific Viewpoint*, vol. 56, no. 3, pp. 365–79.

Clark, M., & May, S.K. (2013). *Macassan History and Heritage: Journeys, encounters and influences*. Canberra: Australian National University Press.

Lloyd, K., Suchet-Pearson, S., Wright, S., & Burarrwanga, L. (2010). 'Stories of crossings and connections from Bawaka, North East Arnhem Land, Australia', *Social and Cultural Geography*, vol. 11, no. 7, pp. 702–17.

McIntosh, I.S. (2006). 'A treaty with the Macassans? Burrumarra and the Dholtji ideal', *The Asia Pacific Journal of Anthropology*, vol. 7, no. 2, pp. 153–72.

Palmer, L. (2007). 'Negotiating the ritual and social order through spectacle: the (re)production of Macassan/Yolngu histories', *Anthropological Forum*, vol. 17, no. 1, pp. 1–20.

Responsibilities that come with and are inspired by adoption in Yolŋu, and other Indigenous systems, are explored in:

Bawaka Country, Suchet-Pearson, S., Wright, S., Lloyd, K., Tofa, M., Sweeney, J., Burarrwanga, L., Ganambarr, R., Ganambarr-Stubbs, M., Ganambarr, B., & Maymuru, D. (2018). 'Goŋ Gurtha: Enacting response-abilities as situated co-becoming', *Environment and Planning D: Society and Space*. doi:10.1177/0263775818799749.

Rose, D.B. (1999). 'Indigenous ecologies and an ethic of connection', in N. Low (ed.), *Global Ethics and Environment* (pp. 1–13). London: Routledge.

TallBear, K. (2014). 'Standing with and speaking as faith: a feminist-indigenous approach to inquiry', *Journal of Research Practice*, vol. 10, no. 2, p. 17.

Bawaka Cultural Enterprises and Lirrwi Tourism are Indigenous-run tourism ventures based in Bawaka and Yirrkala, respectively. Further information about their tours can be found by searching on their names online.

For further information about tourism, intercultural communication, and opportunities for personal transformation in Bawaka and Yirrkala, see the Intercultural Communication Handbook on our website as well as:

Bawaka Country, Wright, S., Lloyd, K., Suchet-Pearson, S., Burarrwanga, L., Ganambarr, R., Ganambarr, M., Ganambarr, B., Maymuru, D., & Tofa, M. (2017). 'Meaningful tourist transformations with Country at Bawaka, North East Arnhem Land, northern Australia', *Tourist Studies*, vol. 17, no. 4, pp. 443–67.

Lirrwi Yolngu Tourism Aboriginal Corporation, & Morse, J. (2012). *Yolngu Cultural Tourism Masterplan: A new way forward for Arnhem Land*. Nhulunbuy, NT: Lirrwi Yolngu Tourism Aboriginal Corporation.

Lloyd, K., Suchet-Pearson, S., Wright, S., Tofa, M., Rowland, C., Burarrwanga, L., Ganambarr, R., Ganambarr, M., Ganambarr, B., & Maymuru, D. (2015). 'Transforming tourists and "culturalising commerce": Indigenous tourism at Bawaka in northern Australia', *International Indigenous Policy Journal*, vol. 6, no. 4.

Wright, S., Suchet-Pearson, S., Lloyd, K., Burarrwanga, L., & Burarrwanga, D. (2009). '"That means the fish are fat": sharing experiences of animals through Indigenous-owned tourism', *Current Issues in Tourism*, vol. 12, no. 5–6, pp. 505–27.

Part 3: Guwak

CHAPTER 1: BEING A MESSENGER

Narritjin Maymuru worked extensively with the anthropologist Howard Morphy and with filmmaker Ian Dunlop. His art, work and stories are recorded in several publications and films, including:

Dunlop, I. (producer) (2018). *At the Canoe Camp*. National Film and Sound Archive of Australia.

Dunlop, I. (director) (2018). *Narritjin at Djarrakpi* (video). National Film and Sound Archive of Australia.

Morphy, H. (2005). *The Art of Narritjin Maymuru*. Canberra: ANU E Press.

CHAPTER 3: THIS IS POLITICAL

The impacts of government intervention on Yolŋu lives have been discussed in many publications. Of particular note is the Northern Territory National Emergency Response of 2007, commonly referred to as 'the intervention', which was arguably prompted by a 2007 Commonwealth Government report entitled *Little Children Are Sacred*. The intervention was very controversial and was criticised for the lack of consultation with Indigenous communities and for the suspension of the Racial Discrimination Act. Following a change in government, the intervention was replaced in 2010 with a similar policy called Stronger Futures. See:

Churcher, M. (2018). 'Reimagining the Northern Territory Intervention: institutional and cultural interventions into the Anglo-Australian imaginary', *Australian Journal of Social Issues*, vol. 53, no. 1, pp. 56–70.
Howitt, R. (2012). 'Sustainable Indigenous futures in remote Indigenous areas: relationships, processes and failed state approaches', *GeoJournal*, vol. 77, no. 6, pp. 817–28.
Keenan, S. (2013). 'Property as governance: time, space and belonging in Australia's Northern Territory intervention', *Modern Law Review*, vol. 76, no. 3, pp. 464–93.
Macoun, A. (2011). 'Aboriginality and the Northern Territory intervention', *Australian Journal of Political Science*, vol. 46, no. 3, pp. 519–34.
Morphy, F., & Morphy, H. (2013). 'Anthropological theory and government policy in Australia's Northern Territory: the hegemony of the "mainstream"', *American Anthropologist*, vol. 115, no. 2, pp. 174–87.
Yunupingu, G. (2009). 'Tradition, truth & tomorrow', *The Monthly*, December 2008—January 2009, pp. 32–40.

Mining has been a source of much pain and prompted the Bark Petitions and other land rights activism in Yirrkala. Further information about the mine and its impacts can be found in:

Scambary, B. (2013). *My Country, Mine Country: Indigenous people, mining and development contestation in remote Australia*. Retrieved from Canberra: http://epress.anu.edu.au/titles/centre-for-aboriginal-economic-policy-research-caepr/my-country-mine-country on 20 November 2018.

In 1963, a lease for mining on Gove Peninsula was announced, without any consultation with Yolŋu people. Rirratjiŋu clan leaders sent the Bark Petitions to the Commonwealth Government stating that their land rights must be respected. The Bark Petitions contained bark paintings of clan 'symbols of ownership, of knowledge and rights' with a typed document, and was sent in 1963 (Marika, 1995, p. 100). An inquiry was conducted into the issue. Although the mine went ahead, the petitions eventually led to the Aboriginal Land Rights (Northern Territory) Act being passed in 1976, and legal recognition of Aboriginal land rights and the establishment of land councils in the Northern Territory. Further information about the Bark Petitions and the land rights movement, particularly around Yirrkala, is provided in:

Marika, W., as told to Isaacs, J. (1995). *Wandjuk Marika: Life story*. St Lucia, Qld: University of Queensland Press.
Morphy, H. (1983). '"Now you understand": an analysis of the way Yolngu have used sacred knowledge to retain their autonomy', in N. Peterson & M. Langton (eds), *Aborigines, Land and Land Rights* (pp. 110–33). Canberra: Australian Institute of Aboriginal Studies.
Wells, E. (1982). *Reward and Punishment in Arnhem Land, 1962–1963*. Canberra: Australian Institute of Aboriginal Studies.

The absence of visible agricultural activity has been used to justify *terra nullius*. See:

Gammage, W. (2011). *The Biggest Estate on Earth: How Aborigines made Australia*. Sydney: Allen & Unwin.
Pascoe, B. (2013). *Dark Emu: Black seeds—agriculture or accident?* Broome: Magabala Books.

CHAPTER 4: THE SPIRITS ARE IN EVERYTHING

Anthropologists and ethnographers have recorded much information about Yolŋu spirituality and love, and the Bawaka Collective has explored the idea of märr and love. See:

Bawaka Country, Wright, S., Suchet-Pearson, S., Lloyd, K., Burarrwanga, L., Ganambarr, R., Ganambarr-Stubbs, M., Ganambarr, B., Maymuru, D., & Graham, M. (2018). 'Everything is love: mobilising knowledges, identities and places as Bawaka', in M. Palomino-Schalscha & N. Gombay (eds), *The Politics of Indigenous Spaces*. London: Routledge.
Berndt, R.M. (1976). *Love Songs of Arnhem Land*. Australia: Thomas Nelson.
Morphy, H. (1994). 'From dull to brilliant: the aesthetics of spiritual power among the Yolngu'. *Man,* vol. 24, no. 1, pp. 21–40.

CHAPTER 5: LIVING IN TODAY'S WORLD

Yothu Yindi, Gurrumul and East Journey are well-known examples of contemporary music that draw on Western, international and Yolŋu influences, and share messages about culture, rights and respect. Do check out their music by searching for them on the internet. The following publications discuss Indigenous music as an example of living in two worlds, as a mode of intergenerational knowledge sharing, and as a vehicle for intercultural communication.

Bracknell, C. (2015). '"Say you're a Nyungarmusicologist": Indigenous research and endangered song', *Musicology Australia*, vol. 37, no. 2, pp. 199–217.
Corn, A. (2010). 'Land, song, constitution: exploring expressions of ancestral agency, intercultural diplomacy and family legacy in the music of Yothu Yindi with Mandawuy Yunupiŋu', *Popular Music*, vol. 29, no. 1, pp. 81–102.
Corn, A. (2014). 'Agent of bicultural balance: Ganma, Yothu Yindi and the legacy of Yunupiŋu', *Journal of World Popular Music*, vol. 1, no. 1, pp. 12–45.

Neuenfeldt, K.W.M. (1993). 'Yothu Yindi and Ganma: the cultural transposition of Aboriginal agenda through metaphor and music', *Journal of Australian Studies*, vol. 17, no. 38, pp. 1–11.

Part 4: Wititj

CHAPTER 1: SETTLING OF THE SERPENT

Yolŋu ideas about boundaries and territory are explored further in:

Williams, N.M. (1982). 'A boundary is to cross: observations on Yolngu boundaries and permission', in N.M. Williams & E.S. Hunn (eds), *Resource Managers: North American and Australian hunter-gatherers* (pp. 131–53). Boulder, Colorado: Westview Press.
Williams, N.M. (1983). 'Yolngu concepts of land ownership', in N. Peterson & M. Langton (eds), *Aborigines, Land and Land Rights* (pp. 94–109). Canberra: Australian Institute of Aboriginal Studies.

Laklak's story is described in detail in our second book:

Burarrwanga, L., Ganambarr, R., Ganambarr-Stubbs, M., Ganambarr, B., Maymuru, D., Wright, S., Suchet-Pearson, S., & Lloyd, K. (2013). *Welcome to My Country*. Sydney: Allen & Unwin.

The protocols and order for sharing knowledge in Yolŋu culture are discussed in a number of publications. Of particular note is the way this contrasts with imperial research agendas that assume the right to know and to discover. For further information, see:

Brigg, M. (2016). 'Engaging indigenous knowledges: from sovereign to relational knowers', *Australian Journal of Indigenous Education*, vol. 45, no. 2, pp. 152–8.
Bawaka Country including Wright, S., Suchet-Pearson, S., Lloyd, K., Burarrwanga, L., Ganambarr, R., Ganambarr-Stubbs, M., Ganambarr, B., & Maymuru, D. (2016). 'The politics of ontology and ontological politics', *Dialogues in Human Geography*, vol. 6, no. 1, pp. 23–7.

See our Bawaka Collective website for more information about our first and second books.

CHAPTER 3: WAPITJA

The story of the Djan'kawu Sisters and their journey has been discussed in numerous publications, including:

Dunlop, I. (director) (1983). *In Memory of Mawalan* (video). National Film and Sound Archive of Australia.
Hutcherson, G. (1998). *Gong-wapitja: Women and art from Yirrkala, northeast Arnhem Land*. Canberra: Aboriginal Studies Press.
Wells, A.E. (1971). *This Their Dreaming: Legends of the panels of Aboriginal art in the Yirrkala church*. St Lucia, Qld: University of Queensland Press.

CHAPTER 4: WOMEN'S KNOWLEDGE AND WISDOM

For many years, universities have been sites where colonial knowledge is acquired and reproduced, and where Indigenous knowledges have been treated as artefacts, exotic curiosities, or absent. In recent years, scholars have explored ways of recognising Indigenous knowledges in universities, and of decolonising or indigenising universities, particularly in terms of research and teaching practice. See:

Christie, M. (2006). 'Transdisciplinary research and Aboriginal knowledge', *The Australian Journal of Indigenous Education*, vol. 35, pp. 78–98.
Hunt, S. (2014). 'Ontologies of Indigeneity: the politics of embodying a concept', *Cultural Geographies*, vol. 21, no. 1, pp. 27–32.
Marika-Mununggiritj, R., White, L., & Ngurruwutthun, D. (1992). 'Always together, yaka gana: participatory research at Yirrkala, as part of the development of a Yolngu education', *Convergence*, vol. 25, no. 1, pp. 23–39.
Nakata, M. (2013). 'The rights and blights of the politics in Indigenous higher education', *Anthropological Forum*, vol. 23, no. 3, pp. 289–303.

Tuck, E., & Yang, K.W. (2012). 'Decolonization is not a metaphor', *Decolonization: Indigeneity, Education & Society*, vol. 1, no. 1, pp. 1–40.

Wright, S. (2018). 'When dialogue means refusal', *Dialogues in Human Geography*, vol. 8, no. 2, pp. 128–32.

Further information about the Dhimurru Rangers can be found on the Dhimurru Aboriginal Corporation website and in the following:

Dhimurru Land Management Aboriginal Corporation, & Wearne, G. (2006). *Yol\ŋuwu mo\nuk gapu wäna sea country plan: A Yol\ŋu vision and plan for sea country management in North-east Arnhem land, Northern Territory*. Dhimurru Land Management Aboriginal Corporation.

Hoffmann, B.D., Roeger, S., Wise, P., Dermer, J., Yunupingu, B., Lacey, D., Yunupingu, D., Marika, B., Marika, M., & Panton, B. (2012). 'Achieving highly successful multiple agency collaborations in a cross-cultural environment: experiences and lessons from Dhimurru Aboriginal Corporation and partners', *Ecological Management & Restoration*, vol. 13, no. 1, pp. 42–50.

Marika, R. (1999). 'The 1998 Wentworth lecture', *Australian Aboriginal Studies*, vol. 1, pp. 3–9.

Muller, S. (2014). 'Co-motion: making space to care for country', *Geoforum*, vol. 54, pp. 132–41.

Yunupingu, D., & Muller, S. (2009). 'Cross-cultural challenges for Indigenous sea country management in Australia', *Australasian Journal of Environmental Management*, vol. 16, no. 3, pp. 158–67.

Part 5: Goŋ-gurtha

CHAPTER 1: KEEPERS OF THE FLAME

Yolŋu leaders and activists, and other Indigenous scholars and activists, have used the idea of 'living in two worlds' to describe being Indigenous in contemporary Australia. See:

Burin, M. (2017). 'Walking in two worlds'. Retrieved from www.abc.net. au/news/2017-04-07/the-junior-ranger/8378336 on 20 November 2018.

Yunupingu, G. (2016). 'Rom Watangu', *The Monthly*. Retrieved from www.themonthly.com.au/issue/2016/july/1467295200/galarrwuy-yunupingu/rom-watangu on 21 November 2018.

CHAPTER 3: THE FIRE ON THE HORIZON

Much Western scholarship privileges a teleological conception of time and history. The readings below explore nonlinear conceptualisations of time with Yolŋu and other Indigenous peoples.

Keen, I. (2006). 'Ancestors, magic, and exchange in Yolngu doctrines: extensions of the person in time and space', *Journal of the Royal Anthropological Institute*, vol. 12, pp. 515–30.

Natcher, D.C., Huntington, O., Huntington, H., Chapin III, F.S., Trainor, S.F., & DeWilde, L. (2007). 'Notions of time and sentence: methodological considerations for Arctic climate change research', *Arctic Anthropology*, vol. 44, no. 2, pp. 113–26.

Perkins, M. (1998). 'Timeless cultures: the "Dreamtime" as colonial discourse', *Time & Society*, vol. 7, no. 3, pp. 335–51.

Porr, M., & Bell, H.R. (2011). '"Rock-art", "animism" and two-way thinking: towards a complementary epistemology in the understanding of material culture and "rock-art" of hunting and gathering people', *Journal of Archaeological Method and Theory*, vol. 19, no. 1, pp. 161–205.

Reid, J. (1979). 'A time to live, a time to grieve: patterns and processes of mourning among the Yolngu of Australia', *Culture, Medicine and Psychiatry*, vol. 3, no. 4, pp. 319–46.

Rose, D.B. (2000). 'To dance with time: a Victoria River Aboriginal study', *Australian Journal of Anthropology*, vol. 1, no. 2, pp. 287–96.

CHAPTER 5: CONNECTING GENERATIONS

Siena Stubbs's book is available for purchase:

Stubbs, S. (2018). *Our Birds: Ŋilimurruŋgu wäyin malanynha*. Broome: Magabala Books.

Index

Page numbers in *italics* refer to artworks and photographs.